D1384906

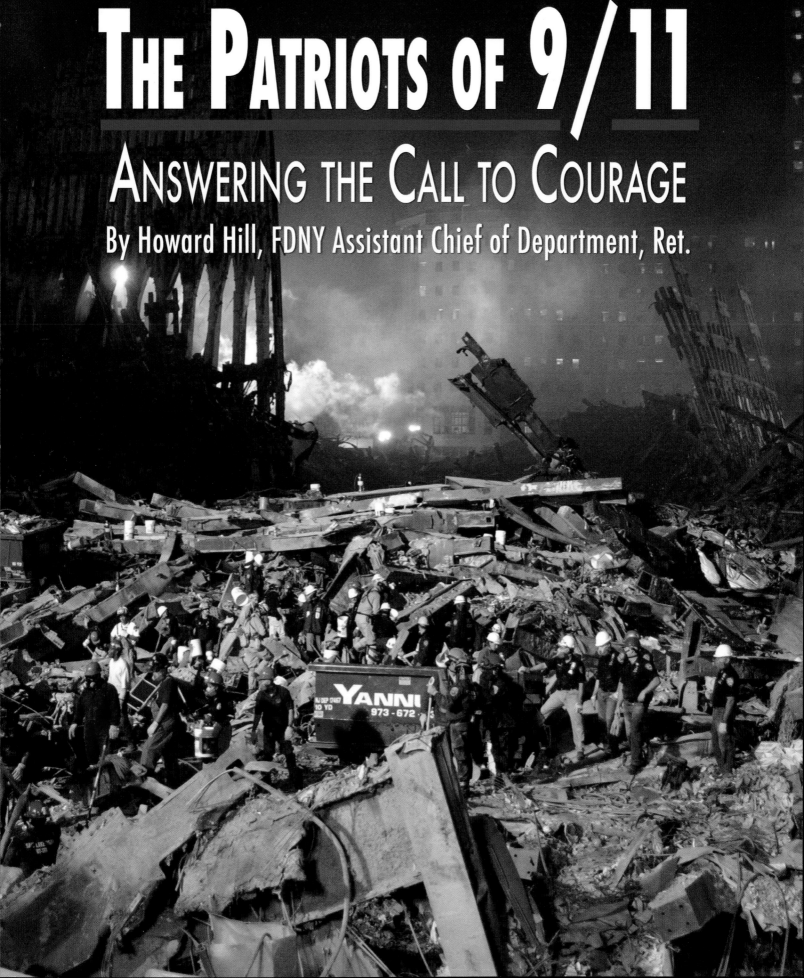

# THE PATRIOTS OF 9/11

## ANSWERING THE CALL TO COURAGE

By Howard Hill, FDNY Assistant Chief of Department, Ret.

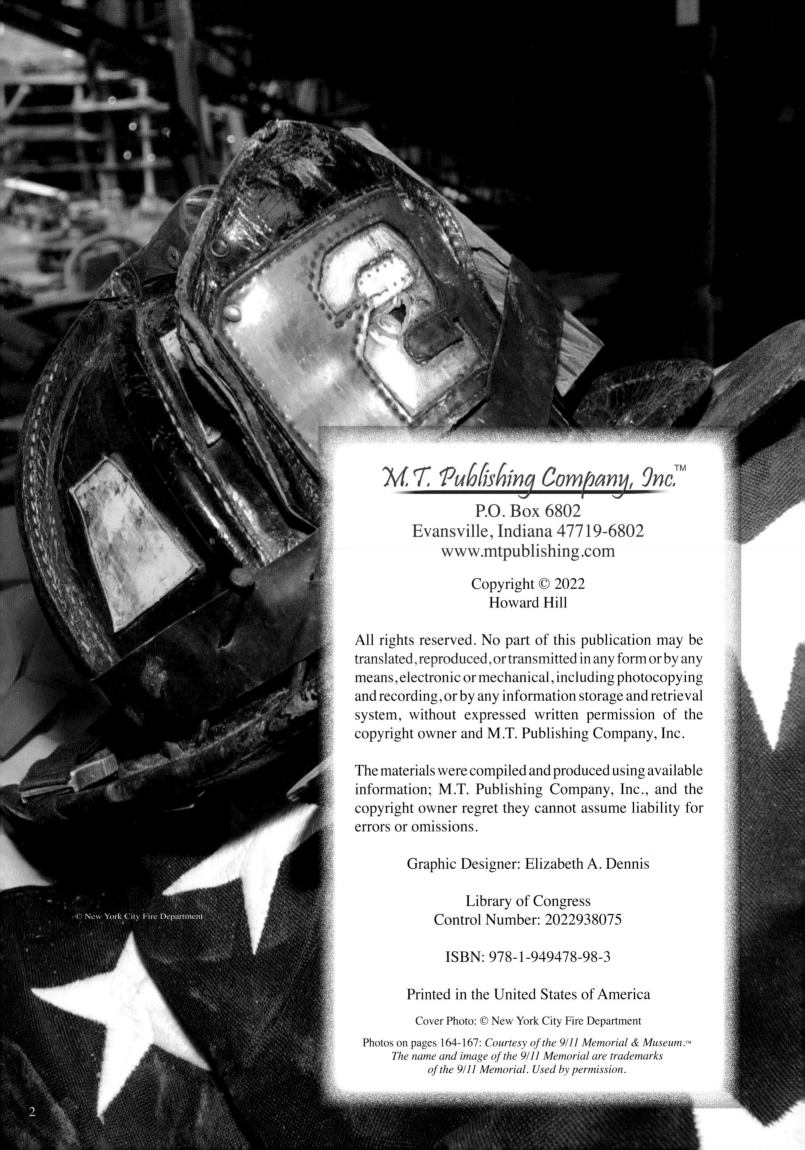

© New York City Fire Department

## M.T. Publishing Company, Inc.™

P.O. Box 6802
Evansville, Indiana 47719-6802
www.mtpublishing.com

Copyright © 2022
Howard Hill

The materials were compiled and produced using available information; M.T. Publishing Company, Inc., and the copyright owner regret they cannot assume liability for errors or omissions.

Graphic Designer: Elizabeth A. Dennis

Library of Congress
Control Number: 2022938075

ISBN: 978-1-949478-98-3

Printed in the United States of America

Cover Photo: © New York City Fire Department

Photos on pages 164-167: *Courtesy of the 9/11 Memorial & Museum.™*
*The name and image of the 9/11 Memorial are trademarks*
*of the 9/11 Memorial. Used by permission.*

# Contents

# Acknowledgements

I started this project in 2019. Over the past three years, it has been my privilege to interview and transcribe the stories presented here. I am indebted to all the interviewees who told me their stories -- terrible to recall and difficult to relive.

I frequently relied on the following sources to accurately portray the events that occurred on 9/11/2001 at the World Trade Center. We wouldn't know the full truth of what happened if it weren't for the scope and detail of the information provided here:

Lynn Spencer's *Touching History, The Untold Story of the Drama That Unfolded in the Skies over America on 9/11*.

*The National Commission on Terrorist Attacks Upon the United States the 9/11 Commission Report* provided insider information on the national response and a thorough analysis of the FDNY operations during the World Trade Center attack.

Mckinsey and Company is the trusted advisor and counselor to many of the world's most influential businesses and institutions. They created the *Final Report* from hundreds of hours interviewing FDNY members resulting in a document that clearly portrays FDNY operations.

*NIST NCSTAR1, Federal Building and Fire Safety Investigation of the World Trade Center Disaster* described how the aircraft impacts and subsequent fires led to the collapse of the towers and included an evaluation of the building evacuation and emergency response operations.

I would like to thank the president of M.T. Publishing Company, Inc. Mark A. Thompson for his immediate support of this project and continuous guidance through the publishing process. And acknowledge the talents of Liz Dennis, the graphic designer, who created a powerful combination of text and photographs.

On a personal note, my wife Maggie counseled and consoled me through the process of writing this book. I don't know if it would ever have been created without her.

Finally, my sons Luke and Adam, 4th generation FDNY members, who grew up on these honored traditions and are answering the call to courage.

This book is dedicated
to all those who follow in
the footsteps of the 343.

# Introduction

This book captures the experiences of the Fire Department of New York City (FDNY) during the attacks on September 11, 2001. I am a third generation FDNY member and on 9/11/2001 was a Deputy Chief assigned to Division 1 which provides fire protection for all lower Manhattan up to 42nd Street. I have focused on the World Trade Center attack because of my first-hand experience and knowledge of this event. Twenty-six individuals were interviewed. Many of them were on site when the two 110 story World Trade Center buildings were collapsing around them.

While researching material for this book I found the initial confusion on the ground was simultaneous occurring in the air as American commercial pilots, the United States Air Force and the White House struggled to understand what was happening during the worst terrorist attack in United States history. We were attacked from outside our borders by terrorist who killed 2,996 people in the United States.[1] This exceeded the number of casualties from the attack on Pearl Harbor.

The FDNY had 343 fatalities which is the most in the history of any fire department's response in a single day. The Port Authority Police Department (PAPD) and the New York City Police Department (NYPD) suffered record breaking fatalities for any police departments in this country for a single day PAPD lost 37 officers and NYPD lost 23 officers.

I learned about American patriotism rising to support one another to face evil and hatred. The enormous help from the civilians in New York City, the rest of America, and people from countries near and far supporting us in our modern era showed the willingness to help by all people of good conscious. I felt amazingly connected and thankful this patriotism was there during the worst days in the history of the FDNY.

> ## I learned about American patriotism rising to support one another to face evil and hatred.

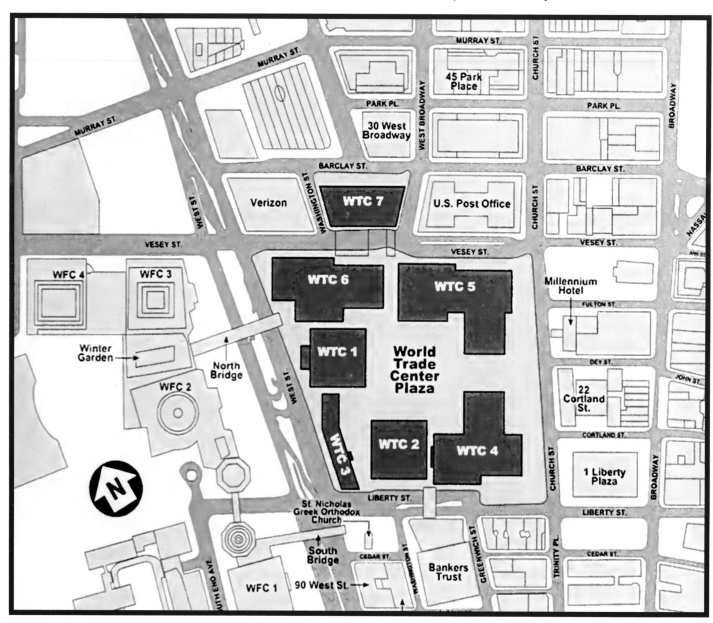

# CHAPTER 1

# The United States is Under Attack

Everyone talks about how perfect the weather was on September 11, 2001. September is the peak month for hurricanes in New York. On the morning of September 11 hurricane 'Erin' had just passed through and was 500 miles off the coast. As hurricane 'Erin' passed by New York on the evening of September 10 it formed a cold front that swept through the area with rain and thunderstorms. New York City skyscrapers were struck six times by lightning associated with thunderstorms developing along this cold front. On the morning of Tuesday September 11, the clear air with light winds created by this cold front leaving the area led to ideal conditions for flying. If this cold front had taken an extra day to pass through New York City September 11 would have had storm conditions adversely affecting the ability to fly a plane and likely would have impaired the hijackers to the point where they might have lost control of the planes. Hurricane 'Erin' could have changed everything.

## In The Air
## American Airlines Flight 11

On September 11, 2001, a Boeing 767, American Airlines Flight 11, left Boston Logan airport for a nonstop flight to Los Angeles. It carried its full capacity of nine flight attendants and eighty-one passengers, including the five terrorists. The plane took off at 7:59 A.M. and at 8:14 A.M. air traffic control instructed the aircraft's pilots to climb to 35,000 feet. That message and all subsequent attempts to contact the flight were not acknowledged. From this and other evidence it is believed the hijacking began at 8:14.[2] About five minutes after the hijacking began stewardess Betty Ong contacted the American Airlines Southeastern Reservations Office using an AT&T airphone to report an emergency aboard the flight. This was the first of several occasions on 9/11

when flight attendants acted outside the scope of their training which was to communicate with the cockpit crew for a hijacking. The emergency call lasted approximately 25 minutes as Ong calmly and professionally relayed information about events taking place aboard the airplane to authorities on the ground.[3]

Passenger Daniel Lewin, who had served four years as an officer in the Israeli military, was seated in the row behind terrorist Atta and Omari and was stabbed in the back

by one of the hijackers who was seated directly behind Lewin. He may have tried to stop the hijackers in front of him not realizing another was sitting behind him.[4] At 8:44 stewardess Sweeny reported "Something is wrong. We are in a rapid descent . . . we are all over the place." She was asked to look out the window to see if she could determine where they were. Sweeney responded "We are flying low. We are flying very, very low. We are flying way too low." Seconds later she said, "Oh my God we are way too low." The phone call ended at 8:46 A.M. when American Airlines Flight 11 crashed into 1-World Trade Center in New York City. All on board along with an unknown number of people in the tower were killed instantly.[5]

## Daniel Nigro
### FDNY Chief of Operations (promoted to Chief of Department and later to Commissioner of the FDNY)

I was Chief of Operations on the seventh floor of 9 Metro Tech on the morning of 9/11. Every morning, around 8:00 A.M. the Staff-Chiefs in headquarters would meet in Pete's office (Chief of Department Peter Ganci) and much like the kitchen table in the firehouse we'd have our coffee and chit-chat about personal lives, solving the world's problems and what's on the day's agenda for the fire department. We broke up around 8:40 A.M. I walked down the hall to my office sat down at my desk to get to work when I heard a noise and thought 'Did somebody on the eighth floor drop a file cabinet or something? What the heck was that noise it shook the building.' Then Pete yelled out "Dan look out the window a plane hit the World Trade Center." We saw this huge cloud of black smoke. We couldn't see where the plane hit, which was on the north side of 1-World Trade Center, but certainly a huge amount of smoke. It was a

> We raced in no traffic. Imagine that 8:50 on a work-day morning the Brooklyn Bridge with no traffic. In the car on the way there I said to Pete "This will be the worst day of our lives."

beautiful clear day and I'm thinking 'How could a plane accidentally fly into the World Trade Center?' First of all, they're not supposed to fly that low in Manhattan. Maybe somebody flying a private plane and I don't why, but I thought of someone doing something they shouldn't be doing like sightseeing hit the building.' It didn't strike me somebody did it intentionally. We quickly decided. I went in the car with Pete so we could talk about strategy on the way there. Steve Mosiello was driving. I told my driver to take then Captain John Sudnik who happened to be on a detail in headquarters to the site.

We raced in no traffic. Imagine that 8:50 on a work-day morning the Brooklyn Bridge with no traffic. In the car on the way there I said to Pete "This will be the worst day of our lives." Pete transmitted a 5th alarm as we sped over the Brooklyn Bridge to Barclay Street, then down West Street and arrived in a matter of minutes after the first plane hit the tower. ❖

## Elizabeth DeFazio
### Secretary to Chief of Department Peter Ganci

I worked for Chief of Department Peter Ganci. I was at my desk in the office doing my morning routines when Chief Ganci yelled out to his Chief of Operations Dan Nigro "Holy shit Dan a plane just hit the World Trade Center!" Everybody went running into Chief Ganci's office.

We looked out the window and saw smoke from a World Trade Center building. I asked him "Did you see it actually happen? Or did you hear it from the department radio?" He said he heard it from the department radio. At the time we all thought it was a small Cessna plane. It was a clear beautiful day as everybody remembers. Then Chief Ganci and Chief Nigro responded to the World Trade Center. Many of the other Chiefs gathered in Chief Ganci's office watching the World Trade Center building burning. Senior Officers were explaining how the people above the fire were going to have a difficult time getting out and if you were below the fire had a good chance of getting out and should be okay. ❖

9

# First Response By FDNY Member:

**B**attalion Chief Joseph Pfeifer assigned to Battalion 1, witnessed the impact of the plane from the corner of Church and Lispenard Streets while investigating a gas leak emergency. He immediately transmitted a 2<sup>nd</sup> alarm.

While responding to the World Trade Center he transmitted a 3<sup>rd</sup> alarm for additional resources and designated a Staging-Area for 3<sup>rd</sup> alarm units. When Battalion 1 arrived at 1-World Trade Center Chief Pfeifer established the Incident Command Post in the building lobby.

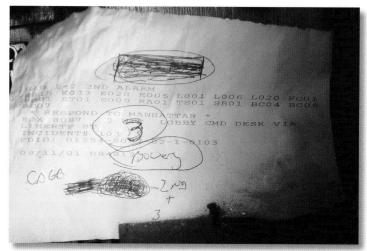

## John Sudnik
### Captain Engine 290 (promoted to Chief of Department)

**9**/11 was a day where everybody remembers where they were. It's like where were you when Kennedy was shot type of moment. But for us—it was worse. Some people were there. Some people were home. Some people were away and wish they were home. Everybody knows where they were.

On the morning of 9/11 I was the Captain of Engine 290 detailed to the seventh floor in Headquarters with three Lieutenants from my firehouse sitting in the office over by the pantry right down the hall from Chief Ganci's office when I saw a couple of people urgently running down the corridor. I walked into Chief Ganci's office where from the window you got a clear view of smoke coming out of 1-World Trade Center's upper floors. I will always remember the look on Chief Ganci's face—straight concern—saying "This is not an accident. No doubt. This was intentional." The early reports on the radio were a small private plane hit the building then as more information came in, they said it was a commercial airline.

Chief Ganci and Chief of Operations Dan Nigro were responding and waiting for an elevator in the ele-vator lobby. When the elevator car door opened, I asked them "What do you want us to do? Do you want us to come with you or do you want us to stay?" Chief Nigro said "Two guys come. Two guys stay back." I jumped in the elevator with Lieutenant Mike Donovan also from Engine 290. When we got down to the parking garage level Chief Nigro told me and Lieutenant Donovan to go in his car with his temporary driver at the time Adam Vilagos. We responded over the bridge in the Chief of Operations' car and Chief Nigro responded in Chief Ganci's car.

> ## 9/11 was a day where everybody remembers where they were. It's like where were you when Kennedy was shot type of moment. But for us—it was worse.

We parked on Church Street and walked to the 'West Street Command Post' on World Financial Center Building 2 parking-garage sidewalk entrance across the street from 1-World Trade Center. I was on an administrative assignment. My turnout coat, helmet, and other gear were in the firehouse so I operated at the Command Post alongside Chief Ganci, Chief Nigro and initially worked closely with Chief Downey doing what I could to help.

I was expecting some kind of collapse from the amount of fire and the building debris falling but I didn't think it would be a total pancake collapse. I thought it would be more localized. I'm sure the Chiefs had conversations about some type of collapse, but I wasn't part of any of those. I was a Captain operating at a Command Post with high-ranking Staff chiefs. We never experienced a collapse of a high-rise building due to fire before so the concept of a total collapse of a high-rise building, no less one of the tallest buildings in the world totally collapsing, didn't seem possible to me at the time. ❖

## In The Air
## Northeast Air Defense Sector

Northeast Air Defense Sector (NEADS) Rome, New York. The NEADS 'Vigilant Guardian' exercise is ready to start at any moment. This training exercise runs several scenarios including a simulated hijacking. There is no way to know exactly when the exercise will begin. At 8:37 A.M. a phone call comes in from the Federal Aviation Administration controller Joseph Cooper to Tech Sargent Jeremy Powell who works on the NEADS Operations floor in support of the senior director in charge of the Weapons section "Hey Huntress," Cooper says using the NEADS call sign "We have a problem here. We have a hijacked aircraft headed toward New York and we need you guys to scramble some F-16s or something up there help us out." "Is this real-world or exercise?" Powell asked looking across the Operations floor to the simulations team to see if he can discern whether this may be one of their tricks for the morning. "No, this is not an exercise, not a test." Cooper responds urgently. Powell bolts up and turns toward the ID section behind him on the Operations floor. "We've got a hijack going on!" Assuming the exercise has begun the leader of the ID section directs her team into action. "We have a hijack going on. Get your checklists the exercise is on." "No" Powell urges "You don't understand. We have a no-shit hijack!"[6]

## In The Air
## United Airlines Flight 175

United Airlines Flight 175 departed from Boston Logan airport for Los Angeles at 8:00 A.M. with seven flight attendants and fifty-six passengers on board. The flight had taken off just as American 11 was being hijacked. At 8:42 A.M., the United 175 flight crew completed their report on a 'suspicious transmission' overheard from another plane (which turned out to have been Flight 11) just after takeoff. This was United 175's last communication with the ground.[7]

At 9:00 A.M. Lee Hanson received a second call from his son Peter "It's getting bad Dad. A stewardess was stabbed. They seem to have knives and Mace. They said they have

## "No, this is not an exercise, not a test."

a bomb. It's getting very bad on the plane. Passengers are throwing up and getting sick. The plane is making jerky movements. I don't think the pilot is flying the plane. I think we are going down. I think they intend to go to Chicago or someplace and fly into a building. Don't worry Dad if it happens it'll be very fast. My God, my God." The call ended abruptly at 9:03:11 when United Airlines Flight 175 struck 2-World Trade Center. All on board along with an unknown number of people in the tower were killed instantly.[8]

## Daniel Nigro – FDNY Chief of Operations

We set up a Command Post in the middle of West Street across from the North-Tower. Chief Joe Pfeifer (Battalion 1 Chief) was already in the lobby with Pete Hayden (Division 1 Commander) and Chief Joe Callan who had taken over as the City-Wide-Commander for the day and took command of operations in the lobby. They were all in the North-Tower with the arriving units of the 3rd alarm that Joe transmitted.

Everybody in their career as a fire officer especially if you reach a certain rank has one fire you look back on and remember. This was it. Kind of wiped out my memory of all other fires.

So, our heads were together. Trying to plan what we were going to do and how we were going to do it. Did we think we were going to put the fire out—no. I said to Pete "No one's ever put out this many floors of fire in a high rise." We thought we could possibly extinguish the fire in one of the stairwells to give people a way to get out of the building and we could get up there and somehow get people who were trapped above the fire out of the building. People below the fire were getting out as fast as they could and as they were going down, we were going up.

That was the plan. Units were streaming in and getting sent upstairs into the building. The elevators weren't working. In the aftermath I found out there was one service elevator somewhere in the North-Tower that possibly went as high as 20-stories and the South-Tower had a shaky elevator working up to a sky-lobby somewhere in the forties.

We were on West Street and decided to move across the street because it was too precarious a location for a Command Post. We went onto a loading-dock driveway area in front of the World Financial Center Building 2 and set it up there. The Field Communications unit came in and went to work. Units were reporting in and being assigned where to go. (Note, the primary Field Communication unit had access to the NYPD's Special operations channel used by NYPD Aviation's, but it was in the garage for repairs on September 11. The backup unit lacked that capability).[9]

Just after we moved across the street, we heard a noise looked up and there was a blur of the United Airlines Boing plane striking into the South-Tower. Moving at over 500 miles-an-hour it was difficult knowing exactly what it was. Our problems had just doubled. Another 5th alarm was transmitted, and those units started responding in. Donald Burns (Assistant Chief of Department) was the relieved City-Wide-Commander who stayed around, and Jerry Barbara (Assistant Chief of Department-Chief of Fire Prevention) was there. We sent them into the lobby of the South-Tower to take command of that operation. They grabbed a couple of people from the Command Post maybe including Orio Palmer (Battalion Chief from Battalion 7) and went to the lobby of the South-Tower where they set up their Command Post. Knowing Donald how organized he was and his abilities to take command of an operation he was running things the way they should be run. He had his extra companies lined up by the Marriot Hotel. Unfortunately, in a spot where most of them were killed when the South-Tower came down. Jerry would be second in command. Donald was senior to everybody and quite the guy. ❖

© New York City Fire Department

## 1–World Trade Center Lobby

The FDNY chiefs in the increasingly crowded North-Tower lobby were confronting critical choices with little to no information. They had ordered units up the stairs to report back on conditions but did not know what the impact floors were. They did not know if any stairwells into the impact zone were clear, and they did not know whether water for firefighting would be available on the upper floors. They also did not know what the fire and impact zone looked like from the outside.[10]

They did know that the explosion had been large enough to send down a fireball that blew out elevators and windows in the lobby and conditions were so dire some civilians on upper floors were jumping or falling from the building. They also knew from building personnel some civilians were trapped in elevators and on specific floors. According to the Division 1 Chief for Lower Manhattan Peter Hayden "We had a very strong sense we would lose firefighters and were in deep trouble, but we had estimates of 25,000 to 50,000 civilians and we had to try to rescue them." The Chiefs concluded this would be a rescue operation not a firefighting operation. One of the Chiefs present explained. We realized because of the impact of the plane there was some structural damage to the building and most likely the fire suppression systems within the building were probably damaged and possibly inoperable.... We knew that at the height of the day there were as many as 50,000 people in these buildings. We had a large volume of fire on the upper floors. Each floor was approximately an acre in size. Several floors of fire would have been beyond the fire-extinguishing capability of the forces that we had on hand. So, we determined very early on this was going to be strictly a rescue mission. We were going to vacate the building, get everybody out, and then we were going to get out.[11]

Between 9:45 A.M. and 9:58 A.M. the ascending Battalion Chief continued to lead FDNY operations on the upper floors of the South-Tower. At 9:50 A.M. an FDNY Ladder Company encountered numerous seriously injured civilians on the 70th floor. With the assistance of a security guard at 9:53 A.M. a group of civilians trapped in an elevator on the 78th-floor sky lobby were found by an FDNY company. They were freed from the elevator at 9:58 A.M. By that time the

Battalion Chief had reached the 78th floor on stairwell 'A' he reported the stairway looked open to the 79th floor. Well into the impact zone. He also reported numerous civilian fatalities in the area.[12]

The highest-ranking officer in the North-Tower was responsible for communicating with the Chief of Department. They had two brief conversations. In the first the senior lobby chief gave the Chief of Department a status report and confirmed that this was a rescue not a firefighting operation. In the second conversation at about 9:45 A.M. the Chief of Department suggested that given how the North-Tower appeared to him the senior lobby chief might want to consider evacuating FDNY personnel.[13]

The first FDNY fatality occurred at approximately 9:30 A.M. when a civilian landed on and killed a firefighter near the intersection of West and Liberty Streets.[14]

**We determined very early on this was going to be strictly a rescue mission. We were going to vacate the building, get everybody out, and then we were going to get out.**

# John Casey
### Division 3 Commander (promoted to Staten Island and South Brooklyn Commander)

I was on medical leave for a few days and on the morning of 9/11 was driving from my home in Staten Island to Division 3 headquarters located in a firehouse on West 77th street in Manhattan to see how everything was going. At the entrance of the Holland Tunnel in New Jersey the radio reported a plane hit one of the World Trade Center towers. I immediately called the Division. Tom Galvin was the Deputy Chief working that day. He told me a plane had hit 1-World Trade center and shortly after that a second plane hit 2-World Trade center. Then said this must be terrorism. Two 5th alarms were transmitted, and he was responding in. When I got through the tunnel I pulled over on West Street. Got out of the car and looked downtown. The World Trade Center buildings were on fire. Everything was in chaos. People were streaming north along West Street. I had to make a decision. Am I going to go down there or am I going to go to Division 3? I didn't have any protective gear and knew they had plenty of people down there now with two 5th alarms in.

On February 26, 1993, the day of the bombing in the parking garage of the World Trade Center's Vista Hotel (later called the Marriot) I was the Battalion Commander in the 1st Battalion and knew from that experience the city was going to be stripped of fire protection with very few units available to respond to other fires. Thinking of that I decided to go to 3rd Division headquarters. This decision probably saved my life.

## It turned out almost every man on those firetrucks from the 9th Battalion died that day.

Some things haunt me as I look back on that day that I find emotionally tough to deal with. As I was going north all the units from the 3rd Division were passing me by responding south. Towards the fire. I saw Ed Geraghty who was later killed in the collapse in his Battalion car shooting down with the all the rest of the units in the 9th Battalion. Sirens and air horns blaring. It turned out almost every man on those firetrucks from the 9th Battalion died that day. I got to Division 3 headquarters. Bill Alford, a Lieutenant who worked as the office-manager, was in the office. He said, "What are we going to do?"

## By now midtown Manhattan had almost no fire companies available to respond to other fires.

Then, the phone calls started coming in from members who came in from home and reported in at their firehouses asking "We want to go down there. When are we going?" I kept telling everyone "Look we'll be down there sooner or later. They got plenty of help now. If they need more, they'll let us know." By now midtown Manhattan had almost no fire companies available to respond to other fires. I told the units that had spare rigs in quarters to man the rigs as best they could with tools and equipment and prepare the apparatus to respond if needed.

That day after the attack started, I can't remember any other fires coming in thank God. We had so few units' in-service to respond to alarms more people could have been trapped in fires. Bill told me Chief Dennis Devlin responded along with firefighter Carl Asaro who was driving Chief Galvin. Both would be killed, and Chief Galvin survived. ❖

---

**In the 17-minute period between 8:46 A.M. and 9:03 A.M. on September 11, New York City and the Port Authority of New York and New Jersey had mobilized the largest rescue operation in the city's history. Well over a thousand first responders had been deployed, an evacuation had begun, and the critical decision that the fire could not be fought had been made. Then the second plane hit.[15]**

# CHAPTER 2
# May-Day Building Collapse

## Daniel Nigro – FDNY Chief of Operations

Once we had everybody situated and people assigned, I said to Pete "I'm going to leave for a minute to walk around the perimeter and see what these buildings look like from the other side." We were cognizant of localized collapse and worried about the members when they got up there because the way this fire was raging, we'd have floors collapsing onto other floors. But as far as the building collapsing no, we did not think they would collapse. We were concerned with floors collapsing within the building. Walking around the perimeter looking at the South-Tower I was shocked to see the corner of the building missing and parts of the United Airlines plane knocked off as it had gone through. Later they found parts on the roof of the postal office on the other side of Vesey Street. That's how bad it was. This made me concerned with the stability of the upper floors of the building.

As I got onto Church Street I wanted to get back to the Command Post quickly and knew if I went through the South-Tower, I could come out of the lobby on the other side into the Marriot Hotel then come out at the Command Post. So, myself and Adam Vilagos my sister's son who was a firefighter in Ladder 175 at the time was on light duty and driving me. We were on Church Street across from Century 21 heading towards the South-Tower when we were stopped by a guy yelling "Chief, Chief." It was Gabe Dela Pena a civilian who worked on the eighth floor in Headquarters. I knew him well enough to know he just had his first child holding his cellphone yelling to me "My wife just went back to work on the 78th floor of the South-Tower. I can't get in touch with her." As much as I wanted to get back to what I had to do I felt I didn't want to abandon this guy and I had a bad vibe he was never going to see his wife again but didn't want to tell him that. I said which was true "Gabe, cellphones aren't working everybody's trying to call they're all overloaded. I'm sure she came down she's somewhere in the area. Get yourself away from the building and everything will be all right." And, as it turned out he did lose his wife and raised their baby girl on his own. I have to say that little delay—saved

Adam and myself from being in the South-Tower when it came down. As it started to collapse, I looked up. My initial feeling was 'I am too close to the building.' You learn about collapse-zones. I have seen five-story tenements buildings where the walls came collapsing down. The height of the wall measured the collapse-zone of the building. I'm looking at a building over a thousand-feet-high collapsing thinking 'I'm too close.' I turned around and tried to get a little further away. We got to Dey Street. Ducked into a doorway. And survived.

When the dust cleared, I decided to head down Broadway to Rector Street then to West Street and the Command Post but before I could do this—the North-Tower came down.

© New York City Fire Department

17

Fires were burning all over and we had water problems. Rescues attempts were being made. Everybody knew people were missing.

© New York City Fire Departmen

© New York City Fire Department

Now we had God knows how many people lost. The feeling of dread you had at this point was... all sorts of 'may-day' and 'urgent' messages were coming over the handie-talkies. I started walking towards the Command Post and met a few people Dr. Kelly oddly enough and a couple of members who were getting back to the Command Post. Dennis Conway a firefighter from Ladder 111 stopped me. He was off duty a good friend to Pete Ganci. He's distraught saying "Pete's missing." Oh, that's bad news. Amongst all the other people I knew would be missing, Pete's missing.

We finally got back to West Street and found a new Command Post at Vesey and West Streets. A lot of Chiefs were there. Some came in from home. Chiefs Frank Fellini and Frank Cruthers had gotten in along with Chiefs Harry Meyers, Michael Butler, and many others.

We started sectoring out the site. Fires were burning all over and we had water problems. Rescues attempts were being made. Everybody knew people were missing. Ladder 6 and a few other people miraculously survived in a stairwell.

People knew where Pete Ganci and Bill Feehan were last seen. They were trying to affect the rescue of Lieutenant Bob Nagel from Engine 58 who survived the collapse of the South-Tower but was trapped and later perished. So, a lot of members went to the area where Bill and Pete were last seen and in a little more than an hour, they uncovered the body. That solidified the fact. I was now the Ranking Chief. The day was bad enough now it got worse.

God knows who else and how many more were dead or trapped. Pete and I had been very close for years. This certainly was not the way we planned anything to work out. But there it was. Al Turi (Chief of Safety), who was a very good friend from back in probie days with Pete and Steve Mosiello had the sad job of going out to Massapequa and telling Kathy Ganci and Pete's three kids that Pete wasn't coming home. That was repeated over and over across the city.

It was a very difficult job determining who was gone. The Command Post was destroyed. We didn't have what we have today where who's working is electronically recorded so recreating the command-board (personnel tracking system) wasn't easy. A lot of people from headquarters and home came in. We worked all night and the next day trying to determine who was missing. That's the term we used at the time. For a week to 10 days it was called a 'Rescue Operation.' Although we kind of knew after the first day we weren't rescuing anybody.

The fire in 7-World Trade Center continued burning out-of-control throughout the afternoon and it had damage on the south side of the building from the collapse of the North-Tower. Having seen two buildings collapse I didn't want a third one to collapse and kill people.

I issued an order to keep all our personnel out of the building and created a collapse-zone. Even though some people with us still wanted to attempt firefighting operations. We created an appropriate collapse-zone and around 5:00 P.M. this 47-story high-rise building did collapse. It would have been the largest building collapse in history caused by a fire. It came down like the other two towers came down. But in this case. We didn't lose anyone. That was the only bright spot of the day.

Once the dust cleared, we were able to get back to putting out fires and looking for people which went on and on and on. I stayed on the site long into the evening. Borrowed a car from Harry Meyers because my car was destroyed. Quickly got home. Took a shower. Changed my clothes and came back. Like so many other people hours and days ran into each other trying to get a handle on everything. Underneath all the rubble active fires were burning until November with intensity.

We were using aerial camera photos supplied to us to capture the high-temperatures in some spots. If you wanted to know what hell would be like. You just had to go down to this 16-acres of destruction. The smell... everything about it for the days and nights afterwards was awful.

And through it all our members showed great dedication. I didn't get the department back on its feet. I was a part of the team trying to make sure the department kept its traditions. And it was fantastic what everybody did. We formulated different plans early on and created new work shifts for the department. We never left command of the site until the end of May.

The work we were doing, as careful as we could, was sifting through every piece of debris they took out of there. Searching not just for our members but for all the innocent victims. We did find remains of about 2/3 of the victims, but still—1/3 of the victims—were never found or identified. Not for lack of trying that's for sure. ❖

# 2-World Trade Center Collapse

At 9:59A.M. the South-Tower collapsed in ten seconds killing all civilians and emergency personnel inside as well as several individuals—both first responders and civilians—in the concourse in the Marriott and on neighboring streets. The building collapsed into itself causing a ferocious windstorm and creating a massive debris cloud. The Marriott Hotel suffered significant damage as a result of the collapse of the South Tower.[16]

At about 10:15 A.M. the FDNY Chief of Department and the Chief of Safety who had returned to West Street from the parking garage confirmed the South-Tower had collapsed. The Chief of Department issued a radio order for all units to evacuate the North-Tower. Repeating it about five times. He then directed the FDNY Command Post be moved further north on West Street and told FDNY units in the area to proceed north on West Street toward Chambers Street. At approximately 10:25 A.M. he radioed for two ladder companies to respond to the Marriott where he was aware that both FDNY personnel and civilians were trapped.[17]

At least two Battalion Chiefs on upper floors of the North-Tower, one on the 23rd floor and one on the 35th floor, heard the evacuation instruction on the command-channel and repeated it to everyone they came across. The Chief on the 23rd floor aggressively took charge to ensure that all firefighters on the floors in the immediate area were evacuating. The Chief on the 35th floor also heard a separate radio communication stating that the South-Tower had collapsed. Which the Chief on the 23rd floor may have heard as well. He subsequently acted with a sense of urgency and some firefighters heard the evacuation order for the first time when he repeated it on tactical channel 1. This chief also had a bullhorn and

## The Chief of Department issued a radio-order for all units to evacuate the North-Tower. Repeating it about five times.

traveled to each of the stairwells and shouted the evacuation order "All FDNY get the f... out!" As a result of his efforts many firefighters who had not been in the process of evacuating began to do so.[18]

After the South-Tower collapsed some firefighters on the streets neighboring the North-Tower remained where they were or came closer to the North-Tower. Some of these firefighters did not know the South-Tower had collapsed but many chose, despite that knowledge, to remain in an attempt to save additional lives. Just outside the North-Tower on West Street one firefighter was directing others exiting the building. Telling them when no jumpers were coming down and it was safe to run out. A senior Chief had grabbed an NYPD bullhorn and was urging firefighters exiting onto West Street to continue running north well away from the WTC.[19]

## Some of these firefighters did not know the South-Tower had collapsed but many chose, despite that knowledge, to remain in an attempt to save additional lives.

## John Sudnik – Captain Engine Company 290

Both towers were on fire and the 'Lobby Command Posts' from both buildings were calling for additional units. I would see who we had available at the Staging-Area and assign units based on the requests coming from these 'Lobby Command Posts' until—the South-Tower collapsed. I saw it starting to come down. It looked like it was a banana starting to peel away. It started near the top then peeled down like you would peel down a banana. Obviously, I didn't wait around too long to watch it come down completely. We were looking for shelter.

I believe most if not everyone went down the ramp into the parking garage. I was 15 feet down the ramp entrance huddled up inside a little wall-cutout area expecting the worst with the—roaring high-level of noise—coming from the building collapse. Then it stopped. And a forced rush of dust and building debris slammed down into the garage ramp. I couldn't see anything and couldn't breathe. There were a couple firefighters one of them had a mask one of them didn't. They were battling a little bit over sharing the face-piece taking hits of air off the mask. The dust was thick and being forced in under pressure. I really thought I was going to suffocate… I knew going further back into the garage wasn't an option because I didn't have an SCBA (self-contained breathing apparatus) to rely on, so I didn't go back deeper into the garage to try and find a door leading into the building. I had no choice but to get out the same way I got in which was up the ramp.

I fully expected to be trapped inside by debris. Enclosed in a high concentration of dust I couldn't breathe or see. I had to get out. I slowly felt my way along a relatively clear path through the rubble leading up and out of the ramp onto the West Street sidewalk where the Command Post had been. I didn't hear anything outside. It was eerily quiet. There was no Command Post and nobody around.

I was stunned waited a moment, and then looked around. It was a little bit easier to breathe because I wasn't in that confined space, but it was still thick enough to inhibit my breathing. The wind was blowing from the North. I went in that direction thinking the air would be a little clearer and eventually worked my way to the new Command Post on the corner of West and Vesey Streets.

I didn't know what happened to and never saw Chief Nigro's driver or Chief Nigro and Chief Ganci. These were the guys I was looking for. Looking back, I always thought 'If I would have walked out and met up with say Chief Ganci or Chief Downey I would have been with them and we know, I probably wouldn't be here.'

**I fully expected to be trapped inside by debris. Enclosed in a high concentration of dust I couldn't breathe or see. I had to get out.**

© New York City Fire Department

© New York City Fire Department

I was a firefighter in Engine 23 in Division 3 and a lieutenant in Engine 235. What strikes me was all the people I knew coming through the Command Post to get their assignments while I was operating there. I saw 23 Engine and 235 Engine and had a brief conversation with Chief Dennis Cross and Captain Timmy Stackpole. People I knew so well who I saw… and then they were gone. This is still very difficult for me. Also, all the people I didn't see at the Command Post but certainly knew from working with them. From time to time, I look at the iconic poster with all the faces and names of the members we lost and think back about the conversations and relationships I had with these people. It's still so sad. All of them gone.

People were operating in and around the new Command Post. I was vomiting dust and used a bottle of water someone had given me to irrigate my eyes and my ears. I spent a few minutes expelling some of the dust out of my nose and my mouth while trying to have conversations with some of the people there. I found Lieutenant Donovan. He was wearing some turnout gear he found on a rig.

We now know truss construction affected the way the buildings collapsed. I was thinking more localized-collapses of floors caused by structural-steel buckling and concrete failing. And I knew the fire would probably have to consume most of the available fuel on those floors before we ended up making any progress towards putting the fire completely out. After the first collapse of 2-World Trade Center there was no command structure anymore on West Street. Obviously, the new Chief Commanders I'm certain were thinking 'We just had one building collapse so there is the likelihood of the other same type of building coming down as well.' I was thinking we had the tallest building in New York City one of the tallest buildings in the world collapse. If it collapsed other than the way it did, which was basically a pancake collapse straight down, what if it fell over, or started collapsing and then teetered towards us. This was going through my mind and then—1-World Trade Center came crashing down.

It was pandemonium. Everyone was being covered by collapsing debris. I found myself again in thick-suffocating dust and blinding smoke. Initially I went further west towards the Hudson River. I didn't have an FDNY radio so I couldn't get a sense of the fire operations going on. I started working my way north again and briefly stopped in Ladder 1's firehouse on Duane Street. Then I walked south and found another Command Post set up on Church Street with a lot of reinforcements and additional units responding in. I never saw anybody who I was operating with at the original Command Post. I had a brief conversation with Jimmy Grasso, Chief Joe Grasso's son, from Ladder 105. I knew him from being a lieutenant in his battalion and said "We've had to lose hundreds of guys."

25

I was in shock. Looking for people I knew for hours and ended up with blisters on my feet from wearing those patent leather dress-uniform shoes. I decided to try to get back home and then get back to the firehouse get my gear and get back to the site to do what I could.

My wife was working on Union Square in Manhattan so she and the whole city, the whole world, was shocked. I thought about her. We didn't have cellphones at the time. When I stopped again in Ladder 1, I did manage to give her a call and told her I was all right. I stared walking towards Penn Station, stopped by her office washed and cleaned up a little bit and said, "Come on, we're getting on a train and going home." I was surprised the Long Island railroad trains were even running. We wound up getting on a train and arriving home sometime that night.

When I got home, I had the wherewithal to call FDOC (Fire Department Operations Center) and said, "This is Captain Sudnik just wanted to let you know I'm okay." I knew Lieutenant Mike Donovan was okay because we were nearby when 1-World Trade Center came down. Certainly not out of danger, but further away from this building collapse than we were when 2-World trade Center collapsed. It was a long day for me.

On September 12, I got up early and went into the firehouse. They already found Timmy Stackpole's body. Timmy was recently promoted out of the Sheffield Avenue firehouse. It was somber. A lot of tears going on in that firehouse. I was the Captain there. As much as I wanted to stay in that firehouse, I felt like I needed to get down to the site and do what I could. I got my gear. Drove to Headquarters. Went to the seventh floor and saw Dan Nigro. The first thing he did was hug me. He thought I was dead.

In the first couple days, certainly not the next morning, we didn't know how many people we lost. We knew—there was hundreds. There was a list going around of who was missing and I was on that list. He probably saw my name and thought 'I told him to get in my car and go to the site.' I suppose that's how he saw it. I never asked him.

Dan Nigro was now the new Chief of Department. I said to him "What do you want me to do," he said, "Well, you know what because we're going to need as much help as we can at headquarters would you stay in Operations and help us out?" I said "Of course." What was I going to say? I didn't feel it was a request. I took it more like this is what I need you to do type of thing. So, that was my assignment. I stayed and worked in Operations.

In the days following we worked on developing some type of family assistance and fielded phone calls from families asking for information about family members who were missing. Obviously, you can imagine how our families were reaching out. They needed information. When bodies were found and identified we needed to notify them and how that was going to happen was a big concern.

Another big concern was taking control of the site. You had emergency operations being performed by people coming from all over the country trying to help and they were on the pile which was extremely dangerous. They needed coordination. Getting control of this was another big concern of the Staff Chiefs in Headquarters.

Then I got promoted to Battalion Chief on Sunday, September 16th, which was that big promotion to replace those we lost in all ranks. I had a bunch of emotions. Obviously, to say it was bittersweet is an understatement. It's always nice to get promoted. But there was no celebrating.

## In the first couple days, certainly not the next morning, we didn't know how many people we lost. We knew—there was hundreds.

In Headquarters it felt like you had to start from scratch and try to deal with something you'd never dealt with before. Everybody wanted to go down to the site and the Staff Chiefs realized at some point everybody's going to get tired and there's going to be nobody able to work at the site or in the firehouses. We had to force people into a schedule where you'd work at the site and maintain a workforce to staff the firehouses. And then you need to go home

An 'AB' work schedule was created 24 hours on, 24 hours off for the people in the firehouses and for the people down at the site. Then we went to the 'ABC' work schedule 24 hours at the site—24 hours off—then 24 hours in the firehouse followed by 24 hours off. This was to insure we had 'continuity of operations' and we were not burning out our members.

The hardest part for me as a Captain was getting promoted out of my company and not being able to be in the firehouse to help support them. Within short order they got another Captain in there. I had a good relationship with Timmy Stackpole. We got promoted to lieutenant together, so I knew Timmy for a long time. That he is gone still bothers me to this day. The Lieutenants in Engine 290 were senior guys. They picked up the leadership role and the truck officers as well. That's a good firehouse. I ended up going down to the pile a couple times on my days off from Headquarters.

I considered myself lucky and fortunate to be alive and a little bit guilty as well. There was nothing I wouldn't do. When they asked, I said, "Whatever you need I'm here." This was my internal thinking. I knew when the Chief of Department asks you to do a job and help out it's because this is where you're needed. You step up. They knew me. I was in headquarters before I got the spot in Engine 290 working on making the necessary changes to our bulletins for the 'Two in-Two out' OSHA standard requirements so I wasn't some random Captain that came out of nowhere. From those experiences I guess they felt confident in my ability to help with navigating whatever issues needed to be taken care of.

After spending a few months in Operations, I volunteered for a 30-day detail and worked down at the site as a Battalion Chief Sector Commander during the month of December. I remember meeting the mayor-elect Bloomberg when he came to the site on the day he was inaugurated. ❖

---

## Elizabeth DeFazio – Secretary to Chief of Department Peter Ganci

---

I was looking at the TV when the second plane hit. Everybody looking out the window yelled they couldn't believe what they were seeing. Even the TV commentators couldn't believe what they were seeing. At that moment everybody realized we were being attacked and people started to leave to help. The City-Wide-tour-Commanders Chief Burns and Chief Barbara were changing shifts early on 9/11 when the second plane hit, and these Chiefs responded like they would usually do for anything that happened. Some other Chiefs working in the building came upstairs and were milling around the office. They wanted to make a plan to go over in an organized fashion. Then, when 2-World Trade Center collapsed the firefighters, lieutenants, captains, and chiefs working in the different offices were all saying "Our guys are over there. We've got to go."

Chief Joe Ramos was very active in the 'Recall' process along with Chief Michael Canty. They were trying to create teams to go over deciding step-by-step how they were getting gear to certain areas. The Staten Island Ferry Terminal was a place gear was sent to. They were telling officers "We'll go, but we have to go in an organized fashion. We have to be a team and work together." As far as I remember none of the commissioners came down to the seventh floor then or from the mayor's office and no one from other agencies like the CIA or FBI came in.

My husband's a firefighter. He was off that day. I didn't want him to go and was pleading with him not to go. What saved him was going as a group. They were waiting for one of the guys who had to pick up his daughter from pre-K and then they all were going together to the site.

Later in the afternoon I saw Pete Guidetti who was Commissioner Bill Feehan's aide wandering around the hallways in headquarters completely covered in dirty-gray dust. I went to grab his arm. He pushed away from me saying "I have to find Commissioner Feehan, I have to find Commissioner Feehan." That's all he kept saying. I said "Pete, it's me Lisa." He pushed away again. He was totally in shock. They told him to take a shower and took his blood pressure. Then I said, "I'll drive you home." Because he lived in Staten Island, and I didn't want him to drive. He took off and left. I didn't think he was able to drive.

## When 2-World Trade Center collapsed the firefighters, lieutenants, captains, and chiefs working in the different offices were all saying "Our guys are over there. We've got to go."

Mostly I sat at my desk during the morning saying prayers with the other girls in the office. I was afraid for my husband who I knew was going there. Most of us were in shock. The building was in 'lock-down.' No one could get into Headquarters without showing ID to the police. We were waiting to hear from Chief Ganci and Chief Nigro. We couldn't get in touch with any of them. The cellphones were out, and we had sporadic phone service at Headquarters. The televisions were on all during the day. I didn't hear from any of the Chiefs.

At approximately 4:00 P.M. Chief Ganci's two sons called and said the television reported 'senior-brass' were missing and then Chief Ganci's daughter called. I said I hadn't heard from him. She was distraught and said, "Find my father. Try to get him on the phone." I tried to reach the Chief and reached out to other people, but I couldn't get through. So many of our phones weren't working.

That whole day was a blur. My parents were in Italy with my sister Karen and my brother-in-law Brian. They were supposed to fly home the next day into Logan airport. I couldn't get in touch and was worried about them. Later my parents told me they were walking the streets of Italy when a man stopped my dad and said, "Are you American?" My father said "Yes." And the man said, "The Trade Center was hit by planes and collapsed." My dad said, "Brian he said that planes hit the Trade Center and the Trade Center buildings collapsed." Nobody could believe it. They stopped in a hotel with a TV in the lobby. Everyone was looking at it. And they saw the pictures of Chiefs Feehan, Ganci, and Father Judge.

Sometime after 8:00 P.M. I was driving home. There were military personnel with machine guns standing in the streets. The roads were dark and empty. It felt like the World Trade Center smoke was following me from headquarters to Staten Island. It was the most eerie feeling. I wasn't in a rush to get home. My husband wasn't there, and my parents weren't around. ❖

## The roads were dark and empty. It felt like the World Trade Center smoke was following me from headquarters to Staten Island. It was the most eerie feeling.

# Patrick McNally
### Deputy Chief Division 14 Queens (promoted to Assistant Chief of Department, Chief of Operations)

I was finishing a night-tour in the 14th Division. This 9/11/2001 was my 25th wedding anniversary. I was planning a nice day of golf with my wife then Peter Luger's restaurant for dinner. I was getting ready to go talking with my relief in the kitchen area watching the *Today Show* when a report came on. A plane hit one of the World Trade Center buildings.

They reported it might have been a single-engine Cessna. All we could see was smoke around the building. I said, "Well a Cessna wouldn't be much of a problem the department should be able to handle it fairly easily." I remembered the WNYF article ('With the New York Firefighters' a quarterly magazine published by the FDNY) about a bomber plane hitting the Empire State Building in heavy fog shortly after the war and how well everything went. I called my wife said, "I'm going to watch this for a minute."

Then we saw the second plane hit and knew this was not an accident and not a single-engine plane. I let my wife know I was going to the site. Got my uniform back on. Told my aide Michael Lashkowski to throw a couple of masks in the back of a suburban and headed on down the Long Island Expressway. Lights and sirens. Made excellent time to the Midtown-Tunnel. Coming out of the tunnel in Manhattan we could see heavy smoke from the FDR and knew this was a major fire.

While we were driving in, I remembered reading a WNYF article about the 1993 World Trade Center bombing saying, "You're not going to go to work right away don't put all your bunker gear on because you're going to wear yourself down quicker." So, I put the lower part of my bunker gear on and slung my mask over my shoulder thinking 'don't put everything on until we're ready to go because this is going to be a long day.' I could see Chief Freddie Scheffold Battalion 12 and Chief Joe Marchbanks Jr. Battalion 12 heading towards the Marriot Hotel. Both later died in the collapse.

I reported in at a Command Post on a wide parking-garage driveway with two big entrances leading under the World Financial Center Building 2 across the street from 1-World Trade Center. Chief Ganci, Deputy Commissioner Feehan, and Chief Cassano were all at this Command Post. I reported in to Chief Cassano. He said "Stand-by, we're trying to put some teams together to go into the buildings." The elevators were out-of-service, and we were estimating how long it would take to walk up with equipment to the 50th floor and based on walking almost a minute for each floor estimated it would take one hour before units could begin attacking the fire. Many of the headquarters' staff was standing by Captain Timmy Stackpole and Battalion Chief Eddie Geraghty. Both men would later be killed in the collapse. It wasn't chaotic. They were organized. Treating it as a fire in a high-rise building. There was a Forward-Command Post in each of the towers and they were coordinating initial tactics with these two Forward-Command Posts. I was there maybe 15 minutes when I put my mask on the ground and — 2-World Trade Center collapsed.

Everybody immediately retreated into those parking garage entrances. Most of them went to the right down the driveway closest to the Command Post. Myself, my aide, and Chief Ray Downey went left. We were being cautious. Going down the ramp a little bit. Because we didn't want to be trapped in there. Hedging our bets and not going down into the garage proper. When the noise settled Ray and I went back up and were able to go out onto West Street. The Command Post was completely blown away. No semblance of it left. On the right side the collapse debris blocked the driveway entrance. Everyone there had to go inside. We were on West Street in the front of the World Financial buildings when Chief Al Turi, who was the Chief of Safety, came by with some other Chiefs. Chief Turi told me to go further north and establish another Command Post out of the collapsed zone. Chief Downey, who later died with Chief Ganci and Deputy Commissioner Feehan when 1-World Trade Center collapsed said "I'm going to wait here for Pete he should be along shortly." He didn't know they ended up having to go out the back way through the whole length of the building. Exit by the Hudson River. Then come back to West Street near Vesey in an area somewhat clear of the debris-field.

I set up the new Command Post on West Street well past the Verizon-telephone-building a block north of Vesey. New people were responding in. Our firefighters were getting their act back together. We started getting things organized. Creating a Staging-Area and planning what we were going to do next. Ten-minutes later Chief Sal Cassano said, "Let's go down and look for Tommy Galvin (a Deputy Chief from Division 3)." He had a pretty good idea where he thought he might be. Before I went with him, I told a Chief "Okay, this is now the Command Post. Try to get everybody organized here." To help I left my aide with the Chief.

Sal and I went south towards 1-World Trade Center. The dust was so heavy from the collapse we couldn't see anything. I remember Sal saying, "I think the whole tower came down." I said, "Well maybe only from where the plane hit and above had come down." We were guessing. I don't know how to describe it. We could see three lower stories of 1-World Trade Center and little else.

As we were walking suddenly 1-World Trade Center collapsed all around us. We were in a bad spot. Right in front of where moments before 1-World Trade Center stood. I think Sal ducked under a truck parked on West Street. I somehow made it to the corner of the World Financial Center Building where I could still hear the building pancake-collapsing rapidly, loudly, Boom! Boom! Boom! As each floor hit the one below it then immediately hit the next floor below. It came down with tremendous noise, wind, and dust. I don't know how you would describe what I was experiencing. Like the world was ending. I was feeling along the edge of a building trying to find an opening for protection from the wind whipping thick-gray dust around like a strong tornado. I couldn't see anyone or anything. Couldn't find a doorway.

Using my hand on the building wall as a guide trying to run as best I could towards the river. Running and slipping on glass still falling from the glass wall that had lined the first floor of World Financial Building and worried I might be shredded by the crashing glass I could hear exploding around me. I kept moving finally finding a marble indentation I immediately curled up into and held on for dear life while everything came blowing by. It was like a World War II movie where the soldier is curled up in the foxhole with bombs exploding around him. That's what it felt like. And, when you see the guy praying, that's what you do. There was so much wild storm like wind force from the continuing collapse. I literally had to tightly hold my helmet on in a curled-up position. Trying to hang on as long as I could by myself. And I didn't think I was going to get out of there.

## It came down with tremendous noise, wind, and dust. I don't know how you would describe what I was experiencing. Like the world was ending.

After a few minutes the noise subsided. I got up. Realized I was near the entrance doorway to the World Financial Center. And bumped into an EMS member. The two of us grabbed a hold of each other and started walking towards the river. It was the blind leading the blind for real. The dust blurred our vision so bad we couldn't see. We were hanging on to each other. The both of us said "If we can get to the river, it should be better over there." And luckily, we did get to the river's edge where Emergency Medical Service personnel immediately flushed our eyes and faces out. After a while we could see again. He started working with his EMS members and I made

27

Photo © 2001 by
Michael Heller

Photo © 2001 by Michael Heller

my way back to the Vesey Street Command Post. I didn't know his name. Never saw him again. But we definitely helped each other get through a tough spot.

I believe Chief Cassano was taken to the hospital. I didn't see him for the rest of the day. As I walked it was now so quiet. From the loudest noise I ever heard in my life accompanied by the feeling of being in a tornado. To stillness and quiet within 20 minutes.

Early on you didn't expect the area to be so quiet. There weren't a lot of firefighters around. I don't remember any civilians. You felt like you were stunned by a blow. Got knocked on your back. And were trying to get up on your feet. A lot of firefighters appeared stunned by the events. It's hard to explain how we did it. But we went right back into the mode of okay, what do we do next?

An off shoot of this. When I first got on the scene, I was talking to a photographer saying, "You know you need to get out of here." But he was set on it and said, "I'm doing my job." Two years later I was in Washington DC where all the National Museums are when somebody told me about a museum called 'Newseum'. Inside was coverage of different big-news events. A whole section on the Vietnam War and a film section on the World Trade Center attack from this gentleman who survived the first collapse. But not the second one. They found his camera. Recovered all his film in good condition. And I'm on some of it.

When I got back there was nobody left from the original Command Post. Fresh troops were coming in and I now worked with Assistant Chief Frank Fellini and Assistant Chief Frank Cruthers who designated this location as the Staging-Area. Chief Cruthers was handling firefighters coming in and assigning them to areas at the site where they were needed. Chief Fellini and I set up a Forward-Command Post and dealt with things as they came up.

We found very few live victims. A handle-talky transmission from Battalion Chief Mike Keenan Battalion 49 reported "We have a victim." I asked "Alive?" He said "No." I said, "We have to leave it there and keep looking for viable live victims." They were doing a surface search through the debris.

It was such a large area, and we were only dealing with the northern half of it. When somebody searching saw a crawl space or an opening where people could have been we'd send firefighters into it. Everything was so fluid. We didn't want people doing things on their own. It

was a very dangerous situation. Poor communications. Fires burning all around. Smoke restricting visibility. Small hills of jagged rubble with towering remains of unsupported steel walls leaning precariously. You wouldn't send in two firefighters. You'd send eight or ten with an officer to make sure nobody got lost, trapped, or injured with nobody to assist them.

Somebody gave a report of a person who survived the blast standing at a window in 6-World Trade Center an eight-story building so heavily damaged in the collapse it had to be torn down. We sent Battalion Chief Mike Keenan in charge of a team to get this victim out. The victim must have been in the bathroom when the collapse happened because he looked like nothing happened to him! His problem was he couldn't get down because the stairways were gone. They found a portable extension ladder from who knows where and got him out fast. He was the only rescued live civilian I am aware of. As people-trapped reports came in we would contact Staging asking for a Chief, Lieutenant, and 10 firefighters to respond.

© New York City Fire Department

A major issue was establishing a water supply to fight the fires. The mains had been damaged. The hydrants were crushed and leaking water underground into the area. I sent a Battalion Chief with three teams to try and establish a water supply from one of our Marine fireboats docked on the Hudson River harbor west of the site. It took a long time to get water. Moving around anywhere was difficult. You had to maneuver over large mounds of unstable debris.

We were able to make sporadic handy-talkie contact with Chief Richie Picciotto B-11 and firefighters with Captain Jay Jonas trapped in the B stairwell. I sent Chief Mark Ferran with a team of firefighters to locate them. It was interesting. Richie's in the 'B' stairwell and he thinks we know where he is. He's saying "Well I'm in the 'B' stair what's the problem? Why can't you find us?" He didn't realize the 'B' stairwell was the only intact thing left of the buildings structure in the entire 16-acre complex. Trying to find them was a major undertaking. Basically, they got themselves out and when they did, we had guys nearby to help them see daylight. Almost no civilians were saved. It was an overwhelming event. You either survived or you didn't.

## It took me 45-minutes to negotiate the one block

We didn't incur a lot of injuries during recovery efforts. One stands out. Captain Al Fuentes of Rescue 1 got himself into a rig to search for a possible victim when debris moved and collapsed on the truck, and he couldn't get out. He was able to talk to the dispatcher on the apparatus radio saying, "I don't know where I am, but I'm trapped in the rig." We found him and got him out.

Chief Brian O'Flaherty was hit with some debris which severely injured his shoulder and was taken to the hospital.

At 1:00 P.M. at the north/west Staging-Area Assistant Chief Fellini said to me "Could you try to get to the south side and see if they could give us any help?" I said "Okay." Because of the huge debris field, I felt it might be better to try to go around the back of the World Financial Center Buildings near the Hudson River cutting thru the buildings to West Street then climbing over the collapse rubble. It took me 45 minutes to negotiate the one block

Deputy Chief Pete Hayden Division 1 was supervising the South part of the site. They were a little luckier. They had a water supply from our Marine fireboats in the Hudson River which was supplying a tower-ladder water-stream operation and handlines. But they also had more fires. They had what probably would have amounted to three, 3rd alarm fires going simultaneously. One involved fire on several floors in 90 West Street. A hotel on the southern end of the site was a 1938 building code heavy construction building which helped contain fire extension. Chief Hayden was standing on a pile of debris operating his Command Post. Pete said, "I don't have anybody to send you. I have enough trouble on my hands right now and I can't help out." So, in other words, you're on our own.

Pete and Frank were not able to communicate with their radios from their respective Command Posts. So now I had to work my way back to Frank and report Pete can't send us any help. He needs everyone he has at his Command Post. On my way back from meeting with Pete Hayden I used some phones in the mezzanine of the World Financial Center buildings to make a fast phone call to my mother my wife was at work, said I'm alive and I'll see you later.

We never got a good water stream. The one hydrant working in our area could barely put out the eight car fires going on at the same time near the Command Post creating a dangerous situation with heavy black smoke severely limiting our visibility. We were able to extinguish a small building fire in the Verizon Building. Unfortunately, we could not address the fire in 7-World Trade Center a 47-story building. We were never able to get enough manpower or water to affect an aggressive attack on it. The front-right corner of the building from the 6th to 13th floor had been ripped out from the North-Tower falling debris. We knew a possibility for collapse existed due to the continuing fire damage weakening the main structural supports. Deputy Chief Terry Roche from the 14th Division made a survey of what would be needed to get a handle on it. He said, "It's too far gone." So, we let it burn.

At 3:00 P.M. Chief of Operations Nigro—who was now in command—consulted with other Staff-Chiefs and decided to pull back and let it collapse. The twin-towers collapsed in a pancake fashion. But there isn't a lot of research on how a 'high-rise building' (a building 75 feet or more in height) will collapse and not a lot of history to study. So, it's a bit of a mystery. We moved our Staging-Area and Command Post a good two blocks towards the river and not too long after 5:00 P.M. 7 WTC did pancake collapse.

The next job was to try to get a handle on casualties. Deputy Chief Tommy Galvin was going to do it, but he was severely banged up missing several front teeth. He had been caught out in the street when 2-World Trade Center collapsed and didn't have his bunker gear because it had been torn from him from the collapse. I think he was now wearing a police shirt.

They asked me if I could help try to get a handle on what the casualties might be. I called the members together said "If you're an engine company get on the right-side of the street. If you're from ladder company get on the left-side of the street." We had some fresh Lieutenants report in, so I told them "I want you guys to make a turn-style and have everyone in the Staging-Area walk through and report to you if anybody they know was definitely dead or missing." I didn't know what else to do. We had to organize it somehow. As the firefighters were being relieved, they were all banged up, the same questions were asked. It took a half-an-hour to get a quick rundown. I went over to a Lieutenant recording the names on a legal pad and the first page is filled. I said, "Well that's not so bad how many 25 or 30?" He says, "Well Chief there's 10 pages." So, we knew we probably had at least 250. I was told they were using phones in

the World Financial Center Buildings to call firehouses and find out who responded. Cellphones were not widespread at the time. I didn't own one. These two efforts were being performed early on at the site to determine some accountability on who was missing.

We had to allow for people self-responding like myself. Which now we would say was a dumb thing to do. But at the time I was available and felt they would need Chief officers. I remember the 1993 World Trade Center attack. A situation like this needs a lot of supervision. You end up needing more Chiefs to do things safely.

Once the initial actions for accountability of who was missing was done, I went back to the Command Post which, after we felt it was safe enough, we moved closer to Vesey and West Street.

It must have been 9:00 P.M. when I left. I couldn't talk. I couldn't see. My eyes were completely shut down. I couldn't function anymore and wasn't much use to anybody. My aide and I hooked up. Went back to the car, which was still where we parked it full of dust with the rear window broken but drivable. I knew I needed to go to a hospital and said to my aide "We'll go to Elmhurst General in Queens and afterwards go back to the firehouse" because I thought the Manhattan hospitals would be overwhelmed.

At Elmhurst General a whole triage center was set up outside to decontaminate people. They didn't want anybody coming into the hospital in bunker gear. They took my gear off. Got me inside and treated my eyes which I couldn't open. They were so sensitive to light. While lying there the top eye doctor in the hospital trauma center was working on me. I said "Gee, thanks I can't believe you're taking care of me like this" and a nurse said, "You're the first victim we've had all day." I got home at midnight. It was all over.

On Thursday I went to the hospital again. I tried to drive myself, it's only eight miles away from where I live, and had to pull over several times. I couldn't keep my eyes open. So, I drove to the 14th Division which was closer, and they took me to the hospital. The same doctor I had seen on Tuesday night was there. He put a different ointment on my eyes, and it cleared them up right away. I worked the rest the afternoon at the 14th Division.

On Friday, September 14th I reported in at the site. Chief Frank Fellini was there and asked me to work with

him again. We did the same thing we had done on Tuesday worked at the Command Post on West and Vesey. Only now it was more organized. And it got even more organized as time went on. I worked 20 hours on Friday. Went home. Slept a couple hours and the funerals started on Saturday. The first funeral was First Deputy Commissioner Bill Feehan and the second one was Chief of Department Pete Ganci. I went to both of those on Saturday.

Deputy Chief Pete Hayden was made 'Incident Commander' of Ground-Zero and set up his Command Post in the quarters of Engine 7 and Ladder 1 on Duane

## After six weeks I'll tell you the truth I was shot. We were going to funerals on the day-tours and working at night.

© New York City Fire Department

Street. Pete was looking to deal with one guy for the day-tour and one guy on the night-tour. A schedule was set up where Assistant Chief Frank Fellini and Assistant Chief Joe Callan on and off handled the day-tours. Deputy Chief Eddie Kilduff and I did the night-tours until early November. Now there was continuity of command. Knowing what was done and what needs to get done brought more organization to the process. Your tour started with a meeting with Pete then meet with the relieving crews and fill them in on what was done and the next shift goals. We couldn't keep sending firefighters all over the place with buckets. Someone was going to get hurt sooner or later doing that.

After six weeks I'll tell you the truth I was shot. We were going to funerals on the day-tours and working at night. It was a crazy existence. Your 15-hour tour would be 17-hours. You couldn't get everything done and then give all your information to your relief in 10 minutes. We wanted to be as thorough as possible. It was important to have some remains for the families. Even today with all the DNA analysis performed around 35% of the families didn't receive any remains of their loved ones. They never had a funeral. They had a memorial service. Consider the emotional damage to the families who only had a piece of a turnout coat to bury.

The Catholic church must have a body or some part of one to have a funeral. Before the attack Safety Battalion Chief Larry Stack donated platelets to a blood bank. Years later his wife was able to retrieve some of the stored blood platelets. So, they had the funeral and buried the platelets he had donated. We recovered a piece of a helmet of a firefighter, and it was all they had —terrible. ❖

# Thomas Galvin
## Deputy Chief, Division 3 (promoted to Assistant Chief of Department, Chief of Training)

I was working the day-tour of September 11th in Division 3 when the first plane hit, and the alarms came in. When the second plane hit the dispatcher called me "There's another 5th alarm you're assigned to respond." I got into the car with firefighter Carl Asaro and Battalion Chief Dennis Devlin. Chief Devlin volunteered to come along to assist us as it would probably be hectic setting up the Lobby-Command Post in 2-World Trade Center. Deciding to have Dennis ride with us was a fateful decision as both Carl and Dennis were killed in the line-of-duty.

While driving down the West Side highway I was writing down the 5th alarm assignments the dispatcher was giving us over the air with Chief Devlin making a second copy. Normally it would take 25 minutes. NYPD had cleared the major avenues of traffic we didn't slow down at any point and got there in 10 minutes.

We were assigned to the South-Tower. I told Dennis and Carl to take the command-board to the South-Tower lobby and I would meet them after I went to the main Command Post on West Street. I reported in to Chief Ganci at the Command Post told them "I'm the Deputy Chief on the second 5th alarm for the South-Tower. Handed in a copy of all assigned units then headed towards the South-Tower by going through the Marriot Hotel on West Street. As I got into the hotel lobby, I ran into Chief Sal Cassano he said, "There's enough people commanding the South-Tower you are now in charge of getting people out of the hotel."

As I was setting up a Command Post in the hotel lobby I made numerous calls trying to get Dennis and Carl to leave the South-Tower and bring the command-board to the hotel lobby. But I never got through to them. As units came in I had them turn their radios from the normal tactical-channel, which was being overloaded with communications, to a spare tactical-channel so we could communicate the status of the evacuation with each other. Then I assigned companies to different floors. We had people running the elevators. In a short time, we had enough units handling the hotel evacuation. I told the later arriving units they could probably be of use in the South-Tower and to go there. Basically, I was running the Command Post by myself. Dennis and Carl never made it back out of the South-Tower.

As we were conducting the evacuation—the South-Tower collapses. The hotel building is shaking. I didn't know what was going on. Fortunately for me I was facing south and started running south through the hotel lobby. Had I'd been facing in any other direction and moved in that direction I probably would have gotten killed. The South-Tower collapse sheared off one side of the hotel and I got knocked to the floor by the collapsing debris and wound up by the elevator shafts. I found out later they reinforced the lower floors near the elevator shaft after the 1993 terrorist bombing in the basement area. I'm lying on the floor in the lobby. It's all black with heavy dust in the air. Trying to figure out what the hell happened when a guy yells out "Can you hear my voice?" I hear some people say, "Yeah, I can hear your voice." The guy says, "Well that means we're alive and we've got to figure a way to get out of the hotel." It was pitch black. Like being in a cave with no light. I got up and started moving falling over furniture and debris and found an exit from the hotel leading to the street.

**If you can hear my voice, come to my voice." And people started coming to me. I told them "Grab the rope and follow it. It will take you outside.**

Outside the exit I found a search-rope somebody dropped. I tied the rope off at the exit and crawled back into the building. You couldn't see. Thick black dust filled the air. So, I started yelling "If you can hear my voice, come to my voice." And people started coming to me. I told them "Grab the rope and follow it. It will take you outside." As the dust starts settling visibility is clearing. I keep moving further into the hotel back towards the elevators when I bump into firefighters from Engine 58 in front of a wall of debris and said, "Hey, follow the rope out." They said "No, our officer Lieutenant Bobby Nagel is trapped behind the rubble."

We could talk to him through the debris. I said, "Hey Bobby, you all, right?" he says, "Yeah, I can't move there's too much debris around me." It's just me and these two guys from Engine 58. I said "Listen, I'm going outside to see if I can get guys with tools, and we'll get people to help you out."

I tied the rope off to a column. Followed it back out and ran into Lieutenant Ray Brown with Ladder-Company 113. I pointed to the general area and said "Listen Ray, you'll find an opening somewhere about 50 feet ahead. Follow the rope and it will get you to Engine 58. Their officer is trapped behind this rubble. We've have to get him out of there. Get in with your guys. Figure out what tools you need, and I'll try to get more people to help you." Later, during the search and rescue operations the rope was found but Lieutenant Nagel's body was never recovered. After 1-World Trade Center collapsed it destroyed most of the hotel and amazingly, the firefighters from Engine 58 and Ladder 113 survived.

I exited the hotel. Started heading south then realized I was moving further away from the building. Turned around started walking north. Looked up, and—at that moment—the top of the North-Tower kicks out as the building started collapsing. I turned and started running. About 150 feet away Ladder 176 just showed up and the officer Jimmy Marketti was calling out to get my attention. I turned and started running towards them. The next thing you know the walls and floors debris from the collapsing North-Tower are streaming down creating a pressure wave. I got knocked off my feet. Tumbled over. My helmet flew off my head. With nothing but dirt and dust in the air there's no-way you could breathe. I turtled into my turnout coat and stayed like that for I don't know how long.

When the South-Tower came down I knew something happened. But I didn't know the South-Tower had collapsed. And then the North-Tower collapses. I find my helmet and struggle to climb over huge piles of debris towards where the towers and the Command Post was. FDNY companies kept responding in.

I met a bunch of guys from the Fire Academy led by Chief Nick Santangelo and Safety Chief Artie Lakiotes and said "Artie, you run this sector. Do whatever you can. Find a water supply and figure out what you can do. I've got to find the Command Post." I trudged along a few blocks and found Chief Frank Cruthers at a Command Post on Vesey and West Streets with EMS and OEM. He said, "Somehow get ahold of SOC (Special Operations Command)." You couldn't get through phones. I gave a message over the radio to the dispatcher saying, "Contact SOC at their headquarters on Roosevelt Island. Chief Cruthers wants everything they have and have them report into the Command Post at Vesey and West Street." I told Chief Cruthers SOC was notified, and he says, "I need you to get to 1-Police Plaza with a list of actions that need to be taken." I'm standing there. Just filthy as can be. Covered with debris. Thinking 'how am I going to get over to 1-Police Plaza?' when a Fire-Marshal offers to drive me.

I walk into 1-Police Plaza lobby. My face is filthy. My helmet and bunker gear are coated with a layer of debris dust. They're looking at me like, what are you doing here? I said, "I was sent here by Chief Cruthers at the site to work with NYPD Chief of Operations." They tell a cop to bring me to their Operations-Center. When I get there a guy sees me in the hallway says, "Stay right here." The way I looked they didn't want me to go anywhere. Chief of Patrol Joe Esposito comes over. I quickly tell him "I'm here from Chief Cruthers. This is a list of things they want to ensure you guys are doing because they can't get in touch with you." Esposito looked at the list and says, "Yeah, we're working on most of this stuff." Then I told him I was here to be the rep for the fire department. He's looking at me and says to someone "Take him downstairs. Get him some new clothes." I put my bunker gear and helmet into a bag with my other stuff just as sweaty and dirty as could be and put on a white NYPD shirt and blue pants. I go into the Operations-Center and there's 10 people from the fire department already there. I asked a Chief "Do you need me for anything?" He said, "No Chief, we're handling the process here." I said "Okay, I'm going back to the site." I got back to the site with my clothes and gear in a plastic bag wearing an NYPD uniform. Later, I had people ask me "Hey Chief, do you have a twin brother in the police department?"

7-World Trade Center is burning out of control. We're waiting for it to collapse. We don't know who we're missing. Several Chiefs were talking about getting accountability and decide to start putting a list together of who's here. I'm still in the NYPD uniform trying to get everybody accounted for.

At around 5:00 P.M. after 7-World Trade Center collapsed and most of the surface searches were completed. It was decided more heavy equipment would be needed to complete the searches. They kept some units and sent some back to their firehouses as they started to develop a search and rescue plan. I was sent back to Division 3 to determine their needs. I go back. Got cleaned up. Put the right uniform on. And am now the on-duty Deputy Chief.

At 8:00 P.M. I got a call from the site Command Post. They tracked down a construction company in Division 3's area who has the drawings for several World Trade Center buildings and directed me to pick them up and bring them to the site. I picked up a bunch of blueprints and delivered them to the Command Post.

I was going to go home on Wednesday night when they called for more Deputy Chiefs to staff the newly created sectors. I said, "Okay, I'll go." and worked till the next morning when Chief Cassano said to me, "Go back to the Division. You're going to be the acting Division-Commander. Your job now is to get the 3rd Division up and running. Find out who you lost and get the equipment and apparatus needed."

Over the next several weeks I worked numerous tours when they needed Deputy Chiefs to staff the sectors, but my primary role was handling the needs of Division 3. I had a great staff to address the needs of the units in Division 3 led by Lieutenant Bill Alford and met regularly with the Battalion Commanders. We needed to ensure we were all on the same page to address each of their needs. We had to know who was lost. How were we taking care of their families. Who was injured. Personnel needs, equipment, and apparatus.

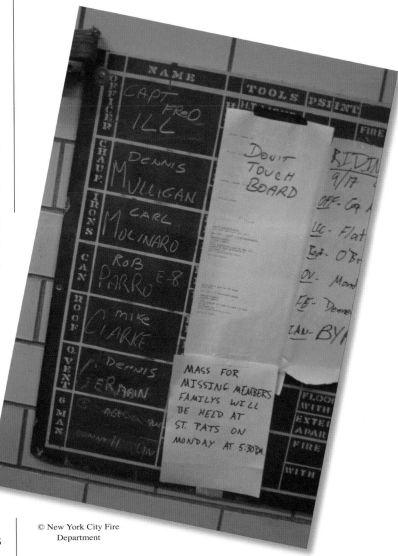

© New York City Fire Department

It was critical to visit each firehouse and let them know we were aware of their needs, and to address any issues, they were having. When faced with the issues we were going through the members needed to hear from their leadership and they also needed to see them. We wanted to provide assurance and keep them focused on the daily responsibilities and issues firefighters deal with every day. ❖

Photo © 2001 by Michael Heller

# Ralph Bernard
## Lieutenant Supervising Fire Marshal, Multi-Media Unit Supervisor

I was working in the Multi-Media Unit in Headquarters when we were notified a plane crashed into the World Trade Center. We immediately got ready to respond to the World Trade Center. As luck would have it, we weren't able to respond right away. Our cars were in the shops for maintenance and by the time we got a car from the carpool 2-World Trade Center was hit by another plane.

As part of our job our unit documents major FDNY operations for training purposes and we thought this is an opportunity to capture learning material in handling a high-rise fire and medical-triage procedures for mass casualty victims. On the other end we were concerned about the loss of life we felt was eminent.

I saddled up with two video cameras and with Steve Chimento a retired FDNY Captain who was consulting with the Department on training initiatives. We responded in an FDNY vehicle and parked on the corner of Vesey and Church Street. Both planes had crashed into the two towers. No buildings had collapsed yet.

EMS personnel were treating people on Church Street performing triage and arranging transportation for victims to hospitals. We were preparing to do some filming then stopped. We didn't have handie-talkie radios with us and thought 'Nobody knows were here. We need to check in at the Command Post.' Then we heard what sounded like jet engines roaring. I looked up and saw smoke coming out of 2-World Trade Center and thought 'let's get some video of the smoke explosion.' It was 2-World Trade Center collapsing.

A dark cloud of smoke erupted all reflective looking from the glass. Like a Christmas cotton cloth with the sun shining on it. I'm thinking 'that's coming at me' and, along with everybody else, I took off running down Church Street. When I turned around everybody was gone. I felt it was surreal because I'm running—but I'm not afraid. I see this open big silver door and ran in. I ran up the stairs into an enclosed lobby with bars above counters. It was the public area of the Post Office. The people coming in behind me were cut-up and bleeding.

Suddenly, in seconds, it goes from being visible to where you can't see anything. Completely black. Not being a good journalist, I shut the video camera off because everybody's yelling "We're going to die, this is it." We stayed in the lobby for a little while.

When the outside started to lighten up a bit we went out the doors and right away, it went from a color world—to a gray and black world. Everything was deep-gray and black. Gloomy monotone. You couldn't see the sky. You couldn't see much of anything. There was four inches of large, fluffy dust, blanketing the ground and falling everywhere.

We're walking away from the site when we heard jet engines and immediately started to scramble for shelter and ran into someone from the FBI who said, "Don't worry, those are our planes." We continued walking when I look to my left and I'm walking with Mayor Giuliani who just came out of 7-World Trade Center with many of his commissioners including FDNY Commissioner Thomas Von Essen. We dropped back and walked behind them towards City Hall. When we got close to City Hall, we got a couple of medical masks from EMS.

Steve and I needed to get back to Headquarters and find out what's going on. We went back to our vehicle started to drive toward headquarters and as I turned the car around 1-World Trade Center collapsed. It was like that scene from the *Raiders of the Lost Ark*—where a big ball is coming at you. I'm looking at this big black dust-cloud rolling behind us. Steve was in the front seat getting as low as he can go as debris came crashing on the back of the car. The dust filled the air. We're trying to get out of there as quick as we could without running anybody over. I could barely see where we're going and slowly made a left on Broadway.

We finally get on the Manhattan bridge and heard everybody saying, "The Twin Towers have collapsed." You can't see anything because the whole sky is full of thick deep-gray dust. We're in denial. We saw 1-World Trade Center it was intact. We were sure it must have been a smoke-explosion on some floors.

As soon as we walk into Headquarters everybody in the Multi-Media Unit was looking at us saying; "You're alive?" We go "What do you mean we're alive?" On the TV we saw a rerun of the North-Tower collapsing and now knew both towers had collapsed. I said, "We've got to get back there and document what's going on."

By 11 A.M. we finished gathering up still and video cameras about ready to leave when the press-office called "We have over 700 members missing. We need photos of everybody." We switched from going back to the site and turned the Units focus on this operation. Everybody's personnel folder has photos of when you came on the job and every time you got promoted. We scanned the pictures and put them into a book for the Fire Marshals and Battalion Chiefs. We had hundreds of personnel folders lined up in the hallway.

Fire Marshals were going to hospitals. Battalion Chiefs were checking in their Battalions calling firehouses trying to identify who responded and who was missing. Quickly we got a bunch of photo scanners connected to a bunch of computers staffed by retired firefighters, firefighters and officers running six scanners and scanned hundreds of photos. The first list had 700 missing members. Our main goal was identifying who was missing. It went on all night and into the next day.

## By Thursday September 13th — we ended up with the final 343.

When confirmation of a missing member was assured, we identified who they were and later—if confirmed alive—we deleted the name and put another updated book together. Every time something changed, for better or worse, we made corrections. Dozens of copies were then given to Operations. Initially we didn't know how many were missing. By Thursday September 13th— we ended up with the final 343. ❖

## In the Air
## Captain Krakowski, United Airlines Vice President of Safety

Captain Krakowski, United's vice president of safety, watches a close-up replay of the aircraft hitting the South-Tower and recognizes the United markings on the underside of the plane and knows for sure: the second aircraft to hit the World Trade Center belonged to United.... [20]

Executives from both American and United Airlines are quickly on the phone to FAA headquarters and the FAA Command Center. They're brought into a conference call that has now been set up with Secretary of Transportation Norman Mineta and Vice President Dick Cheney at the White House. The airline executives inform the secretary they are each dealing with additional aircraft they are unable to contact... They seek guidance, but there is none. The nation is under attack, but there is no plan in place and no guidance is forthcoming from the top as the crisis escalates.[21]

## In the Air
## Northeast Air Defense Sector, Pilots' Orders

Back at NEADS, F-15 fighter pilot Nasypany has already ensured his Weapons Team is prepared to give shoot-down orders. Now he checks if the other pilots are willing to execute those orders. He directs the Otis Weapons controller to radio Duff, another F-15 pilot flying a plane in the area, and with a bone-chilling inquiry asks, "If we get another hijack track, you're going to be ordered to shoot it down. Do you have a problem with that?" "No - no problem with that," Duff responds, somewhat taken aback by the questions. 'If I have a problem with that order,' he thinks, 'I am in the wrong seat.' He's doing what he's been trained to do. He's just never trained to do it over America or against civilian aircraft. But if he gets a legal, lawful order, to take out an airliner, then that's what he's going to do. He knows every other fighter pilot would do the same. It might be hard to live with afterward, but he'll follow orders nonetheless to protect New York.[22]

## Stanley Dawe
### Deputy Chief Division 14 (promoted to Assistant Chief of Department, Chief of Fire Prevention)

On the morning of September 11th, I was on my way to the golf course and stopped in the local deli for a cup of coffee where the TV news was reporting a plane hitting 1-World Trade Center. My initial impression was this would be a major incident and the FDNY members working in the 1st and 3rd Divisions would be in for a long dangerous day. When the TV replay showed rather than the small private aircraft I envisioned a large commercial airliner had been involved I realized all the FDNY was facing a long dangerous firefight.

I headed for the 14th Division in northern Queens where I was a Deputy Chief. I had to drive past the building where my wife worked and decided to stop in to see her. While we were talking the second plane hit 2-World Trade Center. I stayed with her for a couple of minutes then got back in my car and listened on the radio as both towers collapsed. Driving across the Tri-borough Bridge I could see the enormous smoke cloud in downtown Manhattan. I arrived in the firehouse. Got my gear and called firehouses in the area to gather groups together. The Transit Authority was sending city buses to firehouses to take firefighters to the World Trade Center site. I waited for the bus to show up and got there about 1:30 in the afternoon.

FDNY personnel were staging on West Street north of Chambers Street. It was somewhat disorganized. Many individuals had traveled to the location on their own. Some with hand tools or folded hose. A few handie-talkies. But no SCBA (Self Contained Breathing Apparatus). Several officers were working to organize the members into work units. There was not a lot of coordination. Going to the Staging-Area I walked down West Street and ran into Chief of Operations Danny Nigro who was trying to establish a Command Post at Vesey Street. I stayed with him.

Chief Joe Callan reported in completely covered in gray dust. He had been on scene as each tower collapsed. He was disoriented and upon being examined by EMS they determined to transport him to an Emergency Room for further evaluation.

We got a couple of folding tables set up and more Chief Officers started to report in. Chief Nigro wanted to establish communications with Headquarters and the City-Wide Dispatcher. Most of the landline phones in the area were down and Chief Nigro asked me to see if I could find working phones. I went into Stuyvesant High School and found a landline working. I explained to the Manhattan dispatcher Chief Nigro was setting up a Command Post at West and Vesey Streets and to notify units on the handie-talkie channels and apparatus radio.

Dan asked me to see if I could find a location to expand communication capabilities for the Command Post. Captain Ralph Cellentani, who I had worked with in 58 Truck, and I went to a World Financial Center building. On the mezzanine level we found an office that overlooked the site and had several working telephones. Chief Nigro instructed us begin contacting all FDNY firehouses and start compiling a list of members who were known to have responded to the World Trade Center and were unaccounted for. Captain Cellentani went to a local firehouse, obtained a FDNY Phone Directory, started calling the firehouses and recording the names of the members who were in the firehouse and those who were unaccounted for. Ralph called all through the night.

Chief Nigro then ordered me to begin establishing a handle-talkie communications network. I contacted the Chief Officers on the scene and began designating sectors to enable better coordination of FDNY activity. One Chief I was able to contact was Chief Tommy Haring who was supervising fire-suppression in the Deutschland Bank building. I asked him to gather information on what units he had working and in what locations hoping to get an estimate of the resources he had operating in this sector. Tommy and I worked together for several years and his straight-forward response to me was simply, "I have too much fire and too many hose lines in operation to give you an answer."

Chief Nigro called for a meeting with the Chiefs on the scene. We met in the cellar of the Verizon building along with representatives of Verizon. They had emergency generators in the building and were supplying us with portable generators and portable lighting systems which was a priority that night. This meeting's priority was how to re-establish cellular and landline telephone communications in lower Manhattan. Water from broken water mains was pouring into their cellar on Vesey Street hampering Verizon employee's ability to complete this vital task. Several engine companies were assigned to operate educators which helped to control the water flow in the basement.

During the night the FDNY Field Communications unit arrived on scene. I coordinated with them to control the communications systems and assign units to the different operational sectors. Once it got dark it was chaotic, with a lot of handie-talkie traffic. Field Communications got set up and handled the communications. The familiar sound of dispatchers assigning units as they responded in was heartening. I tried to determine if Chief Medical Officer Kelly or any other Medical Officers were on the scene to find out if they had established a triage or treatment site. To the best of my knowledge, it didn't happen on the first night.

## Chief Nigro instructed us begin contacting all FDNY firehouses and start compiling a list of members who were known to have responded to the World Trade Center and were unaccounted for.

Officers and Firefighters were continuing to respond on their own to the site through the night wanting to help in any way possible. We were doing our best to keep them out of the site and report to the Staging-Area where we could organize them into operational-units with an officer and five firefighters and then be given a particular assignment rather than climbing on the pile and moving stuff around with no real objective in sight.

My strongest memory on the 11th was the layer of gray/white dust over everything. Firefighters who had been there during the collapses were completely covered in dust. Walking around looking like ghosts. Their faces, hands, turn-out gear, helmets, everything, covered in a heavy layer of gray/white dust.

I stayed at the site until noon the next day. Chief Butler was now in charge of the Command Post at West and Vesey. I told him Ralph Cellentani was basically done gathering information of who had responded and gave him the twelve-page list Ralph had compiled and said we needed to take a break.

I don't remember eating anything the entire time. The department was using city buses for transportation. We got on one. It took us to the parking lot on Francis Lewis Boulevard where Ralph had parked his car and he drove me to the 14th Division. That ended my first 26-hour day. ❖

# Tom Curti
## Fleet Maintenance Deputy Director

**W**e start work in Fleet Maintenance at 6:30 in the morning. I was at my desk on 9/11 when the first plane hit 1-World Trade Center. A lot of people thought 'Oh, somebody was being stupid flying a small plane and crashed into the tower.' But after the second plane hit it was an obvious attack. I called for a Suburban and with my assistant Andy Diamon proceeded to the World Trade Center.

## We proceeded to the Hudson river's water's edge. Headed up north a few blocks. And then 1-World Trade Center come down.

We drove through the Midtown-Tunnel without incident. The fastest we've ever gone through the tunnel. Arrived in Manhattan and proceeded the World Trade Center site. We parked two blocks away at a bus-stop. Put our bunker gear on. And walked to 1-World Trade Center. As we got closer what looked like a lot of debris coming off the building was—people jumping from the upper floors. Many of them were holding what looked like tablecloths over their head to act as a parachute. Pairs of falling people holding on to each other. We were going to report to the Command Center in the lobby but because of all the people making that fatal decision to jump and landing in the area of the lobby we decided to walk around the building.

We found landing gear. What looked like a pilot's seat. And body parts in the street. I decided we needed to regroup. It was a serious situation. We crossed over West Street and went to the Winter Garden (which is between World Financial Center Buildings 2 & 3 across the street from 1-World Trade Center) when 2-World Trade Center collapsed. I heard the screams from people running towards us—then everything went silent—as a cloud of debris drifted down and surrounded us and everything went black.

It seemed like an hour before we could see again. It was probably ten minutes. We proceeded to the Hudson River's water's edge. Headed up north a few blocks. And then 1-World Trade Center come down. After that collapse we were treated by EMS. My eyes were completely clogged up from the dust and everything else in the air.

We ran into Assistant Commissioner Tom McDonald who was the Administrator in Charge of Fleet Maintenance. He told us to standby until we got additional personnel at the scene. We headed back to the collapse area to see if we could assist in any way and started going around the building rubble to perform an evaluation on the condition of the apparatus. Most of them were totally destroyed.

**Obviously, the loss of life was unbelievable compared to any apparatus. That was our first concern. But our responsibility was to get the apparatus back in-service as quickly as possible and that's what we proceeded to do.**

I have to say something. Obviously, the loss of life was unbelievable compared to any apparatus. That was our first concern. But our responsibility was to get the apparatus back in-service as quickly as possible and that's what we proceeded to do.

I was keeping a guarded eye on 7-World Trade Center which was brightly burning when it collapsed later in the day. I found the Mask Service unit which was heavily damaged. Got it started and was able to drive it a short distance. Then I called out on the radio "We have mask-air-bottles available."

I called the shops (repair center for apparatus) for the tow trucks. We ended up pulling 10 to 15 various apparatus out of the debris with tow-trucks. Lined them up on West Street. Got a police escort and at 11:00 P.M. started our caravan back to the 'Shops.' Most of them were completely covered in thick heavy-gray dust with their windshields blown out. We had to use goggles to drive them. Units beyond repair were picked up by crane and transported to a landfill in Staten Island. Within four days we brought back 80 rigs to the 'Shops' to be cleaned, repaired, and tested. ❖

# James Esposito
## Deputy Chief Division 15 (Promoted to Assistant Chief of Department, Chief of Operations)

9/11 was a beautiful day. I left my house early in the morning to attend a golf outing with the members of Battalion 40 at the Silver Lake golf course on Staten Island. I was a Battalion Chief in Battalion 40 and now a Deputy Chief assigned to Division 15. Our group had just teed off from the first hole. Chopping away at the ball. When suddenly we heard this loud boom reverberating through the sky. We thought maybe Fort Hamilton shot a cannon off saluting some occasion. Soon after the members who had yet to tee off called us back to the clubhouse. A large television screen was showing news about an airliner crashing into the World Trade Center. Being the senior Chief I said, "All right, everybody report back to your firehouses."

My car radio news stations were reporting all FDNY, and NYPD members had been recalled to duty. I took off to the 15th Division in Brooklyn. When I arrived Shamus McNeela, the 15th Division Commander, had ordered all recalled officers and firefighters to report to Division 15's quarters which would serve as a mustering point and transportation hub for our response to the World Trade Center. We needed to make sure there were enough companies in the Division to provide fire protection for the area and simultaneously maintain a sense of command, control, and accountability for members on recall.

We contacted the Brooklyn dispatcher's office and received instructions to use city buses for transportation. Firefighters in Engine 283 flagged down several MTA busses and told the bus drivers the FDNY was 'commandeering' the busses. The drivers were more than accommodating. They discharged their passengers and staged a number of these buses in the designated locations in front of quarters.' I was on the first bus out filled with 'Recalled' Division 15 officers and firefighters.

We were instructed by the Dispatcher to respond to the Brooklyn side of the Brooklyn Bridge. Everyone was in full bunker gear with all available masks, tools, and equipment. On arrival at Brooklyn Bridge Plaza, we disembarked and walked over the bridge.

At around 11:00 A.M. I reported in to Assistant Chief of Department Thomas Haring. He was in command of an FDNY World Trade Center manpower mustering site located at Broadway and Vesey Street in Manhattan. Tom told me how he was deploying members to the site and asked me to take a group of Chiefs, officers, and firefighters to the southern sector. Then known as Liberty-Command. Which later became known as the Church Street-Command.

I was a Lieutenant in Engine 10 and had a good knowledge of the area. Smoke and building debris were thick in the air with papers flying all around. We had some N-95 face-masks available. They clogged up quickly and were useless. It was somewhat difficult getting to the area we were assigned as collapsed rubble and debris were everywhere. There were few civilians on the streets. As we walked south along Church Street in ankle high pulverized moon-like dust. The air was thick and heavy with gusty winds. It was a very active site with multiple car-fires, burning building rubble and gray debris-dust getting on everything.

## It was a very active site with multiple car-fires, burning building rubble and gray debris-dust getting on everything.

Although still standing, 5-World Trade Center at Vesey Street and 4-World Trade Center at Liberty Street had partially collapsed. They looked like burned-out vacant buildings. The Millennium Hotel and One Liberty-Plaza office building located on the east side of Church Street adjacent to the WTC site sustained significant damage.

I established a Command Post for my team on Liberty and Church Streets. A good vantage point to control the search and rescue operations. There were multiple fires in the Liberty Street sector and no available water supply from the hydrants in the surrounding area because of broken water mains. And no available engine company pumpers or ladder company apparatus. So, our initial efforts focused on site assessment with the emphasis on areas of potential search and rescue.

On the corner of Liberty and Church steps led down to a below-ground concourse level where stores and subway stations were accessible. A search team was deployed to search this area as much as possible which was accomplished by members of Ladder-103, Engine-236, Engine-290, and Ladder-107. Over the course of the late morning and early afternoon they were able to assist one civilian who was disoriented and rescue another using available tools to remove debris blocking their egress and brought both to safety.

Another search team was deployed to the Bankers Trust building (AKA Deutsche Bank) located at 130 Liberty Street adjacent to the 10-House (Engine 10 and Ladder 10 quarters). This building was severely damaged and had a raging out-of-control fire in the basement level accessible via Cedar Street. Chief Haring eventually dispatched an engine company to the Liberty Street Command. The unit who reported in found a serviceable hydrant. Liberty Street was impassable. The debris field literally was up to the 10-House firehouse driveway from a sizeable portion of the collapsed north façade of the Bankers Trust building combined with the World Trade Center buildings debris field.

We had a very limited supply of masks. Nevertheless, these firefighters did a remarkable job in containing most of these fires. Stopping them from spreading vertically or horizontally across a 15-foot-wide Cedar Street to involve the 10-House.

I dispatched another reconnaissance team to 90 West Street located on the Corner of West and Liberty Streets. Fire was venting out of windows on several floors of the hotel some more than 10 stories above ground level. I sent in an officer and six firefighters to access this location via Albany Street south of Liberty Street. The orders were to perform searches, rescues, and evacuations. I was not too concerned about the fires in those buildings simply because we didn't have the resources to put them out.

The Greek Orthodox Church on Liberty Street was covered under a giant debris-field with quite a number of voids, so we had search teams engaged there. Accountability was very important. I didn't want to have any secondary incidents with the rescuers needing rescue. It was a very intense day and the hours seemingly passed as minutes.

I had good communications from Liberty Street with Chief Tom Haring who was able to supply me with a tower ladder and a couple additional pumpers. As the afternoon wore on a heavy-rescue company from New Jersey swung over. I told them where to park. We were accessing tools from their apparatus and using them in the concourse level under the smoldering remains of 4-World Trade Center and part of our expanding surface search and rescue efforts that included 2-World Trade Center debris. The debris field in certain locations was very hot from fires burning deep. The dust encased steel beams were very slippery. They created voids many stories high which made these search efforts particularly hazardous. The afternoon passed quickly. The landscape was surreal.

> We had a very limited supply of masks. Nevertheless, these firefighters did a remarkable job in containing most of these fires.

49

Via my handie-talkie radio I was monitoring a developing situation over on the north side of the debris field involving 7-World Trade Center which was in danger of collapse. Search teams were being pulled back from the immediate area and safety zones were being created. I was similarly concerned subsequent collapses could cause vibrations and movement in our debris field. So, I too removed all Liberty Street Command search and firefighting teams off the debris field. We left and all waited in a Staging-Area. 7-World Trade Center collapsed at approximately 5 P.M. To my knowledge there were no injuries from this collapse. As the sun was setting generators started powering portable tower-lights in the immediate Liberty Street sector debris field.

© New York City Fire Department

**Those firefighters and fire officers worked so tireless and diligent throughout that day and night know who they are and, as I tell their story I will never forget their truly heroic efforts.**

Then a significant incident happened. Firefighters in the North Sector reported a trapped police officer in the middle of the debris field and initiated a rescue operation. This rescue was a long and arduous operation. I was monitoring radio calls from personnel on scene requesting masks, hurst tools, cutting tools, then handlines to protect the rescue effort. Fires were threatening the rescuers and obviously the trapped police officer. Our Liberty-Command sector supported this operation with all available resources for much of the night and into the early morning hours. The only reliable source of

water in the Liberty Street sector was up on Broadway by Thames Street. I designated a water-resource officer to conduct a water-relay operation with two pumpers supplying water into tower ladder-124 whose boom was fully extended up onto the debris pile. We used this tower ladder to transport hose, portable ladders, tools, and equipment as far up the pile it could reach. We also attached a hose line to its nozzle that provided a critical water supply. The boom allowed us to negotiate the debris pile climb more easily.

As the rescue operation continued thru the night, we set up a bucket line to carry heavy hose and equipment because negotiating the debris pile was too dangerous. We passed along rolled lengths of hose to the forward stationed firefighting teams. Climbing portable ladders were often necessary to negotiate twisted, fallen steel beams hovering above deep smoldering collapsed areas. Officers were assisting their teams in these efforts and provided me with critical resource requests.

When my handie-talkie radio batteries started failing I positioned myself up on the pile near this operation using a bullhorn to communicate with my Command Post/ Resource Officer at the Liberty-Street Command Post. The stretching of this line took hours and was an extremely difficult, labor-intensive operation. Nevertheless, it was all worth the effort when we eventually heard "start water" and finally, the successful removal of the trapped police officer.

In retrospect, with the available personnel, tools, and equipment, we operated the best we could that day and night. At the height of the Liberty Street Command operations with the on-going rescue efforts of the trapped police officer we had 75 to 100; Chiefs, officers and firefighters working to save that life.

Morning was upon us in a flash. Deputy Chief Tom Dunne from Division 7 relieved me early in the morning with a fresh crew of firefighters and officers. We were exhausted with nothing to drink or eat throughout the previous day and night. We never even thought about eating. Those firefighters and fire officers worked so tireless and diligent throughout that day and night know who they are and, as I tell their story I will never forget their truly heroic efforts. I am honored to have served with them and to be forever with them as part of the FDNY family. ❖

# CHAPTER 3
# What's Going On

## The 911 Commission Report

The deputy-fire-safety-director in the North-Tower told us he began instructing a full evacuation within about ten minutes of the explosion. But the first FDNY Chiefs to arrive in the lobby were advised by the Port Authority fire-safety-director, who had reported to the lobby, the full-building evacuation announcement had been made within one minute of the building being hit. Because of damage to building systems caused by the impact of the plane the public-address announcements were not heard in many locations. For the same reason many civilians may have been unable to use the emergency intercom phones as they had been advised to do in fire drills. Many called 911. The 911 system was not equipped to handle the enormous volume of calls it received. Some callers were unable to connect with 911 operators receiving an 'all circuits busy' message. Standard operating procedure was for calls relating to fire emergencies to be transferred from 911 operators to FDNY dispatch operators in the appropriate borough. In this case Manhattan. Transfers were often plagued by delays and were in some cases unsuccessful. Many calls were also prematurely disconnected.[23]

The 911 operators and FDNY dispatchers had no information about either the location or the magnitude of the impact zone and were therefore unable to provide information as fundamental as whether callers were above or below the fire. Because the operators were not informed of NYPD Aviation's determination of the impossibility of rooftop rescues from the Twin Towers on that day they could not knowledgeably answer when callers asked whether to go up or down. In most instances, therefore, the operators and the FDNY dispatchers relied on standard operating procedures for high-rise fires. Civilians should stay low. Remain where they are and wait for emergency personnel to reach them. This advice was given to callers from the North-Tower for locations both above and below the impact zone. Fire Chiefs told us that the evacuation of tens of thousands of people from skyscrapers can create many new problems, especially for individuals who are disabled or in poor health. Many of the injuries after the 1993 bombing occurred during the evacuation.[24]

Although the guidance to stay in place may seem understandable in cases of conventional high-rise fires FDNY Chiefs in the North-Tower lobby determined at once all building occupants should attempt to evacuate immediately. By 8:57A.M. FDNY Chiefs had instructed the PAPD and building personnel to evacuate the South-Tower as well because of the magnitude of the damage caused by the first plane's impact. These critical decisions were not conveyed to 911 operators or to FDNY dispatchers. Departing from protocol several operators told callers that they could break windows and several operators advised callers to evacuate if they could. Civilians who called the Port Authority police desk located at 5 WTC were advised to leave if they could.[25]

Most civilians who were not obstructed from proceeding began evacuating without waiting for instructions over the intercom system. Some remained to wait for help as advised by 911 operators. Others simply continued to work or delayed collecting personal items, but in many cases were urged to leave by others. Some Port Authority civilian employees remained on various upper floors to help civilians who were trapped and to assist in the evacuation. While evacuating, some civilians had trouble reaching the exits because of damage caused by the impact. Some were confused by deviations in the increasingly crowded stairwells and impeded by doors that appeared to be locked but were jammed by debris or shifting that resulted from the impact of the plane. Despite these obstacles the evacuation was relatively calm and orderly.[26]

It is not known whether the order by the FDNY to evacuate the South-Tower was received by the deputy-fire-safety director making announcements there. However, at approximately 9:02, less than a minute before the building was hit, an instruction over the South-Tower's public-address system advised civilians, generally, they could begin an orderly evacuation if conditions warranted. Like the earlier advice to remain in place it did not correspond to any prewritten emergency instruction.[27]

# Henny Dingman
## Chief Dispatcher Fire Dispatch Operations, Headquarters 9 Metrotech Brooklyn

On the morning of 9/11 I was at a golf outing in Silver Lake Golf Course on Staten Island. We were one of the last groups going out when we saw TV reports of a plane hitting one of the World Trade Center buildings. We yelled to the groups at the tee to come inside then heard the explosion of the second plane hitting the building. People out on the golf course said they saw the second plane fly over low and wobbly. Next thing we knew the word was out 'Total Recall'. We all headed out to firehouses or wherever we were assigned.

> **We had a Staten Island fire company respond with the mutual-aid-company to be a their seeing eye dog while responding, especially with engines because the FDNY couplings, hose threads and hydrant threads, were not compatible with the New Jersey fittings.**

I figured the best move would be to go to the Staten Island Dispatcher's office which was five minutes from the golf course. I got there and oversaw what was going on. We started by getting a count on what units responded to the World Trade Center site. I spoke with Deputy Chief Teddy Goldfarb in Staten Island's 8th Division. He had a pre-plan for initiating 'Mutual-Aid' with New Jersey Fire Departments and getting fire companies from outside the city to help. Chief Goldfarb used to teach 'Fire Science' in Union County New Jersey had this relationship and said, "We will use them." We contacted the Union County fire department and other fire departments in New Jersey, and they agreed to send fire companies to Staten Island.

Battalion Chief Richie Olivieri was the FDNY Operations liaison with the Communications Office. He worked with me in the Dispatchers office and communicated with field units. I started looking at holes in fire protection and filling empty firehouses with mutual-aid-companies. We had a Staten Island fire company respond with the mutual-aid-company to be a their seeing eye dog while responding, especially with engines because the FDNY couplings, hose threads and hydrant threads, were not compatible with the New Jersey fittings. Doing this provided decent fire protection coverage in Staten Island.

There were no Staff-Chiefs in Fire Department Operation Center (FDOC), so we were making decisions on our own. I talked with the Director of Dispatch Operations John Porcelli and Deputy Directors Joseph Higgins and Ivan Goldberg who were in the Manhattan Fire Dispatch Office in Central Park. And with me showing up in Staten Island we had a Chief Dispatcher in each borough which worked out well.

One thing we got going with Deputy Chief Goldfarb, along with EMS Officers, was to dispatch a load of Emergency Medical Service personnel and firefighters to the Staten Island Ferry terminal to receive victims. All three hospitals on Staten Island were ready to go. Everyone was surprised when no victims came. Not one.

NYPD responded very quickly. Secured our Dispatcher center with a full lockdown status making sure nobody could get in without ID. We even had a couple of national guardsmen on the street with NYPD. But at my level we were not communicating to a large degree with the NYPD.

The street alarm-box system and the voice-alarms communications in the firehouses continued to work because of our own backup emergency power. When power is lost in an area the voice-alarm battery system

53

and power backups for the alarm circuits power put out the required electricity. Which helped because, the cellphone sites were so overloaded you couldn't use your cellphone. The only guaranteed way for a civilian to get help was using a street alarm box.

There were a lot of fire companies calling up our dispatcher's office volunteering to go to the site. The Chief and Dispatch Personnel at the Communications Office told them to stand-fast in their firehouses and only respond to local alarms. After the buildings came down one company thanked us for not sending them.

Every borough Dispatcher Office received calls from people still in the buildings asking for guidance. We told them what we always did "Stay where you are. Let us know how you are doing, and we'll relay it to the fire department units. If you have smoke put wet towels or something at the bottom of the door. And keep the doors closed to separate you from the fire." These were the—Standard-Guidance procedures—we believed would protect them.

After 9/11 the legal division listened to all the tapes and heard us giving these directions. They were afraid of future lawsuits and made changes to our procedures. Now we must notify the Fire Department's 'On Scene Incident-Commander' and ask, "What should we tell the person who's trapped to do?" That became official procedure not long after 9/11. We use these procedures now. We also came up with a form that lists the time we got the call, who we told at the scene, and when the Incident-Commander got back to us with specific information such as 'we checked out apartment two-John, that condition is taken care of' and whatever. Then we update the form with the information. Sometimes we have missing-person notification incidents. We give this information to the Incident-Commander with the missing-person's apartment number to be checked and request to know if the missing person has already gone. These procedures ensured every notification gets checked and all the callers on the scene are contacted. If, due to a high volume of callers there are delays in checking apartments and they couldn't check out an apartment promptly the dispatcher will contact the Incident-Commander again to get a status on each of the searches.

During the day when I wasn't involved in Staten Island issues I was listening to Brooklyn and Manhattan dispatch communications. Staten Island fire-duty was minimal that day. Another thing there was only one 10/45 code (report of a civilian deceased or seriously injured at the fire/emergency scene) citywide for about 10 days after 9/11. When you consider how thin our resources were that's amazing. We had mutual-aid-companies in the city for days because of all the destroyed apparatus. We were pushed to the limits. I don't know if people were more careful but thank God, we didn't get anything major or significant. Some 'All-Hands-Fires' (routine fire handled with initial units responding on the alarm) and an occasional multiple alarm, but none of great magnitude.

All the people of New York City did so much to help us get through it. The 911 attack brought the city together. Got the whole nation together for a bit there. It was a good feeling. And it was such a tragic thing. Which you know, is kind of strange.

I stayed in the Staten Island office until one in the morning then went home and slept for four hours. In the morning I went to the Manhattan Communication Office instead of going to Headquarters at 9 Metrotech where I was normally assigned to have a Chief Dispatcher present in the Manhattan Communication Office on the morning of September 12th.

The atmosphere in the Manhattan Communication Office was somber. We were going through the list of who was missing and who was unaccounted for. I knew a lot of these people. It was quiet…. solemn. We were in a state of shock.

Regarding giving directions to people who called the Manhattan Dispatchers office that day. I listened to all the tapes of the calls. And we truly believed the firefighters were going to get them out. We never had a building come down like that. We were telling the people the firefighters will get you out of there. That was the only guidance to give that made sense. Don't panic. Try to keep yourself separated from the fire by closing doors. These procedures worked time and time again in the past. People talking to us said "You're probably the last person I'm ever going to be talking to." Yeah, there were some very emotional calls. "I have to get home for my kids and my family." Some tear jerkers. I think everybody did well. In Manhattan a new person was on the radio. He was doing fine, and they gave him frequent breaks. It was so overwhelming. We had the right people in the right places.

I'm working as a peer-counselor now talking to people about 9/11 and it's been good. We had mass causalities before like the 'Happy Land' fire. When you get something like that as a dispatcher you have to think 'Could I have done something better?' During the World Trade Center attack, I don't think we could have done more than we did. It's difficult to hear those people in that situation and absorb those emotional impacts from people in distress. I say, "As long as you know we did our best. That's as good as it will be."

I was overseeing operations in the Manhattan Dispatcher Communication Office doing 14 hour-tours every day for the next week or more. Making sure we had adequate fire coverage and talking with our people. Acting like a counselor with the counseling unit telling them "Hey, we did nothing wrong." But they felt bad because they were telling people the firefighters would be getting them out. We believed it! We didn't tell them anything wrong. Who knew the building was going to come down. And they had a good chance to be saved if the buildings hadn't come down.

After a while we went back to our normal staffing which was 12-hour tours. We didn't have a problem get-

**All the people of New York City did so much to help us get through it. The 911 attack brought the city together. Got the whole nation together for a bit there. It was a good feeling. And it was such a tragic thing. Which you know, is kind of strange.**

ting personnel. People showed up and some called up "What do you want me to do?"

In downtown Manhattan the communication line repair-crews were out in full force assessing and repairing communications wires and street-alarm-boxes circuits that were knocked out. Phillip Berger who was one of the supervisors of these repair crews died from a 9/11 related cancer.

After 9/11 we talked about how EMS and FDNY were on different computer dispatch systems. Medical alarms requiring an engine company response were handled in a normal manner from our dispatch office. It would have been much better if we could have communicated with their personnel in the Fire Department Operations Center (FDOC). That was all solved afterwards. Now EMS has Chief Officers in FDOC 24/7 which facilitates communications with our dispatcher's offices better.

Within communications we came up with a new process for a major event. Either the Director or one of the Deputy Directors would go to the borough where the incident was. The second Director would go to FDOC. We used it couple of times. Once was when the plane crashed on East 72 street in Manhattan, and another was the plane on the Hudson.

I didn't go to the site for over a year. We were working so hard. And I didn't want to look at it. In the years afterward on 9/11 I went to the Headquarters ceremony. Now I go to the 57th Battalion mass with my son, he's in Ladder 102.

Unfortunately, so many people who worked at the site for months are sick now and it's a shame. They were exposed to everything and with some of them it isn't being recognized as job related. Dispatch Personnel's PTSD was recognized as a 9/11 related illness. I never filed anything. I've had four o'clock in the morning dreams. Woke me up right out of a dead sleep in a cold sweat. I dreamt planes were pressuring me. Crashing in front of me. Getting closer and closer and finally crash right where I was. They are so weird. So strange. So realistic for a dream. ❖

## Richard Olivieri
### Battalion Chief Battalion 23

I was temporarily on light duty assigned to Division 8 in Staten Island on 9/11. As I pulled into the quarters parking lot, I heard on my car radio there was a smoke condition at 1-World Trade Center. When I entered quarters, I asked the house watch (on duty firefighter who is responsible to turn out the companies when alarms are transmitted and greet any visitors) "What's going on?" He said, "A plane just crashed into the World Trade Center." I said, "What are you watching a King Kong movie?" He said, "No Chief really, a plane crashed into the World Trade Center." I instantly ran up the stairs to the Division office and saw a couple of Chiefs watching the news on the television. Chief Ted Goldfarb the 8th Division Commander came in from home as soon as he heard the first reports of the attack. We thought the first plane was an accident until the second plane hit and then we all realized this was no accident.

Chief Goldfarb took command of the situation. Everyone was reporting into the Division on 'Recall' and wanted to go to Ground Zero. Chief Goldfarb said, "Not everybody can go there." But some officers and firefighters didn't listen and left for Ground Zero. That was a weird thing. Firefighters not obeying the Chief's orders because they felt they had to do something about this awful occurrence.

Chief Goldfarb knew I had worked the past last two years on the Starfire project to improve dispatch performance with units and ordered me to take command of Staten Island's Communications Office and find out what was needed to provide fire protection resources for Staten Island, Manhattan, and the World Trade Center site. There were no precedents or procedures for doing this. The whole occurrence was something new for everyone. I drove from the 8th Division to the Communications Office and informed the Chief Dispatcher I was going to be in command. An odd thing was in the 24 hours I was there no serious fires were reported in Staten Island. This shows you in a crisis everyone is focused on one thing and nothing else happens. Phone calls were coming in constantly. People asking, "My

daughter or son is in Manhattan what do we do?" I said "tell them to stay where they are. Don't go south towards lower Manhattan." My daughter worked on 34th Street in the Empire State Building. She called me numerous times to find out what she and her co-workers should do. I told her "Stay where you are, don't start traveling now." There were a lot of things happening. My son was on the ferry going to work when he saw the plane hit. When he got off the ferry he was in shock and didn't know where to go and walked with numerous people over the Manhattan Bridge to Brooklyn. They all feared the buildings would be falling on them. He walked along with another man who was on his way home in Brooklyn who took him into his home. My son stayed with him and his family until the end of the day when it was safe, and he was able to find transportation home. I didn't know where he was the whole day and worried, he might have been a casualty. Luckily, I heard from all members of my family who were safe.

Chief Goldfarb knew a lot of Chiefs in New Jersey and made phone calls to have New Jersey fire apparatus respond in Staten Island since we had a lot of Staten Island companies responding to the World Trade Center. When the New Jersey companies came over there was no way for our dispatchers to communicate with them. Their radios were on different frequencies. Some of the Staten Island companies could respond at the same time with them. The problem was how was a Staten Island unit going to tell a New Jersey unit what to do since the radios weren't compatible? I came up with a suggestion of switching one firefighter with a handie-talkie to ride on each apparatus. So an FDNY firefighter rode on a New Jersey apparatus and a New Jersey firefighter rode on a Staten Island apparatus which helped. These tactics were unprecedented, New Jersey companies working in Staten Island. There was no pre-planning or procedures on how to do this. At least twenty New Jersey fire companies were available to respond to alarms in Staten Island with many others standing by near the Communications Office.

It was hectic. Many questions were coming up. One report said a thousand people were killed in the attack at the World Trade Center and body bags were needed. I called FDNY headquarters and told them who I was and said, "I want to immediately order a thousand body bags." Headquarters said, "We'll order them right now." None of them were used since everyone in those buildings was disintegrated.

Since I was on light duty, I didn't get to Ground Zero that day. I spent forty hours straight at the Communications Office and didn't know when I should leave when to my surprise a Chief reported in to relieve me and I went home.

I spent the next days working on light duty in Division 8 scheduling duty assignments at Ground Zero and ascertaining what equipment was damaged and needed replacement. I was scheduled to report to the medical office the following week and when I reported there, I

## Retired Chiefs were giving orders which was unprecedented. It was a crazy day.

insisted on being placed on full duty effective immediately. The doctor at the medical office didn't hesitate I received full duty.

I went to the World Trade Center site the next day for a 24-hour tour. A carpool of Chiefs from Division 8 was going to Ground Zero. Everyone was on edge. That first tour was actually scary. We were all very jittery. You didn't know what you were going to see. It was like a war zone. Cops were lined up around the perimeter and the streets were deserted. I couldn't believe the destruction.

I worked at a Command Post with Chief John Casey. Firefighters were searching and finding body parts. Everything had to be recorded when and where the body part or personal items were recovered. Retired Chiefs were giving orders which was unprecedented. It was a crazy day. In the weeks following the attack things were done that weren't in our normal procedures or training. Our work schedule even changed to an ABC chart with three 24-hour shifts one shift in the firehouse, a day off and then one shift at the site.

A lot of guys were in shock and exhausted from working down there. On occasions a Chief would start tearing up myself included saying "I can't do this anymore let's go take a break." It was hard. I thought about my good friend Chief Jerry Barbara who was killed in the first collapse. I went to see his wife. I was so choked up I couldn't say anything to her. It was so sad. Going back after the first day was overwhelming. Seeing body parts all day long affects you. It has to. You're never the same after that.

I remember a football player and a hockey player coming over and saying, "Do you need a hand?" I said, "No thanks." They weren't in the way, and they gave a little moral support. The actor Steve Buscemi came down and searched. He helped out. When I met him, I said "You were a firefighter in 55 Engine." He said "Yes, I worked there with Faust I'm an actor now." Firefighter Faust was one of the first firefighters killed at the WTC site.

## Going back after the first day was overwhelming. Seeing body parts all day long affects you. It has to. You're never the same after that.

You couldn't stop people from coming into your area of operations. There were fathers retired from the job looking for their sons. You were not going to say you can't go in there. We did not have total accountability. Team assignments were given to me. When they wanted relief. They told me at the Command Post. I was making sure I knew where the guys were, and everything was reported. Construction guys were working all around us. There weren't many accidents which was surprising with all the noise going on from active heavy equipment moving around lifting large pieces of heavy steel.

The people on top of the chain of command in the FDNY like Commissioner Feehan and Chief Ganci were killed. They were experienced Chiefs replaced by new Chiefs under extreme continuous stress trying their best. I think there were no real serious injuries to firefighters because we had a lot of Chiefs coordinating at the site. Chiefs like myself and John Casey made sure not too many guys went out on the pile at one time, and they had the right equipment. That was our job. To make sure those firefighters did not get hurt. There was a lot of safety in mind especially after what we went through losing 343 firefighters. We we're not going to lose anymore doing searches.

## The memory of the firefighters who were killed made me think about how important it was to do the job right.

The memory of the firefighters who were killed made me think about how important it was to do the job right. Making sure those firefighters search the right way like they were supposed to. That's the vision I had. Knowing the names of the firefighters that were killed made me think "We got to get this done right."

I meet up with a group of retired firefighters weekly and we were talking about how after 9/11 the NYPD made cards with a barcode on the back for retired cops that read 'Actively retired'. It's an oxymoron as far as I'm concerned. How can you be actively retired? Those cards show you're retired but could go to work. I thought it was a good idea. Something we should have.

Some guys have guilt myself as well and I think 'Why was I on light duty and not down there too?' The biggest impact is how the hell did we lose thousands of people and 343 firefighters? And it may happen again. That's the thing I'm really worried about. Not for me but for my children and grandchildren. Every year on 9/11 I go to the 23rd Battalion in Staten Island to be with all the guys I used to work in that firehouse and hear the names read of the fallen from 9/11. I haven't missed a year. I do it because it's a way of acknowledging that we're not forgetting. That's how I cope with it. ❖

## The 911 Commission Report

The 911 Commission commented on the protocols in place on 9/11/2001 for the FAA (Federal Aviation Administration) and NORAD (North American Aerospace Defense Command) to respond to a presumed hijacking:

• The hijacked aircraft would be readily identifiable and would not attempt to disappear.

• There would be time to address the problem through the appropriate FAA and NORAD chains of command.

• And the hijacking would take the traditional form: that is, it would not be a suicide hijacking designed to convert the aircraft into a guided missile.

On the morning of 9/11, the existing protocol was unsuited in every respect for what was about to happen.[28]

Regarding military notification and response, the 911 Commission went on to report: Boston Center did not follow the protocol in seeking military assistance through the prescribed chain of command. In addition to notifications within the FAA, Boston Center took the initiative, at 8:34 A.M. to contact the military through the FAA's Cape Cod facility. The center also tried to contact a former alert site in Atlantic City, unaware it had been phased out. At 8:37:52 A.M. Boston Center reached NEADS. (Northeast Air Defense Sector) This was the first notification received by the military at any level that American 11 had been hijacked. F-15 fighters were scrambled at 8:46 A.M. from Otis Air Force Base. But NEADS did not know where to send the alerted fighter aircraft and the officer directing the fighters pressed for more information. "I don't know where I'm scrambling these guys to. I need a direction, a destination." Because the hijackers had turned off the plane's transponder and the plane couldn't be readily located. NEADS personnel spent the next minutes searching their radar scopes for the 'Primary Radar-Return.' American 11 struck the North-Tower at 8:46 A.M. Shortly after 8:50 A.M. while NEADS personnel were still trying to locate the flight, word reached them that a plane had hit the World Trade Center. In summary, NEADS received notice of the hijacking nine minutes before it struck the North-Tower. That nine minutes' notice before impact was the most the military would receive of any of the four hijackings.[29]

The first indication that the NORAD air defenders had of the second hijacked aircraft, 'United 175,' came in a phone call from New York Center to NEADS at 9:03 A.M. The notice came at about the time the plane was hitting the South-Tower. By 9:08 A.M. the mission crew commander at NEADS learned of the second explosion at the World Trade Center and decided against holding the fighters in military airspace away from Manhattan.[30]

Clarifying the record, the 911 Commission goes on to state: We do not believe that the true picture of that morning reflects discredit on the operational personnel at

NEADS or FAA facilities. NEADS commanders and officers actively sought out information and made the best judgments they could based on what they knew. Individual FAA controllers, facility managers, and Command Center managers thought outside the box in recommending a nationwide alert, in ground-stopping local traffic, and, ultimately, in deciding to land all aircraft and executing that unprecedented order flawlessly.[31]

On the national level the 911 Commission found: Most federal agencies learned about the crash in New York from CNN. Within the FAA, the administrator, Jane Garvey, and her acting deputy, Monte Belger, had not been told of a confirmed hijacking before they learned from television a plane had crashed.[32]

When they learned a second plane had struck the World Trade Center nearly everyone in the White House told us they immediately knew it was not an accident. The Secret Service initiated several security enhancements around the White House complex. The officials who issued these orders did not know there were additional hijacked aircraft, or that one such aircraft was in-route to Washington. These measures were precautionary steps taken because of the strikes in New York.[33]

About 9:45 A.M. the President told the Vice President: "Sounds like we have a minor war going on here, I heard about the Pentagon. We're at war . . . somebody's going to pay." About this time, 'Card' the lead Secret Service agent, the President's military aide and the pilot were conferring on a possible destination for Air Force One. The Secret Service agent strongly felt the situation in Washington was too unstable for the President to return there and 'Card' agreed. The President strongly wanted to return to Washington and only grudgingly agreed to go elsewhere. The issue was still undecided when the President conferred with the Vice President at about the time Air Force One was taking off. The Vice President recalled urging the President not to return to Washington. Air Force One departed at about 9:54 A. M. without any fixed destination. The objective was to get up in the air—as fast and as high as possible—and then decide where to go.[34]

The 911 Commission reported how the details of what happened on the morning of September 11 are complex, but they play out a simple theme. NORAD and the FAA were unprepared for the type of attacks launched against the United States on September 11, 2001. They struggled, under difficult circumstances, to improvise a home-land defense against an unprecedented challenge they had never before encountered and had never trained to meet. At 10:02 that morning, an assistant to the mission crew commander at NORAD's Northeast Air Defense Sector in Rome, New York, was working with his colleagues on the floor of the command center. In a moment of reflection, he was recorded remarking that "This is a new type of war."[35]

# CHAPTER 4
# Recalled to Duty

There have been three 'Recall to Duty' events I have responded to during my career in the FDNY. One for the 1973 firefighters strike, another for the 1977 Blackout and 9/11. All of these Recalls were announced over public radio and news stations and required all 'off-duty firefighters' to report to duty immediately.

The Chief of Department directed issuance of a recall of all off-duty members which was broadcast by public media outlets and dispatched across FDNY radio channels. Thousands of off-duty firefighters and EMS personnel left their families to help the city and the FDNY. The initial recall order did not include specific directions on where firefighters were to report. Recalled firefighters responded to multiple locations, including directly to the incident area, the firehouse closest to their location at the time of the recall, their own firehouse, or to recall staging areas which were established and communicated later in the morning.[36]

## Rick Gimbl
### Firefighter Haz-Mat 1

I was home when my wife called and said, "Turn on the TV." I saw the news about the World Trade Center burning. Got dressed and drove to my firehouse Haz-Mat Company 1. As soon as I got their Special Operations Command had a Battalion car to take me and three other firefighters from the Haz-Mat company who also came in on 'Recall' to the site. There were no spare

## Thousands of off-duty firefighters and EMS personnel left their families to help the city and the FDNY.

masks in firehouse. We had our bunker gear. The mood was solemn in the car, quiet, with little talking. 1-World Trade Center, the second collapse, occurred a short time before we got there.

The dark-gray cloud of building debris was still coming down from above. Falling all around us. It was horrific. I knew the area from having been to the World Trade Center buildings several times for alarms. Now, I had no idea where I was or what street I was on. The destruction created a totally confusing scene. People running all over the place. Running away from us. We were going in. Initially I don't remember what we did. I tried grabbing a firefighter getting away from the collapse, but I couldn't grab him fast enough. He just kept running out. It was a maze. Something unfathomable.

Being in Haz-Mat and going on 'Special Operations' responses I've been to a lot of weird calls in the city. But never like this. You had to put your head together. Think small thoughts. Go in and do what you had to do. Dead people were lying all over the rubble. All I can say is it was so horrific you had to tell yourself 'Keep your head straight. Don't get caught up with this. Keep going.' None of us turned around. We all went in. We didn't know what to do but we went forward. We tried to find our unit and couldn't. We kept going until we met a Chief with some other firefighters we knew. There wasn't a Command Post. It was confusing. The low dark gray dust-filled air limited our visibility and was still falling all over us. We could see 7-World Trade Center lit up with fire. We were thinking on how we could get there and help put this fire out when a Chief yelled to us "Forget it. You can't put it out. Let it go." The Chief was right. We had no apparatus and no water in the hydrants.

We kept walking through the twisted rubble in two-feet-high piles of ash. Saw a lot of destroyed fire apparatus, all kinds of vehicles. You would think it was a Hollywood set. I was in awe. Couldn't believe what was happening. A lot of ladder-trucks lay on their side bent

and twisted. Crushed engine-pumpers all over the place. It was horrific. Words cannot explain it believe me. The more we looked for live victims the more we found exposed dead bodies. There was no hope. Most were probably civilians who jumped. A total chaotic site. Not because of what we were doing. It was the way it was. Cars on fire all around. 7-World Trade Center's upper floors burning as plain as day. It felt like all hope was gone.

We began walking across this high wide pile and when we got to the other side there was a park bench. I sat down on the bench to take a break and saw a Scott mask frame without a bottle all bent up. I don't know why. I leaned over picked it up and saw it was marked as Haz-Mat Company 1's. What made me sit there and then pick that up? It was so weird. It rocked the hell out of me—just amazing. In my firehouse we lost all our guys: Haz-Mat 1 lost 11 and Squad 288 lost 8. It took me two years to even talk about it.

I have no recollection what happened after we sat on that bench. It's totally out of my mind. Time passed. We found a couple of tools laying around and a stokes basket. Put everything in it and started across the pile searching for victims. We met three other guys in my unit. They came in by themselves and were at the same spot. An amazing fluke. How we got together in a 16-acre area that had been destroyed and in all this falling-gray-dust and smoke and other responders. It was weird how we met up. All trying to find our rig.

There wasn't much conversation. I don't know how to explain it. You're living through something we never experienced before. And we'd been through a lot of multi-causality accidents, emergencies, and fires. I worked in Rescue 4 when we lost one of our guys who was my locker partner, and it was nothing like that. I can't explain it. I lost a lot of hours of memory. Have no recollection until 4:00 P.M. when I saw our USAR (Urban Search and Rescue) New York City-Task Force 1 which I was on setting up a base camp. I worked with them.

At 5:00 P.M. I was with a guy from Squad 1 when we heard this loud noise and thought 'Oh shit, another plane's coming in.' Looked up. Saw windows popping-out of 7-World Trade Center as it was collapsing. Pushing out a huge dark cloud of smoke from where the building used to stand. We dove to the ground as this menacing debris-cloud came right at us. Put our coats over our heads. Laid down right where we were. And

the collapse cloud stopped right before us. Never hit us. Weird. A lot of weird stuff. We got up and the building was gone. Completely collapsed. A pile of smoking rubble left.

From there we went back to setting up with the USAR team. As the night came on, I was trying to find a place to lay down and take a break when I found a phone, called my wife, and told her I was okay. That's when I realized what was going on around us. Military people were controlling intersections all over the place. I thought 'Oh my God what the hell is going on?'

There wasn't much conversation. I don't know how to explain it. You're living through something we never experienced before. And we'd been through a lot of multi-causality accidents, emergencies, and fires.

I don't remember eating anything. It's totally blacked out. Somehow, I got back to Haz-Mat then slept at the firehouse. You have to understand. I've been through firefighters being killed but it wasn't the same as this.

I slept for a little while in the firehouse. Awoke on Wednesday the 12th. Went back to the site. This time I reported into a Command Post on West Street and went to work with groups of firefighters and officers searching for someone alive. Finding only the remains of victims in the pile. I wasn't with anyone from SOC (Special Operations Command). I was in a crew with firefighters

from different companies. We were all trained to work in a confined space and to search through collapse rubble. I worked on a bucket-brigade with them sifting through the rubble. Yeah, that was Wednesday the 12th.

Nighttime came went back to the firehouse and slept. On the morning of Thursday, the 13th got in a Battalion car and went back to the site. I was with SOC firefighters. We worked as teams and did the same thing we did on Wednesday the best we could. I can say that because I told it to the wives I was involved with. I believed these guys might be still alive. There might be a void someplace we have to get to. For some reason I believed. I had faith. 'Yeah, we could.' Maybe because I worked at other collapse sites where we found people. I found a girl when her hand came through some rubble—right where I was kneeling and digging—and she lived. I had a feeling we're going to find people still alive. But it never came true. The wives' husbands were never found. None of our guys were found.

There's a picture of the firefighters in Squad 288 coming up to the site. You never saw a firefighter's face like that. You could tell by their faces they knew this ain't good. The whole crew didn't survive.

The SOC van took us back to sleep at the Haz-Mat firehouse and on the next day Friday the 14th the same thing happened. Woke up. Got in a van. Drove to the site. Got there and kept looking, digging, and searching.

A lot of memories of what I did are lost. I found a few dead victims in the debris on the first day but after that there wasn't many. Though we kept digging and digging. Found one or two. But I have no recollection of what I did when I found them. This is what's been both-

ering me and why I had to seek counseling. I couldn't remember. And I wanted to remember. I wanted to know what I did. I wanted to know why. Why was I saved. That's my guys I worked with for 18 years. Why was I saved? It was bad. It was very bad—really bad. That night the SOC van again took us back to sleep at the Haz-Mat firehouse.

On Saturday morning I was helping the covering Captain in Haz-Mat record what occurred in the Company Journal when he said, "Look you've got to go home." I said, "I really don't want to go home. I want to find our brothers." This Captain insisted "Rick, you've got to go home. I'll go home with you because I want to see John Crisci's wife." I said, "Okay, fine." John was my neighbor. We carpooled together going to work. I drove in my car and the Captain followed me home. That trip was horrible. I was crying half the way home. Seeing the people with signs and American flags flying on the bridges and roadways. It was a bad time. So, the Captain followed me home. Met my wife. Then I took him to Lieutenant John Crisci's house to see his wife. Later, since there's three of our widows living near me, I was assigned to these wives. To visit them and see what they needed. I never went back searching the pile after that.

I was on medical leave before 9/11 happened. I went back to the medical desk on Monday. Got therapy approval to get my ankle fixed. Spent a week on that. Went back to full-duty. I had to get back. We were decimated. I didn't care how I felt. I just wanted full-duty.

The 'anthrax attacks' occurred one week after 9/11 on September 18th. We worked the ABC chart, 24 on 24 off. On our time off we didn't go home. We were training on anthrax releases. People were complaining about powders, and we were responding. We found 'anthrax' in the NBC news building where the first letter containing anthrax arrived in the city. I was working in Haz-Mat that day and when testing for it we found it was positive.

This caused a whole new big thing. We formed the 'Hammer-Team Task Force.' The task force consisted of a Haz-Mat firefighter and a cop. We responded to anthrax suspected incidents and there were many of them. We had to be fully encapsuled in 'Level A' protective suits that you couldn't get out of without assistance. Enter the suspected contaminated area. Find the substance and test it. These Hammer-Teams got busier and bigger. So now on our off days we were training for and responding to suspected anthrax releases. My wife says I was home—one night a week—for five months. Working 90-hours a week. That's how busy it was.

I couldn't put it in my mind. We lost all these guys. They never came out. Helping the widows was hard. One wife was having a rough time. She had a two-year old plus three other kids. In the beginning I visited all three wives once a week. I sat there with them. Talked with them. Trying to give them whatever help I could. We were working so many hours. After a while I didn't see them for two weeks at a time. Being with the widows helped me somewhat because we love to help people. That was a benefit in a way. It kept me a little sane helping. I wanted to help them as much as I could.

We had some tough times. We found the remains of one of our guys and had the funeral. I was the liaison to get things set up. Finding a funeral home. Working with the funeral director to get a casket. It's what all of us were doing.

## There was no question of getting up. Going to work. Doing what needed to be done. You did it.

The next time I went back to the site I was working my normal tour in Haz-Mat and responded for a gas-leak emergency right in front of what was left of 7-World Trade Center. We mitigated the situation. Stayed a little bit. And went back in-service. It was a clear pile. No huge steel remains of walls sticking up. No fires burning. A low pile of rubble. I don't know where that bench was. Never saw it again. My memory of it was dream-like. And when I was looking around, I had a brief thought 'Was I dreaming this?'

What kept me going was the brotherhood. We had to find our people. And family of course. I hate to say this but mainly I wanted to be with my brothers. There was no question of getting up. Going to work. Doing what needed to be done. You did it.

But when it slowed down then it started to hit you. Working the long hours on the ABC chart we tried to

keep ourselves somewhat happy. I like smoking cigars, so I made everybody smoke a cigar with me and have a picture of that too. My firehouse was solemn. Quiet the whole time you're working.

We had a couple of new people coming into Haz-Mat Company 1 and we were doing a lot of training with them. Showing them the new testing equipment. How things work and how to operate in suspected-contaminated-environments. The city needed us to respond to these events and protect them from the effects of the anthrax.

Mostly it was the remaining members of our Haz-Mat company who did the work. Then at night—there were the nightmares. You'd hear firefighters in the bunkroom screaming in the middle of the night. It was a bad time man, bad time. You didn't want to go to sleep. I was afraid to go to sleep. I'm sure everybody else was too. We didn't sleep much during those many months of working 90 hours in a week. We had guest come in. The cast from the Sopranos TV 'woke us up' and made us laugh. They kept our minds off what we were going through and were the first ones that made us laugh in the firehouse. We didn't laugh much anymore.

People were advising us to retire because we couldn't freeze the overtime money for our pension and retire later. That wasn't allowed. I wanted to spend a couple more years on the job. My daughter was in college. I knew we would never make that kind of money again, so I retired earlier than I wanted to.

The only thing that makes me feel guilty all the time is I'm alive and these guys aren't. 'Why was I saved?' I get to enjoy my family and even to this day when I see my grandkids I always think 'Gee those guys didn't get to see their grandkids and I'm seeing mine.' I think about that all the time. I can deal with it now. I've had good counseling. I knew Chief Ray Brown and he became my counselor. I'm happy about that because he helped me through it where the other counselors didn't. For a time, I quit going to those other counselors and my wife said, "You've got to get back for counseling," and I did. My wife stood by me the whole time. She's still with me and I thank her to this day. And I thank Ray Brown.

In the years afterwards when I was retired and lived in New York I went back to my firehouse every 9/11. I would never miss it. My daughter would meet me there and visit with me. To see your brothers and being with the brothers is the best thing. I have to be with my brothers. I'm living in North Carolina now. I meet up with the brothers down here on 9/11. The church gives us a service and from there we go to a college with a 9/11 monument made with steel from the site on campus and have another service there. I would never, ever, not be with my brothers on 9/11. Sometimes I don't want to do it. But you have to. When I get there and I'm with the brothers the pain goes away. You feel more relieved. I know it's hard to explain but being with the brothers— makes the difference. ❖

## John Casey – Division 3 Commander

We kept contacting department headquarters for more orders or information and instructing units to stand-fast in quarters. Some of the firefighters who came in on 'Recall' ignored our orders to stand-fast and went to the attack site on their own. That's the way it was. They were frustrated seeing this damn thing on television and wanted to do something. We knew we lost hundreds of firefighters along with maybe, thousands of people.

Finally, at 5:30 P.M. we got the word from headquarters "Go down and start relieving those still on scene from this morning." We used the spare chief-car to drive in. Officers commandeered city buses and loaded them full of firefighters. If I could do over again, I would've kept a roster of everyone responding at that time. God help the ones that were down there and survived.

So many firefighters came in from home and all the civilians and different agencies. As we're responding to the site on the West Side highway people in the streets were holding up signs and cheering us. We never experienced stuff like this. What the heck are they cheering us for. The guys down there are dead. It was unbelievable that early in the evening so many people lined the streets to do that.

Arriving at the scene was coming into utter chaos. How do you control this situation? We're used to pretty good control at a job even at a major 5th alarm. Everything is well controlled. Even though people may think its chaos. You know where your people are and what they're doing. We roll into this site suddenly we're getting covered with that dark-gray dust and powder. Sixteen acres of destruction was unreal. There was nothing to compare it to.

7-World Trade Center had already collapsed. I worked downtown in the 1st Battalion for many years and to see it like this—oh my God. Rigs crushed. Walking on structural steel columns that paved the streets.

I reported into a Command Post on West Street near Vesey Street and was assigned to supervise all operations across from the World Financial Center Building on West Street. We're searching through the debris with columns of smoke from the fires burning beneath the steel rising around us. No one is finding any victims. Buildings on the perimeter near Liberty Street are still actively burning. We're almost in shock thinking, 'How are we going to do this? This is beyond our capability.' We needed cranes to pick up the large-heavy-steel. You certainly couldn't move this steel without the right equipment.

The only way you could get through the rubble was to start from the perimeter. Move along the edges of the steel and keep working your way in. We did that all night long. I remember thinking 'I'm going to fall off this steel and wind up breaking my legs.' but well, hey, this is what you got to do. The hell with it. You fall, you fall.

I'll always remember how some of the steel columns penetrated the street. Like an arrow driven right in standing tall. We kept looking for any signs of victims. As it turned out by early evening there was nobody left who survived.

© New York City Fire Department

On the morning of September 12th this massive 16-acre area. That you could hardly walk in with fires burning around you. Organization was slowly developing from the chaos. It wasn't perfectly organized but firefighters knew what they had to do and were doing it. Staying together. Looking after each other. You thought 'How the hell are we going to clean this place up.' Holy geez, look at the destruction. Oh my God. We're at war now. Who did this? We knew it was probably the same Muslims from 1993 who targeted the Trade Center. Back then we thought that was the most horrific thing that the fire department would ever see. And look what happened. Something worse.

We left at noontime in the 3rd Division car very tired. I can't remember eating any food only drinking some water. We drove back to quarters and then I went home. I had tried calling my wife, but the cellphone service was still out. I felt bad that I hadn't talked with her earlier. I was still very upset. Shocked and tired. I went to bed and slept till the next morning then back into the Division on Thursday, September 13th. ❖

# Eileen Sullivan
## Paramedic, EMS Station 43
## (promoted to Lieutenant)

I took my big-yellow lab to the dog park near Kingsborough Community College in Brooklyn on this beautiful morning of 9/11. There was another Russian gentleman in the dog park with his rottweiler who I got to know. He didn't speak too much English and always had a transistor radio with him. He walked over to me and said, "Plane hit at World Trade Center." I was either 'A' he doesn't know what he's talking about, or 'B' it's probably a tiny little plane. A few minutes later he comes over and says "Bad." I called my Station. They said, "If you can come in. We're recalling everybody." I called my dog. "All right buddy, let's go." Drove to my house. Got my uniform on and reported in at my Station 43 in Coney Island Hospital Brooklyn.

All of Station 43's ambulances, staff vehicles and apparatus towing equipment were assigned to the World Trade Center site and in the process of leaving the Station. Off-duty EMT's and Paramedics personnel like myself didn't have an assigned ambulance so they loaded us onto a small bus. The driver of the bus was an older civilian. He drove 20 of us in this small bus down Ocean Parkway to the Brooklyn Battery tunnel. By now it's 10:30 A.M. There wasn't a lot of traffic. At the tunnel entrance there were no regular cars being let in. The driver stopped. He didn't know what to do. I jumped out walked over to the Emergency Service Unit cops and told them we were responding to the World Trade Center collapse. Immediately they said, "Okay. Go, go, go."

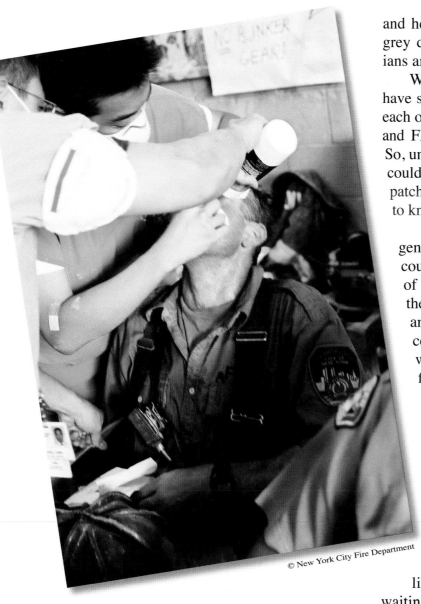

© New York City Fire Department

I was a Paramedic active in Emergency Medical Service since 1977. I worked in Manhattan, Harlem, and the Lower East Side. I was not a supervisor then, but I knew I was the senior person on the bus. As we were going through the tunnel, I told everybody "Listen, you probably are going to see things that you've never seen before. We've got to stick together." There were only a few emergency service vehicles in the tunnel.

We came out at 10:45 and drove right into the collapse area of the World Trade Center site in lower Manhattan. I had no idea where we were. It looked like the whole landscape was turned upside down. We couldn't make the right turn on West Street to drive north. There was no West Street. Everything was covered in building collapse debris. We drove west up on the sidewalk towards the Hudson River. The poor man driving the bus was terrified. I didn't know where I was. Both buildings had collapsed. Everything was covered in concrete dust with paper flying around, obscuring your vision of what was around you. You couldn't tell what block you were on because there were just piles of rubble. The bus driver was going over firehose lines trying to make his way north towards the west side of World Trade Center site. We ended up getting off the bus somewhere near there. We had our bags with us our medical equipment

and helmets and immediately started washing out the grey dust-filled eyes of the first responders and civilians around us.

We didn't have an ambulance vehicle, but we did have some handie-talkie radios and were able to talk to each other and our dispatcher. At that time EMS, NYPD and FDNY didn't talk on the same radio frequencies. So, unless you had an FDNY or NYPD radio you really couldn't communicate with each other. The EMS dispatch was telling us to stay where we were and wanted to know how many EMS personnel we had there.

They told us they were assigning a Mobile Emergency Response Vehicle (MERV) to us. It showed a couple of hours later with stretchers, a whole bunch of oxygen leads, and other equipment. We didn't see the devastating injuries or anything like what I had anticipated. Almost everyone had perished in the collapse. We treated a lot of police officers who were covered head to toe in thick gray dust. The first responders we treated for dust inhalation or eye injuries were dazed and quiet.

The general public, guys running around in suits or women with no shoes on, were more hyped. But no real hysteria that I remember. Basically, the civilians wanted to get out of the area. As we treated them, they were like "Can you wash my eyes out? I got to go. I've got to get out of here." After a while I realized you're not really getting a train out of here. But they were like "I'm going to the 'A' train." I was like 'All right.' A woman told me "My husband's waiting for me near the trains." And I'm like 'I don't think he is.' Mainly that's what we did. We had no critical patients. None.

It was very chaotic. The radio was going crazy. Lots of radio-chatter back and forth. "Any ambulances available over there? Who's where and with what supervisor? Do you have logistics vans? How many backboards does your vehicle have?" People on the Brooklyn Bridge needed assistance. I was assigned to this stationary MERV and couldn't go anywhere. It took a while for EMS to get traction and get Logistics, Triage, and a Transportation Sector set up.

Later a lot of New Jersey EMT's and Paramedics started showing up. They were letting ambulances into a clear area out of the collapse zone on West Street. Fire engines were going back and forth. You couldn't drive north or south like you usually did. An incredible sight. I knew we were going to be there for a long time. It started to get crowded with first responders. EMS Chiefs and Captains were showing up in their vehicles checking on who was where. Asking how many personnel *did* you have? How many do you have *now*? Trying to make sure all our people were accounted for. Somebody came in from out of nowhere and started handing out apples, oranges, bananas, and sandwiches. We treated a lot of firefighters.

Around 5:00 P.M. we were positioned near 7-World Trade Center watching it burn. I didn't particularly notice anything until we heard over the radio "7-World Trade Center is going to come down. Everybody move back." A lot of people started going towards Vesey Street when suddenly—7-World Trade Center collapsed. Let me tell you I took off running. It sounded like a loud 'whoosh' with a big, big, swarm of dust, and the building was gone. Most of us started crying. I was like holy crap. This is too real. That was scary.

Most of the day I didn't really treat any critical injuries or use any of my paramedic skills. Co-workers were caught up in who died. Who's missing? We stayed in the site through the night sleeping in our blankets outside on West Street. Thank God it was nice out. Yeah, it was very somber, sad, and quiet. You could see ironworkers doing their thing cutting steel with their torches. Firefighters and police officers doing their thing searching everywhere. We had our thing, treating injuries. It was like, everybody went about his or her business in a weird quiet way.

In the late afternoon they reassembled us into groups of five willing to go with the firefighters in the pile to stand-by outside the voids they were searching to assist them if they got hurt or if they found a victim that needed medical attention. This way they wouldn't have to say, "Go get EMS." Only one group at a time was allowed on top of the pile. They would stay there for an hour then switch off and let another team take over. We had many EMTs and paramedics on standby.

## We stayed in the site through the night sleeping in our blankets outside on West Street.

I worked emergency services since 1977 and it never felt so disorienting like that was. The next day September 12th, we left at four o'clock in the afternoon. When I got home, I took a shower and slept straight through till the next day.

After the first couple of days a schedule was set up where after working your own regular shift at your Station you were able to go to the World Trade Center site and be on standby. For me that first day back in the World Trade Center site after 9/11 was more impactful than the day of 9/11 itself. At first, I thought, I'm not doing this again. By that time, we knew who died and going back knowing how many people had lost their lives right there and how many more victims we were going to find, was overwhelming.

On my first day off I went to an outdoor pizzeria in Brooklyn with my friends. It was crowded. There was a woman with her family sitting at a table near us. The woman said to her family, "If George didn't come home, I don't think George is alive anymore." That's what you heard. We left our table and went over to talk with her. She told us her nephew worked in the World Trade Center. It was now two days later and "George didn't come home." Things like that were like 'wow' how many people has this affected? So, when I went back to the pile, yeah, it was difficult.

A month later they had brought in trailers and set up an onsite morgue with a Medical Examiner at the site. The pile was now the pit. It was difficult when they found parts of bodies. We would be called to drive an ambulance onto the ramp that went down into the pit. Deep into the foundations of the WTC buildings. After the body parts were removed from the rubble they were put in a stokes stretcher and placed in the back of the ambulance. We tried to respect these remains as best we could. Before bringing it into the morgue we cover a woman's leg or some other person's body part with a sheet. When you walked into the Medical Examiners trailer with these victim remains—everyone would stop what they were doing—the doctors, clerical workers, our supervisors, and stand up. We would wheel it in, dead quiet. They would take it and put it on a morgue slab. Then tag it and we would leave. I probably did that 30 times. Yeah, I did that a lot. I mean, it was bad enough to see what I saw on the first day but the going back was more difficult.

Yet you felt like you had to do something. So, on your day off it was like 'I'll go.' I was drawn back. You wanted to be back. Yeah. Emergency Medical Services learned a lot that day. Communications needed big improvements.

Once you learn to be an EMT or Paramedic let's face it you know what you have to do. But if communications with other people are impeded you can't do all the patient care you might want to do. As a paramedic I must get to the patient. Assess the patient. Then figure out where I'm going to take that patient. If my commu-

## On that day I knew there was this job to do. And it was a huge job. I knew inherently—inside—that whatever it was I was going to do it.

nication is limited my knowledge of what's going to be the next step after treatment is extremely limited. Which makes my options limited. Like I said that day it took EMS a little while to get traction.

Yet, EMS—we did all right. Honestly, we did all right. I went to a couple of locations at the World Trade Center site and even when they were putting us into different groups. You could see people were helping each other. I don't know how to explain it. EMS personnel can be 'Me, me, me. Take, take, take'. This brought us together. It showed us that we could work together. As a result of this I think as a whole group EMS is now more cohesive. We were really cohesive that day. People were asking what do you need me to do? Where's the patient? I'll go there. That was a big difference. For a lot of us we learned to work better and more effectively together.

I've always had that sense of responsibility. A sense of duty. On that day I knew there was this job to do. And it was a huge job. I knew inherently—inside—that whatever it was I was going to do it. There was this big need and I saw that need. On routine responses sometimes you go on calls and find people who really don't need an ambulance. It's discouraging. But that day there was a sense of, I'm needed. Whatever it takes. I'm here for the duration. It was kind of exhilarating. Yet, very sad. Co-workers and everybody else there were checking on each other and it made that day much easier.

If I could have changed anything that happened that day, I'd wish I was working and had an ambulance. And I'd wish FDNY had not set up command in the lobby of the building. That was so sad.

The biggest impact from my experiences that day was a feeling that I was equipped to face anything after that. A sense of, not accomplishment, but it showed me yeah, you're not a phony. You know what you're doing, and you can be ready to face anything.

In January of 2002 I was promoted to Lieutenant and that experience readied me for the rest of the years I worked for EMS. In the years afterwards I would sign up and volunteer to work the 9/11 commemorative ceremony. I was a boss by then and helped supervise EMS personnel working that day. Somebody's always assigned to the mayor or other big shots that show up. I did that for a quite a few years afterwards. Once retired sad to say I didn't attend many ceremonies. I acknowledge the day. It's always a sad day. But I try not to get pulled down into the remorse and sadness. I watch the events on TV. See the reading of the names but then I have to get out of the house. It's—I've got to go on. ❖

## Nick Lorenzo
### Firefighter Engine 67

On 9/11 I was off and like most firefighters working my second job which was a licensed welder for a pile driving company putting a crane together on Willow Street in Hoboken New Jersey. I was looking towards Manhattan when I saw smoke coming over the brownstone buildings lining the streets below. I crawled up to the top of the crane so I could get a better point of view and noticed smoke from the first plane attack on 1-World Trade Center. I yelled down to the guys working with me "Boys, my guys are getting their ass kicked today." That's when I saw the second plane come in. I didn't see it hit the building. It come in sight then it dipped below the brownstone's houses in front of me and suddenly a big plume of smoke rose over the brownstone houses. I knew the plane hit the building.

It wasn't more than a minute later when a radio report went ballistic about a second plane crashing into 2-World Trade Center. I came running off the crane. The guys in the street were asking me "What are you going to do?" I said, "I'm not sure yet." Then suddenly News Radio 88 came on and said "We've just been handed a message from the mayor's office of the city of New York. A city-wide recall has been issued for all police officers, firefighters, and emergency medical personnel. They are to report to their commands." I looked at my boss and said, "I got to go." He said, "Really?" I said, "Yea, I have to go, that's my job." They wished me good luck.

I was a firefighter in 67 Engine on West 170th Street in Manhattan. I thought the Holland Tunnel is near the World Trade Center and might not be open I'll head up towards the Lincoln Tunnel. I drove my white Chevy Astro van to the tunnel entrance. I had to go through five layers of police officers to get there all asking "Where you going? Turn around." I had my driver's license, my badge, and my fire department ID out and told them "I have to get in. I'm a fireman there's a recall." And they let me through. At the tollbooth four officers jumped out "Where are you going?" I told them went through the

tollbooth and saw sand-trucks blocking all the entrances to the tunnel. I drive slowly. My flashers on. Both hands out the window steering with my knees.

As I approach the sand-trucks six Port Authority cops jump out guns drawn screaming. "Get out. Stop that truck. Stop" I said, "I'm a fireman on the job." They yelled back "I don't care who you are. Get out." I said, "Yeah, whatever you want." I open the door got out. Immediately one cop had me by the collar and another cop had me by the arm with my IDs and everything in my hand. They put me face down on the ground. One cop has his foot on the back of my throat and the other cop has a gun right on my head while they're searching my van. Going through my toolboxes making sure I didn't have a bomb.

I was thinking 'I understand they are not taking any chances. I'm not going to get killed because I'm not the bad guy and they're not the enemy.' I was in the Marine Corps in Desert Storm. I know who the enemy is and it's not these police officers. After they searched my van, they picked me up saying "Sorry, really sorry." I said, "It's okay, look there's a recall I got to get in." They moved a truck to let me through and I asked the sergeant "Could you do me a favor, could you get on the radio and let somebody know that I'm coming through? I don't want to get shot on the other end." I know at the other end they're not looking for people coming out of the tunnel they're looking for people trying to come into the tunnel and anybody surprised or unsure you know the deal, shoot first ask questions later. I got through the tunnel and the uptown streets were jam-packed with traffic. I pressed my way to the firehouse and made it to Engine 67 at 11:00 A.M.

About 20 firefighters were gathered up and the Captain of Ladder 45 had us go to Amsterdam Avenue where we commandeered a bus. While heading south we stopped at the quarters of Engine 84 and Ladder 34 on West 161st street and picked up more firefighters and that's where a Chief said, "No, don't go yet. We need to get a handle on this. Everybody get your stuff off the bus and leave it here." There was a high level of frustration. But there was nothing you could do. This firehouse was our staging area.

At 3:00 P.M. ambulances showed up with firefighters who were there when the buildings came down. They tried taking them to the hospitals, but the hospitals had no place to put them, so they were bringing them to firehouses. They brought us one guy from Engine 227 in Brooklyn. He was in hospital clothes telling us his story of not finding anyone. You felt for this guy. I don't think you felt sorry for him. You felt his anguish and frustration.

At 6:00 P.M. they loaded a bunch of us up and we went down to the World Trade Center staging site where they divided us up and into teams. They put us to work on a hose-line pouring water into a hole leading to a deep-seated large fire below the surface rubble. Steam and smoke were constantly pushing out of the hole drifting out over the site.

Victims were spread out over the surface rubble. One that stuck out in my mind was a body with all the skin burnt off it. The eyes were open. There was dust and debris covering the wounds. It looked like someone had rolled them in sand. And there was this woman's leg, a beautiful leg. She had a nice flat pump on and an ankle bracelet. It was perfectly severed halfway up the thigh lying there. There was a little red marker flag where two hands were sticking out of the rubble. Not together. Nine inches apart. One facing one way, one facing the other way. That stays in my mind.

Joe Esposito, a firefighter from Rescue 5, I saw him crying. I always thought of him as one of the toughest bastards in the world. He believed his brother got killed and was crying. I had 14 years of military service and these people inspired me not to show my emotions. That gives me faith to be strong. Fire officers too. You went down that smoke-filled hallway. Got to the fire apartment door. And they'd say "Okay, we're going in. We're going to go past two doors. It's the third bedroom on the left, okay? It's going pretty good so we're going to stay tight. We don't want to open up the line until we get close to it. You got it? Everybody's good? Everybody ready? Here we go." Boom, calm and efficient.

The cellphone system wasn't working. It wasn't until 8:00 at night when I got a chance to call my wife. We had just moved from Staten Island to upstate New York. I had her in a rental apartment with our one-year-old and three-year-old. She had no clue where the hell I was and didn't know what was going on. I explained everything.

At 6:00 in the morning they relieved us, and we went back to 67 Engine. I stayed in the firehouse and within 24 hours was back to the World Trade Center site searching and on bucket brigades moving rubble around. I remember finding a credit card. I said to a firefighter "Hey, it's a credit card," he says, "What good is that?" I said, "Don't you understand there's a name on it that proves this person was here. This is evidence." I brought it over to where they were gathering personal stuff.

One of the things that frustrated me was I could use a torch. I had a G-38 welding license. I told our Chiefs I'm a licensed welder and can use any steel cutting equipment. They said "Oh, yeah, go with those guys on the search teams." I can't really criticize a Battalion Chief or a Deputy Chief. The command structure just got wiped out and now they had to reestablish order and the chain of command. That takes time. The guys they were on the job with for 30 years were now dead. Don't think they weren't upset, or their feelings weren't hurt, or they weren't in shock.

I was there to do what I was told. I wasn't there to ask questions. I stayed with my group an officer and six firefighters. Digging in the rubble and mov-

ing it out in buckets. Still, if there was a torch available, I would take it. When we found a small portable air torch in a fire truck buried under the rubble, I used it.

There were trade ironworkers cutting steel all the time. Anytime we got a chance we would grab a torch and use it. Initially the ironworkers weren't getting paid. They all jumped in. Right off the bat bringing torch carts with oxygen and acetylene. Emptying job sites of all they could. After a week or so construction contractors came in and the ironworkers started getting paid. A contractor's business agent came to me and said "Hey we need people. Come on down to the site and work for us." I said "Are you kidding? How could I go down there making double-time when there's guys down there digging for nothing? I can't do that."

After the first couple of weeks, we got back into the firehouse routine. They were looking for volunteers to go to the site. Sometimes I would go. I felt bad I didn't get to go down there more often. We were working 24 hours on 24 hours off during that period. All the fires that you walked away from and said "Holy shit. I can't believe we got away with that one. I can't believe we

world. He also survived the Beirut bombing in Lebanon. I knew Gary Geidel from Rescue 1 my whole life. I don't know if I'm saying it right. Don't get me wrong. There were times when I was thinking, 'Holy shit, I can't believe this is happening.'

What I loved about the whole 9/11 experience was how the country came together and was so generous to us.

I think about how circumstances protected me. I transferred from 54 Engine to 67 Engine six weeks before 9/11. Engine 54 lost four firefighters along with the whole 9th Battalion on 9/11. I knew them all. There are a lot of other guys who took a last-minute mutual and came into work for somebody and didn't come home and some guys that would have worked were off. For me it was the simple fact that I transferred to Engine 67 only six weeks before 9/11.

The worst thing about being a firefighter is putting out fires. One minute you're having a meatball hero on a Sunday afternoon and the next thing you know you're going into hell. Knocking on Chernobyl's door.

Now I'm retired and don't have to do that anymore and that leaves me with a sense of gratitude. I'm glad I'm retired and lucky enough to get a check at the end of the month. I'm happy and people look at me and say, "You know you're always happy. You got a good attitude." I thank God I'm still healthy and I get to be with my children. I think about the guys who I knew who aren't here anymore. They didn't get to say that.

There are many things in life that I'm not getting upset with. It could be worse. My father is retired from the job. The joke we have is when I say, "Hey Dad you know the one thing we have in common. We know what it's like being a fireman pouring water on a vacant building from a tower ladder bucket on Christmas morning." Thank God I don't have to do things like that anymore. When I play golf people look at me and say, "Wow, you're awfully young to be retired." And I say, "Well, I married wisely."

On the anniversary of 9/11 I rarely wear my fire department uniform. When I mention to some people that I'm a firefighter the questions come. "Oh, where? What happened to you during 9/11?" I don't mind talking about it with other firefighters. I try not to say anything to anybody who is not a firefighter because I don't know if they can understand it. They can't understand the leg. The guy with no skin. There are a certain number of guys who lost somebody on 9/11 that I call to say, "Hey how are you? How are you doing? How's your family?"

Down here in North Carolina the retirees have a 9/11 ceremony. I went to a couple of them up in New York. Now I try to keep a low profile on the anniversary of 9/11, but I think about it all the time. ❖

put that one out." Then something like this happens. The most important thing for me was to get up every morning and keep going.

What helped me get through that day was this wasn't the first time something like this happened to me. I was almost in a mass casualty incident while in the First Battalion, 8th Marines, in Beirut Lebanon on October 23, 1983. For some reason I got picked out of a formation when the gunnery sergeant said, "I need five volunteers." I just happened to be number four. The rest of those guys stayed in our Beirut headquarters. Later that day a terrorist-driven truck laden with compressed gas-enhanced explosives blew up the headquarters building. The resulting explosion and the collapse of the building killed 241 Marines, Sailors, and Soldiers. I had emotional feelings then. But I'm alive and have to do my job to make sure we continue. You can't crumble. You take losses in a combat unit. Being in the military helped with 9/11.

There are times where I'm driving in the car and something stupid comes on the radio that reminds me of somebody and I start crying. I still do that every once in a while. One of the guys killed was John Chipura from Engine 219. John was one of the greatest guys in the

## The Department of Labor's Occupational Safety and Health (OSHA) Report

- More than 30 cranes, including some of the largest in the world, were at work in uncomfortably close quarters inside the green line (work area). In what has been described as an intricate balance of motion and timing, the cranes lifted loads of twisted steel and compacted rubble in an environment fraught with the potential for accidents. High winds, rain, unstable ground, and uncertain loads added to this dangerous mix.

- The potential for explosions was always present at the site. In one case a fuel tank with tens of thousands of gallons of diesel fuel was buried seven stories below ground. With smoldering fires, a rupture could have been disastrous.

- Building 6, the former site of OSHA's Manhattan Area Office, housed many federal agencies, including the U.S. Customs Service. More than 1.2 million rounds of their ammunition, plus explosives and weapons, were stored in a third-floor vault to support their firing range.

- The parking garage under the WTC held nearly 2,000 automobiles, each tank holding an estimated five gallons of gasoline. When recovery workers reached the cars, they found that some had exploded and burned while others remained intact.

- Another danger involved the high temperature of twisted steel pulled from the rubble. Underground fires burned at temperatures up to 2,000 degrees. As the huge cranes pulled steel beams from the pile safety experts worried about the effects of the extreme heat on the crane rigging and the hazards of contact with the hot steel.

- Huge underground tanks held more than 200,000 pounds of Freon stored to cool the seven buildings of the WTC complex. This had been the largest air-conditioning system in the country. OSHA personnel were concerned that workers entering areas below grade could be exposed to Freon gas, a known heavier-than-air, invisible killer.

- Collected more than 6,500 air and bulk samples to test for asbestos, lead, other heavy metals, silica, and various organic and inorganic compounds.[37]

## Tom Cashin
### Deputy Chief Division 1 (promoted to Assistant Chief of Department, Operations)

I started my assigned vacation on September 9, 2001. It was an ideal time to be on vacation. Summer was ending everyone was back to work and the weather was still great. On the morning of September 11th, I was home in the middle of a small project when about 9:30 A.M. the phone rang. It was my wife telling me some planes crashed into the World Trade Center. I turned on a TV saw the reports of the attack on the World Trade Center put on my work duty uniform and left the house. I knew from listening to the news the subways weren't running and thought 'taking my car would have me stuck in a great big traffic jam.' So, I went to the closest firehouse near me Ladder 109 and Engine 241.

A couple of firefighters were there but they were unsure of what to do. I suggested we go over to Ladder 114's quarters to see if a messenger van or some sort of transportation could take us into Manhattan. When we got there, we were met by a few more firefighters but again, there were no plans or transportation to get to the site.

I saw a bus driving by waved it over and told the bus driver "I'm commandeering your bus. All the passengers have to get off. I need you to drive the bus to the World Trade Center site." Right away the bus driver told the passengers they had to get off the bus. Surprisingly, no one complained. I told him to drive down 4th Avenue. The bus driver did exactly what I asked him to do. He did not make a fuss or ask any questions. It was obvious he was willing and proud to do what he could to help us out. Along the way we could see the huge smoke cloud rising above lower Manhattan. I called the 11th Division and told them I was driving down 4th Avenue in a city bus picking up firefighters at firehouses along the way. We filled the bus with firefighters.

On the bus there was quiet chatter among the members. We were all in the middle of our own personal struggles trying to deal with what we were witnessing. I

gave out what little information I had and explained that we would be going to a Staging-Area before going to the site. From the questions I was being asked I could tell the members wanted to get to the site as soon as possible. They did not want to stand by. They wanted to go to work.

When we arrived at Division 11's quarters in downtown Brooklyn the Chief on duty directed us to go to the Staging-Area at Ladder 119's quarters in Williamsburg. When we got there, we were told the Staging-Area was shifted over to the Brooklyn side of the Manhattan Bridge. Arriving there we found the Staging-Area had changed again to the base of the Brooklyn Bridge. At this Staging-Area a task force was being setup consisting of firefighters, buses, and other means of transportation all waiting to get the okay from NYPD to go over the bridge into Manhattan. After a short wait NYPD escorted us over the bridge. The bus driver left us off in front of city hall. I think he felt like he was part of the response team. Whatever I asked of him he did the best he could to get it done.

A short distance from city hall we reported in to the Secondary-Command Post. It was chaotic as plans were still being made on how to get organized and safely manage the release of members down to the site. One immediate problem was so many water mains were broken in the enormous collapse zone. Many areas of lower Manhattan did not have water. The Department of Environmental Protection brought water main maps to the Command Post and with the aid of city engineers we tried to figure out which water mains were still in-

tact and if it was possible for our fire boats to feed the water mains near the collapse zone.

At the same time groups of firefighters and their fire engines from upstate towns were arriving and wanted to help. We worked out a plan to track these volunteers and their resources. There was a lot going on and time was passing by quickly.

Several hours passed when we heard rumors 7-World Trade Center, another enormous high-rise building, had been burning for hours and was in danger of collapse. Firefighters were desperate to get involved and frustrated at standing fast. Saying we could put this fire out. They were more than willing to go into a burning building even after all that happened. We sent a Chief from the Secondary-Command Post down to take a quick size-up. He came back saying "No way anyone is going near that building. We are not going to fight that fire. There is no water. You're not going to be able to put this fire out. It will collapse." Not long later sure

**The bus driver left us off in front of city hall. I think he felt like he was part of the response team. Whatever I asked of him he did the best he could to get it done.**

enough 7 World Trade Center came down. Something never seen in this city before. The total collapse of a modern high-rise building caused by the out-of-control fire intensely burning inside.

It was now early evening, and we were still sending groups of firefighters down to the collapse zone. Communications between our Command Post and the site were poor. There was not much information coming back on the progress being made.

I decided to go down to the site. Walking down Broadway in the early evening darkness gray dust and paper were floating around everywhere. Nearing the collapse zone, I found myself alone on a deserted street leading to the World Trade Center. It felt so eerily quiet. Serene, like being in a snowfall. Only it was gray dust. I never really understood or appreciated the term 'surreal' but here I was in an area I had often passed through always full of people and activity. Now unrecognizable and empty. This was surreal. I will always remember this impression.

Ironworkers were bringing in torches cutting large sections of steel columns. Volunteers started moving collapse debris around to help the searchers gain access to void areas they thought might hold a victim. We didn't have any set procedures organized yet. Everything was sort of ad hoc.

I had a handie-talkie radio and directed a Chief who also had a radio to go out on the rubble pile and let me know where they were searching and the resources they needed. We just started out with basics tactics for a collapse rescue operation. Which all firefighters are trained for.

## It was amazing how many people were showing up. Firefighters from all over the country

Heavy equipment was coming into the site, but it would take time to set up, so it was the efforts of the firefighters and construction workers digging with what they had. We did that all through the night. Rumors were coming in people would be found. This encouraged everyone to keep digging. Focused and determined to find victims.

There were a lot of people down there. Mostly FDNY, construction and ironworkers, working together in separate areas of the debris field. We were gradually extending FDNY's control over the site and the construction workers were deferring to us for directions. It became all about using buckets to move debris away from where we were digging. FDNY supplied the personnel, and the construction workers supplied the buckets. Everyone was working hard and trying to stay focused. But it wasn't easy. We all knew guys that were missing and heard names mentioned. There was a lot of denial and a lot of sadness.

I remember one retired guy who I came on the job with come up to me wearing an old turnout coat. He looked exhausted. I knew he had a son on the job, and I asked about him. That son was okay. But he had another son who worked for one of the brokerage firms in the World Trade Center. It was late. He said, "I guess I should stop looking." He was so disoriented. Oh man—it broke me up. That was a big part of the day. Realizing all the tragedy that took place and trying to deal with getting things done.

In the early hours of September 12th FDNY Staff officers set up procedures for having firefighters and officers normally scheduled to work on September 13th come in and work 24 hours at the site. Sometime in the morning of September 12th I got relieved and joined some Chiefs in a department messenger-van that took us out of the site and went home. That was the end of my first day. I don't remember eating anything during the day or night. My whole family was waiting for me. I stayed home for the rest of the day and got ready for the morning of the 13th.

On September 13th I went to the site. It was a beautiful sunny day. We were organized into four Command Posts around the perimeter of the site. I was responsible for operations on the west side of the site. My Command Post was on West Street near the World Financial Center. Other command posts were on, Liberty Street, Church Street and Vesey Street. I tried to set up my command post location someplace where I could keep track of what was going on and saw a very large I-beam laying parallel to the ground with its tip pushed up by a pile of debris. This gave me some height to see my area of responsibility. I walked out to the tip of this I-beam and people started coming over. From this vantage point I was able to direct firefighters to where they were needed. It was amazing how many people were showing up. Firefighters from all over the country. A whole contingent of Staten Island firefighters came over on a ferry.

I had Chiefs dispersed over the debris pile deciding specifically where to dig and directed incoming volunteers to the Chiefs locations to assist in the searches for trapped victims. We integrated Port Authority PD and NYPD search and rescue teams with teams from various states who came in. We all became part of the search and rescue operation. Everyone worked very well together. Unfortunately, it was still mostly surface digging.

The biggest challenge was not thinking about all the tragic things that happened. It was horrible. You kept hearing names. Guys would come over "I'm looking for my brother." Fathers, one a Chief I knew, calling out for their sons. Every moment was difficult down there because as busy as we were you could not escape the sadness. It was horrible. Trying to stay focused and not get caught up in that. Doing what you had to do to make sure everything was coordinated, and everybody stayed focused and safe. When evening came, I went to Division 1 headquarters and worked there until morning.

I think everybody was subconsciously affected for the rest of their lives. When you recall the event. All the individual gruesome things that happened. It's very upsetting. All these memories are pushed back into the subconscious. And when they come into conscious thought it's very difficult not to get caught up in the way it was. This memory stays with me the longest. The commitment of the members. In spite of all the danger and chaos around them. I'm proud of the department for what they did and the membership, the people, the way they handled themselves. I will always remember that.

© New York City Fire Department

As the days rolled on, we were alternating working one day at the site and one in the Division. 24 hours on with 24 hours of shifts. This was later reduced to a 12-hour day or a 12-hour night shift to limit the stress at the site. The 1st Division lost 99 firefighters. There was such disarray. FDNY firefighters from all over the city were working shifts in Division 1 firehouses so the firefighters who lost people could constantly go down to the site. It was decided that the Chiefs assigned to the 1st Division would stop working shifts at the site and focus on getting the 1st Division back together again. Replacing destroyed apparatus, organizing the available manpower, and having firehouse routines established to operate effectively. And at the same time, we had all those funerals going on. All the firehouses had to be visited frequently. I talked to the guys to find out how they were doing. Some tough times. It was difficult.

The firefighters were great. This is when you saw the root, the true metal of the department. A big part of it was the funerals. I was amazed at how well they put things

## Another thing that impressed me was the construction industry. The ironworkers and owners of construction companies.

together. The eulogies they did. The companies pulled together especially the Captains. They all did a great job. They stood up and lead the firefighters through it. It was a very tragic time. A difficult time. And the individual companies they're the ones. They pulled it all together.

Another thing that impressed me was the construction industry. The ironworkers and owners of construction companies. They had the true knowledge of the site. One guy from Rockland County with a bunch of his equipment was at the site every day. We were tearing things apart. Digging deeper into the building's foundation with heavy equipment searching for victims. There was a lot of concern about the 'slurry wall' which held back the Hudson River from flowing into the site. To prevent the 'slurry wall' from being breached it had to be rebuilt to make sure it wasn't weakened or damaged in critical areas. I didn't know what they had to do. They explained to me what they were doing and how they were doing it which was very helpful. I got to know some of these guys, good people. They were the patriots. They came to a dangerous place to help the country with their knowledge, expertise, and equipment. Without anyone telling them to do it. All out. Getting a very difficult job done safely.

Another thing I remember was late one night at the site when a civilian walked over to my command post and said to me "We're going to get you help. The military is coming in and we're bringing in the National Forest Service." I didn't know who he was. Some kind of Government official. I said, "The Forest Service?" he goes "Yeah, they're going to help you." And sure enough they were the ones who helped us set up our Emergency Incident Management procedures which really helped us get organized. A big deal.

So, yeah, that's the way it went. The thing that helped us to keep going was the commitment. Welcome to the team. Where everybody is helping each other do the best job they can.

My job was to be in command and that was important to the teams I was working with. Many of them didn't know me. We had to stay connected with so much going on around us. They needed to know I knew what they were doing, and I was there to keep them safe and give them the resources they needed to do their job. All you had to do was tell someone what needed to be done and they would do it in a heartbeat. I don't want to say it was an easy command, but that kind of effort made it easy. Helped me. Because everybody was committed to their job.

On the anniversary of 9/11 I go back to the fire company where I was a Lieutenant Ladder 3. They lost 1 Captain, 1 Lieutenant and 9 firefighters that day. When I was a Lieutenant there, I broke in some probationary firefighters along with a lot of other officers. I was very proud of them. They made me look good as a lieutenant. Exceptional people. They did such great things. A big part of 9/11 to me is these guys. It was such a shame. All the memorial events occurring simultaneous during that day. I want to make other events. I try to get to Ladder 105 where I worked as a firefighter. They lost their Captain and 5 firefighters on that day. But it doesn't always work out. So, for many years I always made it a point to be in Ladder 3 on 9/11. ❖

# Edward Kilduff
## Deputy Chief Division 3 (promoted to Chief of Department)

On September 11th I was off on a mutual with Tom Galvin a Deputy Chief Division 3. He was working Monday night into Tuesday day September 11th, and I was working Tuesday night into Wednesday day. I was going to a golf outing for the Lynbrook Volunteer Fire Department on Tuesday which was the reason Tom did the first half of the mutual. We were at the Lido Golf Course at the end of Long Beach Island on the third hole when across Jamaica Bay looking at the Manhattan skyline a column of smoke was coming from the North-Tower. We decided a helicopter proba-

bly miss-landed on top of the Trade Center and maybe crashed but when we saw the South-Tower with smoke we knew there was a serious situation going on.

There were a few FDNY firefighters at the outing. We all scrambled to our cars and headed home. Cellphones were not common back then. We had to depend on listening to the car radio for news. I knew I was going to be gone for a few days. Grabbed a whole lot of uniform shirts and pants jumped in the car and headed to the 3rd Division headquarters on West 77th street in Manhattan with the intention of getting my bunker-gear and then heading downtown to the site.

By the time I got into Manhattan both buildings had collapsed. At the 3rd Division the instructions were do not respond to the Trade Center. Stay back until you are ordered to respond. I spent the next hour listening to the department radio and finally heard Tom Galvin's voice. He was there for both building collapses requesting some assistance. So, we knew he was alive and were greatly relieved. After the collapses he ended up in One-Police Plaza and we wanted to get him back to the Division. So, I went to One-Police Plaza and consequently became the fire department representative basically for OEM (Office of Emergency Management). They were set up in the operations center of One-Police Plaza because OEM was based in 7-World Trade Center, and it was destroyed in the attack. I arrived at One-Police Plaza early in the afternoon.

The most vivid memory I have involve the two families who lost one son in the NYPD and one in the FDNY. John Vigiano's family lost Joe an NYPD officer and John from Ladder 132. The Langone family lost Thomas an NYPD officer and Peter from Squad 252. I'm now in One-Police Plaza doing my liaison thing in a large room with a hundred different agency reps when a cop says to me "Deputy Commissioner Joe Dunn and Commissioner Kerrick want you to come with them for a minute." I stand up. Walk down a hall. Get in an elevator with Commissioners Kerrick and Dunn and Kerrick says to me "We're going to meet some of the families and there's fire department families there too." Then Kerrick looks at me and says, "How many people do you think you lost today?" This is 7:30 P.M. on 9/11. I said, "Probably several hundred." His face dropped. The look he gave was like 'Oh man!' At that time, we knew the cops were talking in the 20's, maybe 30's. So, the elevator door opens and there's John Vigiano (a retired FDNY Captain).

John looks at me while the cops are trying to give him some information and says, "Ed, what can you tell me? What do you know?" I really felt bad because I hadn't worked at the site yet. All I could tell him was "We're looking John, we're looking. If anybody is going to make it out of there John and Joe will. Give it a little time John and we'll find them." He then said "What do we know? What's going on? Where are we going to get information?" I was friendly with John, so this was quite an emotional period.

Then I walked over to the Langone's. The mother and others from the family were crying and I said, "Don't worry we're going to find a lot of these folks. It's going to take time. They're trapped in subway stations and in basements. We're going to find them." I tried to give them some hope. This is the thing I remember most. Meeting those families. That wasn't easy. But somebody had to do it and I was glad we had a fire department presence in One-Police Plaza so I could give them some words of encouragement. So that's what I remember most of September 11th. That and the frustration of not being able to be physically at the site early on.

I stayed in One-Police Plaza until 5 A.M. Wednesday when I was relieved by Chief Hill. As soon as I got out of there, I grabbed a ride from an FDNY Division van going by. Got off at City-Hall Park and did a lap-around the World Trade Center site to see what was going on. Then reported into the Command Post.

My scheduled day-tour in the 3rd Division was Wednesday. I spoke with Frank Cruthers (Assistant Chief of Department) and asked, "Would you like me to stay here and relieve somebody, or go to the 3rd Division and work there for the day?" Frank said "Go to the 3rd Division. Get yourself settled. Then we'll figure it out." Obviously, there was a threat of more damage being done. The city was raw and exposed. He wanted to put members in place in case something else happened. At 9:30 A.M. I was back in the 3rd Division and stayed there all day.

We were reconciling lists of people who were working with people unaccounted for. Driving to firehouses to ascertain what their situations were. Was the apparatus damaged? Who was around? I hit the 8th and the 9th Battalions more than any place else because they were located closer to the World Trade Center site. More of their units responded and they had higher causalities.

All the light-duty folks in the 3rd Division were making calls to help us reconcile who we lost. Families started coming into the firehouses with a lot of questions. It became a situation where you wanted to show some type of presence from a management leadership perspective. I traveled around to a few of the firehouses with the goal of trying to find out who was unaccounted for and to speak with their families.

I was relieved later that night. Went back to the Trade Center and did a few hours of supervision in one of the four quadrants until after midnight and when everything got a little bit quiet. Then I went back home.

On Thursday morning I got placed into the manpower taskforce the department set up. Drove to Shea Stadium parking-lot and from there rode a bus to the Trade Center and reported into the Command Post with bus-loads of people.

I was put in charge of the quadrant in front of 10 & 10 (Engine10 and Ladder 10) quarters on Liberty Street. I had a gaggle of firefighters from all over the place. Some FDNY guys but a lot of out-of-town firefighters

who had gear and helmets on. There was at least a hundred of them. We got 10 & 10 cleaned out with the intent of setting up a 'medical-trauma area' to evaluate victims before transporting them.

Collapse debris had penetrated this firehouse which was directly across from the South-Tower. Grapplers and trucks were moving huge pieces of steel to clear Liberty Street. They had to get an ambulance out of the way. An excavator grabbed into it, even though it was a perfectly fine ambulance, dropped it on top of a flatbed truck and hauled it off.

We had expectations of finding people trapped in the debris. All we had to do was keep looking and we were going to find survivors. That was the idea. Move as much large debris as we could. Look into any void's underneath. And find people.

So, cleaning 10 & 10 out was one task and we coordinated people as quickly as possible to start looking for voids. A lot of bucket-brigade work took place. Moved a lot of debris and performed searches. But we did not find anyone alive.

Two full days afterwards the buildings on Church Street were still shifting. There could be more collapses in the immediate area and there was still a threat of some other type of attack. We were looking for anything unstable including in the hotels across the street. A lot of people were afraid there was going to be another event.

# We had expectations of finding people trapped in the debris. All we had to do was keep looking and we were going to find survivors. That was the idea. Move as much large debris as we could. Look into any void's underneath. And find people.

From a personal perspective a couple of firefighters I knew well were there straight through from Tuesday. Still standing. Still working. Still trying. And they were shot. I'll never forget the looks on those guys' faces. I was saying to them "Stay here with me." or "Sit inside 10 & 10." That was the task. Keep people focused. And keep them safe.

The scene was overwhelming. Smoke pumping-up out of dozens of different areas. Hand-lines ineffective. It was understood you wanted to extinguish as much fire as you could to facilitate searches. But that was a difficult assignment. I don't want to say it wasn't something we couldn't eventually accomplish but the amount of debris was remarkable. We're the most resilient people in the world. But looking to coordinate operations with command and control in the early stages was not an easy thing.

I thought people at the highest-level of command The Cruther's, the Cassano's, the Callan's, Frank Fellini. The small core of City-Wide-Chiefs that were still around did a good job of making themselves available to the troops providing leadership and comfort. The people in charge were there. Hands on. Actively trying to coordinate.

The first few days there wasn't much coordination between the four quadrants other than having bullhorns to blow in case an imminent collapse. Each quadrant had maybe a Staff-Chief or a Deputy Chief who operated independently of each other without much coordination between them other than asking for resources, 'can you send a tower-ladder over or, we need to stretch a few hand-lines.'

> ## The small core of City-Wide-Chiefs that were still around. Did a good job of making themselves available to the troops providing leadership and comfort.

With an event of that magnitude, I don't know what else could have been done to pull it together. I believe the presence of the Staff Chiefs, the Deputy Chiefs, and the Battalion Chiefs provided direction and leadership to make things happen. But the inexperience with an event of this nature clearly hampered us for the first few days.

And the other aspect was the emotional effect of everybody knowing somebody not accounted for. Everybody being all-in. 'I've got to find Joe or Bill.' 'I've got to do something here.' That energy and emotion was hard to marshal. You had to bridge the gap between what management and leadership was looking for and what was going on with the people who were crawling over the debris.

For the next five days we all mobilized at the Shea Stadium parking lot with some Red Cross and other folks. Jumped on the half-dozen buses and were taken to the site. In the mornings everybody onboard was always gung-ho on the way in.

At the Command Post they effectively divided personnel into groups. A Deputy Chief with several Battalion Chiefs, company officers and firefighters assigned to teams. You got assigned a quadrant. Started the bucket-brigade work. And over those five days you did see some progress particularly access into the pile itself. For me it was stay back and let the Battalion Chiefs run the individual areas.

But you always had people on their own working in each of the quadrants because they knew where their guy was last seen, and they weren't giving up until they found them. The fathers of firefighters and brothers of firefighters would not leave the area where their brother or son was last seen. You gave direction the best you could. First surface-searching then removing selected debris and seeing what we could find underneath.

At 11:30 P.M. we'd get on the buses. On the way home it was quiet. Everybody was beat.

Over the next weeks and months, you learned the Chief's primary role. Keep firefighters safe. Out of trouble and danger. That was always on my mind. It was a massive collapse-zone. You almost didn't know where to start. When you turned people loose, they started climbing, ducking under steel. There was always apprehension. Somebody was going to be seriously hurt. It was always two-steps forward, one-step back. We deputized officers as 'safety-observers' which helped to some degree.

© New York City Fire Department

In the immediate days afterwards one of the best resources we had were the light-duty folks in the 3rd Division. We lost Dennis Devlin (light-duty Battalion Chief) and firefighter Carl Asaro. They were both wonderful people. Unfortunately, they were never found.

Our folks worked from 6:00 A.M. until 12:00 P.M. Got up again and worked and worked. Besides the site itself there was always the dynamic of what was going on in the Division. You needed to set the companies back up. Replace apparatus. Replace equipment. Get manpower in to fill-out the companies. Decide how the mutual-aid help was going respond and structure them correctly so everybody was on the same page. The folks in the 3rd Division were key to pulling all of this together. Chief Tom Galvin was very instrumental in restructuring and building the 3rd Division back to being a capable response group again.

What helped me was the relationships I had with some of the Staff-Chiefs and many of the Deputy and Battalion chiefs. As the days went on the conversations between the Staff-Chief and officers at the Trade Cen-

ter was productive. Defining what the goals would be for the day. The current dangers and liabilities. Communicating the status of certain on-going searches. The status of resources and personnel. And being involved with the families who were asking questions. There was a lot of cross-communications going on.

It was also how Headquarters was functioning. There was a lot of confidence in people making good decisions for the right reasons. For the fire department and for our concerns. People were resolved to understand. There were a lot of individuals lost. We needed to keep going as a department to meet the situation as well as we could. The Chief officers were always positive in the sense of we own this. It's our job. And we're going to make sure the fire department has a strong, credible, safe presence at the site.

Early in the third week Sal Cassano came to me and Chief Pat McNally and asked us if we'd be the site 'Night-Commanders.' We did that for a month. It was rewarding and satisfying from my perspective because I got to watch the entire site and saw how things were going. Monitoring the progress. During the day Pat and I went to funerals. Many times, I would leave the site at 7:00 A.M. go home, jump in the shower, put the uniform on, and go to a funeral some place. We did that almost every morning after we finished our night shift.

I appreciated Sal, who was the Chief of Operations, for the confidence he had in Pat and me to take on this responsibility. We both knew many of the firefighters, officers, and chiefs down there and I think we kept it moving along nicely. Occasionally we had to adjudicate a few issues between the NYPD and the PAPD. But basically, we had good relationships with everybody and made good progress.

We stayed on the site till May. Providing what was needed was the whole key to the World Trade Center operation and with all the emotional recovery and physical recovery. Having resourcefulness and resilience. There were people not digging in the rubble contributing just as much. If not more. In structuring and providing family support by being 'family liaisons.' Those people were just as important and resourceful as somebody driving an excavator or trying to deliver tools at the World Trade Center.

## We needed to keep going as a department to meet the situation as well as we could.

I felt I did a good job providing a presence in the firehouses and finding out; How are you doing? Where are your problems? Who are you having the most problems with? How are you addressing them? And are you keeping an eye on each other?

How many firefighters took it upon themselves to be Radar O'Reilly the tool guy. The go-to guy. And they became the go-to people. Yeah, a firefighter who you didn't even know was asking "Chief, what do you need? Chief I can do this. I can do that." And in Headquarters too. Individuals who without coordination from supervisors took on tasks beyond what was normally required.

I have so much pride in the resourcefulness firefighters are known for. When five firefighters get off a rig and walk into a building there's nothing they can't fix. Well, the Trade Center comes down and the attitude of the fire-

**Trade Center comes down and the attitude of the firefighters is we can do this. We can fix this. We can make this right. That was a tremendous thing to witness and a great thing to be part of.**

fighters is we can do this. We can fix this. We can make this right. That was a tremendous thing to witness and a great thing to be part of.

There's a lot of good that came out of it. Clearly the best thing that happened, something we can all be proud of as Chiefs, nobody suffered a serious life-threatening injury. Not only our folks but all the construction workers, cops, and everybody else. Nobody suffered a serious life-threatening injury and believe me there were plenty of opportunities for somebody to get in trouble and get hurt there.

Pier 94 was in the 3rd Division's administration area. It fell on us to provide a daily presence of people to pull together the family-support services at Pier 94 for the fire department. They provided a tremendous presence. Clearly a lot of compassion for everybody. And the FDNY got that set up in three days from nothing. Again, the resourcefulness. The most important element to the whole recovery. Chief Galvin spent quite a bit of time at Pier 94 and provided them with needed resources.

I felt my role on the 9/11 anniversaries was to provide comfort, so people knew the leadership cared about them. I always made it a point of remembering who the family members were so I could call out to them making

sure I went to each family member in particular firehouses where I had a relationship. I felt it was my job. Providing empathy and compassion to the parents who lost their firefighter at the Trade Center. And being we were the same age we had a common bond of being parents. I know it was very important to Sal Cassano. To know who the family members were. And to know their concerns over the years not just immediately afterwards and continue to understand how they were doing. I always made it a point to know them and spend some time with them. And I enjoyed that. I relished the opportunity to do that and make the bond and connection with them. To try and make them understand these individuals are important and the department still relishes the service of that member and their family.

The year after the Trade Center many of us may not have been quite ready for prime time but we got thrown into leadership roles. And as you are learning your new role you still had to address the repercussions taking place from the World Trade Center attack. Making sure the firefighters' and new officers could carry out their roles. We had a whole new cadre of leadership from company officer to Staff-Chiefs. I always took pride in how we were able to stand up and provide the training. Helping people accepting new positions and rebuilding the department. Afterwards I was made the Brooklyn-Borough-Commander. I felt my primary role was visiting the Brooklyn firehouses that suffered the most losses.

On the anniversary of 9/11 I made sure to go to two masses usually Ladder 105 and Rescue 2's. And I would always make sure I got by Ladder 132 because John Vigiano would be there for their ceremony. Then get myself to the Headquarters ceremony for Pete Ganci, Jerry Barbara, Donald Burns and Bill Feehan. Finally, I'd either end up down at the Trade Center with the band or go home and have a quiet night with my wife.

My wife will always be grateful for the Lynbrook Volunteer Fire Department Golf outing occurring on Tuesday. It can clearly be said the outing possibly saved my life. I'm not being dramatic. I'm saying it's possible. You just don't know. Tommy Galvin was in the hotel for the second collapse and survived. Where would I have been? ❖

# Anna Schermerhorn Collins

## Firefighter Ladder 9 (promoted to Lieutenant)

On the morning of September 11th, I was home in Riverdale the Bronx and was just awake when my phone rang. It was my sister-in-law. She asked if I had turned on my TV. I said "No why? What happened?" She said, "Anna just turn on the TV." I turned on the TV saw the image of 1-World Trade Center on fire said goodbye, hung up and saw the second plane fly into 2-World Trade Center. Then a message rolled across the TV screen: 'All police, emergency medical personnel and firefighters are being Recalled to Duty.'

My firehouse Ladder 9 is located on Great Jones Street in Manhattan's Lower-East village area. I didn't have a car at the time and went to the number-1 subway station on 231st Street and Broadway in the Bronx. When I got there, I saw a train go by and was like okay great the trains are running. I asked the token booth clerk and she said "Yes, the trains are running as far as Chambers Street." I went on the platform and noticed people on their cellphones trying to make calls. Nobody was getting through. After a half-an-hour wait we were finally told no more trains were going into Manhattan.

I tried to catch an express bus. An express bus driver heading out of Manhattan told those of us waiting at the bus stop there were no trains or buses going into the city. I knew Metro-North wasn't going to be working either.

I decided to walk into Manhattan across the bridge at 225th street into Inwood and find a way to get in from there. The police had all bridge traffic shutdown. As I walked over the bridge a firefighter from Ladder 25 in a pickup truck was waving his hands telling the police officers he needed to get through. I called out to him said I was a firefighter trying to get to Ladder 9. He said jump in. We drove to his firehouse on West 77th Street. On the way there he told me both World Trade Center towers had fallen. I didn't know that. From there I jumped in a cab and arrived at Great Jones Street at around 11:20 A.M. That whole process took a long time.

Firefighters coming in on 'Recall' were arriving in waves. We knew Engine 33 had responded on the 2nd alarm and Ladder 9 responded on the 3rd alarm. Earlier some guys went over to Great Jones lumberyard across the street from the firehouse and were able to get one of their trucks to drive them to the site. There's a photo somewhere of the firefighters from 33 and 9 on a flatbed lumberyard truck heading into the World Trade Center site.

Fifteen of us were waiting in the firehouse when we were directed to responded to the quarters of Battalion 6. We collected all the tools from the tool locker in the basement, emergency medical equipment, whatever we could grab and got on a flatbed lumberyard truck which drove us to the quarters of Battalion 6 and Ladder 3 on West 13th Street. Many members from the 6th Battalion were there.

We tried to account for who was working. Because this happened at the change of the tours, and everybody jumped on the rigs we had no idea of the extent of how bad it was. I remember looking at Ladder 3's running board (a chalkboard-list of who's working and their position/tactical duties for the tour) and seeing Captain Paddy Brown's name on the board. That hit me. I don't know why it hit me so hard. I had known Paddy from when I was training to get on the job through mutual friends and it shouldn't have surprised me. He was on duty because I knew. No matter where he was. He would've been there.

We realized both Engine 33 and Ladder 9 were riding heavy. The probie (probationary firefighter with less than a year in the field) in Ladder 9 worked the night-tour and was not supposed to be on-duty during the day. We found out later that he had jumped on the rig after being told by the senior guys not to jump on the rig.

At 1:30 in the afternoon the 6th Battalion Commander told us to get a city bus to go down to the site in. We commandeered a city bus. Got on the bus with all the tools and equipment. We're ready to go when the 6th Battalion Commander walked on the bus, looked at us with a heavy face and said, "I don't know how to tell all of you this but we're not going anywhere." We were angry. We wanted to go. And I knew he knew we wanted to go. But we were ordered off the bus and went back in quarters again waiting for further orders.

At some point Richie Meehan who was a firefighter in Ladder 3 came walking into the firehouse. Richie had not been on-duty. He had gone down to the site on his own. When he walked into Ladder 3's firehouse I realized this was so much worse than any of us could imagine. We were still thinking firefighters knew about the possible collapse were given warnings and were out of the buildings. Richie was caked over from head to toe in gray dust. I looked at his face. His eyes were glassy, emotionless. There was nothing there. He walked up the stairs. Not saying anything to anyone. That's when it really hit us.

We called our firehouse on Great Jones Street to find out if anyone had shown up. Ladder 37 from the Bronx was covering alarms in our firehouse. They said there was one guy Burt Springstead. We asked Burt "Have you seen

anybody? Do you know if anybody's okay?" He was able to account for a few of the guys from Ladder 9, but nobody had heard anything about anyone from Engine 33.

In the afternoon I was sitting in the house watch when the Chief asked me if I had called my parents and as bad as it sounds, I never thought to call them. I feel bad about that. It was the furthest thing from my mind. All we were thinking about was trying to figure out who from Great Jones Street and the Battalion were alive. He said, "You need to call your parents." My parents lived in Minnesota. They had no idea of what my status was.

At 6:00 P.M. further instructions came in stating those who are scheduled on-duty for the night-tour should work and stay until 09:00 hours. Anyone who was not scheduled on the night-tour would start in the morning. So, we now had a new work schedule. The Chief told us to return to our quarters and stand-fast until further orders.

Walking down Lafayette Street towards our firehouse an NYU security-van driver asked us if we needed a lift anywhere. The lieutenant said yes. Looked at us, defying the Chief's orders said, "Do whatever you need to do." We all jumped in the van. South of Canal Street power was out for most of downtown and the streets got progressively darker. We got out at City Hall Park where a mustering of Chiefs were at a staging area. Ironically the first person we ran into was the 6th Battalion Commander who had ordered us to go back to our quarters. He looked the other way.

Then twelve of us from 33 and 9 started trudging our way towards the World Trade Center site. We passed Ladder 9's rig on Church Street and searched the rig for whatever tools were left. The front of the cab was totally damaged. We took a few ten-foot hooks, the torch, and the maul. We found Engine 33's apparatus on West Street hooked up to a hydrant still chugging away and looked into Engine 33's compartments to see what tools we could find. I climbed into the cab and found the riding list for the 6 by 9 night-tour. I put it in my pocket to take back and give to the senior guys of Engine 33. I felt it was important for me to grab that piece of paper.

Destroyed rigs were everywhere. Ladder 3's aerial ladder looked like twisted spaghetti. Ladder 101 and Ladder 105's rigs were crushed underneath the pedestrian bridge that went over West Street.

We were at the World Trade Center site for a few hours trying to search the pile for victims. We didn't have shovels. It wasn't effective. We weren't accomplishing much. At some point we knew several of us would be starting on the morning shift and we needed to go back to quarters and regroup somehow. Some stayed and some went back to quarters. That was my first day. I slept in the firehouse.

The next morning, we were not in-service as a Ladder company. We needed a rig, tools, and equipment. We were still trying to account for everybody who was missing.

They sent us down to the World Trade Center to work in teams doing victim recovery. That shift we were split up amongst Lieutenant LaRocco and Lieutenant Acevedo. I was with Lieutenant LaRocco. At first it felt like a lot of hurry up and wait. Then while sitting around the Staging-Area someone called out "Does anybody have a saw?" Lieutenant Acevedo saw it as an opportunity to get on the pile. He gathered us up and off we went.

Going through the Winter Garden (public space in the World Financial buildings complex) everything was brownish gray. Like a snowstorm. Windows, floors, walls, covered in dust. Finger-written messages in the dust, concerning missing members, were all over the site. I saw the names of firefighters missing from Engine 235 Nick Chiofalo and Larry Veling. I worked with them when I was on probationary-firefighter-rotation. Their being unaccounted for stuck out in my mind.

Day into night we worked as two teams searching in the pile doing our recovery effort. No photograph. No movie. Nothing portrayed compared with the enormity of 16 acres of destruction. It was overwhelming.

The bucket brigades on the first day and the days immediately after were chaotic. Firefighters were little dots. Little ants on a huge hill strewn with rubble and black smoke pushing up from the fires below. Where do you even begin? Lieutenant Acevedo would pick a spot and say, "We'll dig here." and we would start digging.

At one point during the evening digging on top of a huge mound of rubble we were recovering human material. While looking for a new place to dig the ground was spongy. Steve Spellman from Ladder 9 said, "We're going to dig right here." We started digging and unearthed a dead man who was intact. He didn't have a shirt on. He had pants on with a pager and was obviously deceased. While clearing him out of the rubble to put him in a body-bag I was trying to make sense of how this individual was still in one piece. Was he from the top of the building and rode it down during the collapse? I didn't know how this could be. That these enormously tall buildings could collapse in a way we would find someone whole. In one piece. We put him in a body-bag. Got him on a long-board and carried him out.

We were sent back to quarters for the night to sleep and start another day. Steve Spellman was former military. Very sharp and very aggressive. He had a sense of duty. Didn't want to quit. When we were told to return to quarters he stayed. Lieutenant Acevedo was looking for his best friend another lieutenant who was unaccounted for stayed. And firefighter Mike McGuire who responded that day and survived the collapse was driven by having survived also stayed.

There was a heated debate concerning when Ladder 9 would go back in-service. A few members said, 'No way we're not ready to go back.' They wanted to continue searching. There was the anger. "How can we go back in-service when we're missing people?" They felt it was their duty to go the site. I think some mentally, weren't prepared to be in-service. I felt we needed to get back in-service. I wanted nothing more than to get back on our rig and start responding to runs. Going to fires, emergencies, whatever.

Ladder 9's apparatus was destroyed, and the replacement apparatus was our old Ladder 9 rig which had been used as a city-wide spare apparatus. I was in the firehouse and saw it coming down Great Jones Street and immediately knew it was our old rig. A chauffeur in 33 Engine Carl Oreggia was meticulous about the maintenance of our apparatus and adorned our rigs with gold stars. When that old Ladder 9 Mack truck with the gold stars on it came down the block it was like seeing an old friend. It felt so good seeing that rig. We went back in-service and started taking in runs again. That was the best feeling after being in all this chaos.

Deep in the Pile steam, smoke, and heat was coming up from the last of the fires that were still burning for weeks afterwards. Our time was now split between responding to alarms from our firehouse and being assigned to the WTC site because our 95 foot tower-ladder could reach into inaccessible areas.

For a long time, we were operating in the tower-ladder bucket, dumping water on 7-World Trade Center's burning building rubble.

The odor that permeated the site remained. The funny thing about the smell was at first, I hated it. Yet as the weeks turned into months and that smell started to go away in a weird way, I missed it. Because for me it finalized it. There was no one left alive. The rigs were being cleaned and the air at the site started to clear and that was so sad. Once the smell was gone it was the end of any hope. Even though I knew that second night when we were digging, we weren't saving anybody. I know other people going deep into the voids felt that there was still a good chance of finding people. Working on top I felt there's no way. There can't be anyone alive here.

Every day you kept hoping there'd be a story about somebody being rescued. But it didn't work out that way. Instead, what we got every day was the names of those who were identified as deceased. Still, there were many that weren't accounted for.

Our guys from 33 and 9 were getting out of 1-World Trade Center. They were almost at the bottom when it collapsed. Some of the members from Ladder 9 did make it out. But no members of 33 Engine other than the chauffeur survived. We didn't start finding body parts of our missing members until January, February, and March when the digging progressed, and the pile became the pit.

Afterwards, I struggled with the fact it took me so long to get to the firehouse on the morning of 9/11. I wish I had been able to do more that day. Even when I was there at the site trying to be effective. It didn't feel like it was making a difference. And I know that's silly because I think every little bit helped and it takes everybody to try to make it better. But as one individual I didn't feel I had done anything important or extraordinary, or valuable, when there were so many people who gave everything that day.

Getting back in-service was important. And I think what also helped me was our team-leader Lieutenant LaRocco. He and I had a good talk that first night. He had close calls in his career and was being very sensible and practical saying "This is our job. This is what we do." He was a guy who believed in fate. He believed we are here to do a job and stay focused. That was important to me. He kept me grounded. I felt this is the guy I want to keep working with.

We had guys who survived the collapse in the firehouse who were not doing so well. The chauffeur (a firefighter who drives and operates apparatus) was the only one from Engine 33 who survived. When he came back to work after many days searching for victims, he couldn't do it anymore. He worked in the firehouse for one night and that was it. He was done. I don't blame anybody for any of that. I can't even imagine what it would've been like to be there when those buildings collapsed and survived.

I took the 30-day-detail to work at the World Trade Center for the month of April. That was important to me because finally I felt I was making a valuable contribution. Spending a month there going through rubble raking and digging for body parts. Getting nearer to closing the site. That was probably the most important month of my career.

I had been studying for lieutenant's promotion exam and stopped studying after the attack. I was going to scrap the whole thing when I decided a couple of weeks before the exam I might as well take it. Thankfully, from all the studying I did before the World Trade Center attack, I ended up getting a high enough score to become a lieutenant.

Going through all of that had a big impact on me as an officer. Being responsible for the safety of my crew and knowing at any time anything could happen. September 11, 2001, started off just like any other beautiful day. And it doesn't have to be a terrorist attack. It could be a fatal fire. It could be any type of unforeseen events. My takeaway is expect the unexpected. At any point things can radically change. And it's my duty and obligation to ensure that my firefighters are prepared and as safe as they can be while we complete the duties we have to do.

> ## My takeaway is expect the unexpected. At any point things can radically change. And it's my duty and obligation to ensure that my firefighters are prepared and as safe as they can be while we complete the duties we have to do.

I had a conversation with somebody years after 9/11 about how some can absorb it a little better every year. Not that it's ever going to be healed. But you process it better. For me it's the opposite. As I get older, and more time passes the significance of 9/11 has been greater every year. I think about it more especially with fewer and fewer people on the job now who were on the job then.

If I am working on the eve of the anniversary of 9/11 I talk with the young firefighters and do a presentation with the other firefighters and officers in the house who were on-duty during 9/11 to educate and share with the young firefighters our experiences. It helps to talk about it and share with them. But yeah, it's a funny thing. I thought it would get easier as time goes by too and now, I don't think it will. We're reminded all the time by some retired firefighter or active firefighter who has died from cancer after logging in hundreds of hours at the World Trade Center site and you wonder. When is it going to happen in my future? But that's the risks we take doing our job. We know when we sign up there's a risk. It's a dangerous job. But we love our job and it's worth it. I wouldn't want to do anything else. ❖

# Howard Hill
## Deputy Chief Division 1 (promoted to Assistant Chief of Department, Chief of Fire Prevention)

I was promoted to Deputy Chief on July 7, 2001, and assigned to Division 1 an area which encompasses all of lower Manhattan up to and including West 42nd street in Midtown. A few days before 9/11 I checked in with Chief Pete Hayden the Division 1 Commander to schedule our next 24-hour tour. I took the night of Sunday September 9th into the day of September 10th he took the night of September 10th into the day of September 11th. If I had worked the second half of our mutual and it had been me instead of Pete working on 9/11, I believe I would not be writing this now.

**If I had worked the second half of our mutual and it had been me instead of Pete working on 9/11, I believe I would not be writing this now.**

On the morning of September 11, 2001, after dropping my youngest son off at school I was jogging along the water near the Verrazano Narrows bridge in Bay-Ridge Brooklyn. When I finished jogging, I drove to my bank. In the street I sensed a strange buzz. People were quietly talking to each other, almost whispering, about a fire in a high-rise building in Manhattan and a plane crash. I decided to drive down to the 69th street pier where I could get a good view of downtown Manhattan from across the harbor.

When I arrived, there was a large crowd on the pier. I could plainly see both 1 and 2 World Trade Center buildings burning. People were saying it was a terrorist attack. I knew someone with binoculars and asked to use them. Through the binoculars I saw either parts falling off the building or people jumping out of broken windows I couldn't tell. Many on the pier were saying it was people. I was mesmerized by what I was witnessing. I was willing myself to leave but couldn't pull myself away. Totally immersed in what I was seeing.

Suddenly a massive cloud of dust burst out rolling over the water, obscuring all of lower Manhattan. I knew a building had collapsed. I fell to my knees and grabbed the pier railing. I was still hanging onto that railing when the second collapse occurred. The lower harbor was now enveloped in a mountain of evil-looking smoke. A gigantic dust cloud blotted out the skyline. Briefly, I saw a gap where the Twin-Towers once stood.

I was now desperate to get home, change into my uniform and get to the scene. Faces of firefighters I knew in Division 1 were reeling in my mind. I knew for certain Pete Hayden was in the collapse area.

I raced to my car. As I drove through the traffic clogged streets I saw a car with five firefighters packed in one of them holding his helmet on the hood of the car honking its horn. I felt as if we were being attacked and were now at war. It brought to mind a scene in a movie about Pearl Harbor where the civilians and soldiers were trying to come to grips with what was happening as Japanese planes roared overhead.

I got home, immediately called the FDNY Operations Center, and made myself available in whatever capacity was needed. I anticipated the need for managing this unthinkable World Trade Center buildings collapse. I told them I was a covering Deputy Chief in Division 1 and asked, "What do you want me to do?" They needed a Deputy Chief to be in command of Division 1. I was hoping to be running a Command Post at the World Trade Center site.

I called my wife at work to let her know I was going in. She was in her classroom and all she knew was parents were coming in to pick up their children. Our oldest son was already being picked up by a relative from his high school on 16th Street in Manhattan. Maggie would get our youngest son from his elementary school when she finished work. I knew my family was safe. My wife told me to be careful and call her later to let her know how it was going. She asked me "What the hell is happening." I told her I loved her, and I'd call her as soon as I could.

I drove onto the Brooklyn-Queens Expressway. It was devoid of traffic. The NYPD allowed only emergency responders on the highways. This was why the streets were jammed with cars. I got to Division 1 in 30 minutes, record time. When I walked into the Division office a large group of officers were standing in front of the desk with a Battalion Chief sitting behind it looking from face to face as they all tried to talk at once. So many firefighters came in on Recall. I had to manage the influx of personnel so we could have accountability.

I had the officers start organizing members into teams. We taped large, flip-chart size sheets of paper on the office wall, listing what units were available in the Division. We organized teams and put the names of the 'recalled' officers and firefighters of each team and posted that on the office wall. It quickly became apparent. We had a lot of people but no apparatus and little equipment for them. Almost all of Division 1 responded to the attack. Their firehouses apparatus was gone. A few 'relocated-units' from other Boroughs in the city were filling the empty firehouses but not enough to control a multiple-alarm fire or significant event.

I gave Operations a status report describing the limited amount of fire companies available to respond resulting in a lack of adequate fire protection. They told me to do everything I could to organize a response force and it looked like they might need fresh firefighters to go down to the site at 3:00 P.M. and to call back then.

We went to work getting updated reports on who had come in and informed the Battalions to stand-by until further orders. And, most importantly not to go down to the site unless ordered by the Division.

We consulted the 'Emergency Command' manual for procedures involving civil-riots and improvised on those guidelines. There were no specific procedures for a situation of this magnitude. A major problem was trying to keep the members in the firehouses. Many had come to Division 1 headquarters. Quite a crowd had gathered on the apparatus floor. I called them together and explained how we were organizing teams, and no one was to leave. I appealed to them to be professional and at 15:00 hours I was going to call Operations to see if they could be assigned to respond to the World Trade Center site for relief purposes.

They were watching volunteers working bucket-brigades on TV while they were being told to remain in quarters. This was hard to take. They had friends and family in that death filled rubble. Most stayed. Everyone was stressed-out. I completely understood how they felt. I wanted to work at the site too, but the situation mandated we follow orders and be prepared to protect NYC the best we could.

I drove to firehouses to support the Battalion Chiefs with their efforts to have the firefighters remain in quarters until further orders.

I went to the collapse site. Everyone looked ghost like covered in the gray dust. 7-World Trade Center was burning vigorously with flames out windows on several floors and no apparatus or members fighting the fire.

At 2:00 P.M. I checked in at the Command Post on West Street to find out if there were any procedures for responding into the collapse area in the event immediate assistance was required. I was informed of the access points to get through areas blocked by the collapse rubble. The streets without water due to broken water mains and the locations where FDNY fireboats were providing a water supply. My orders from the Staff Chiefs were 'Respond to all alarms for fires and emergencies outside of the immediate 16 acres collapse area.'

I called Operations at 3:00 P.M. sharp. They told me keep all members available to respond to alarms and maintain a state-of-readiness in Division 1's response area. I explained how members were witnessing volunteers working at the site while they sat in firehouses, and this wasn't fair. Operations response was "None of that mattered. Do not send units down to the site unless ordered." I acknowledged.

Everyone in the FDNY wanted to respond to the site. I went back downstairs. Called all the firefighters together again and said I regretted I could not order them into the World Trade Center site. There was only so much persuasion I could muster to keep them in the firehouse. Some were leaving the apparatus floor and going to the site as I was talking. Battalion Chiefs in the Division were telling me they couldn't keep the 'Recalled' members in quarters much longer.

Late in the afternoon there was one brief good moment when Chief Pete Hayden returned to the Division 1 office with his son. At least one person I feared dead was alive. His face was caked-over with a thick layer of gray powder. His eyes were ringed in blood. I told him I was doing the best I could to get the Division back in operational condition. He then left to get some medical attention.

The day became night and with it came the wives, brothers, daughters, fathers, mothers, friends. They all came to the Division wanting to know where their loved ones were. Headquarters couldn't provide this information nor could anyone else. I could only answer with uncertainties on who was alive or dead. I knew for certain many firefighters had died and there was no official casualty report yet. Frustrated family members said to me "How can it be that you, a Deputy Chief in Division 1, has no information?" All I could do was be respectful and as honest as I could. I told them I truly didn't know and to come back later, tomorrow perhaps, when we might have the information, we all wanted.

## None of the companies who responded to the attack, which was approximately 95% of Division 1 units, came back in-service that day—none.

Through the night I visited firehouses trying to strengthen their spirits. I would gather the members together and tell them that even with our tremendous losses I knew we would respond when the alarm sounded. It was essential to let them know their leadership was aware of what they were going through and doing everything possible to support them.

The phone never stopped ringing. I wanted to throw it out the window. The same types of problems kept coming up the need for personnel accountability, tools, and apparatus. I never had more than a skeleton crew of companies available to respond to alarms. None of the companies who responded to the attack, which was approximately 95% of Division 1 units, came back in-service that day—none.

FDOC called at 5 A.M. I was told to be the FDNY representative detailed to NYPD's Command Center in One-Police Plaza. The NYPD command center became the temporary headquarters for the Office of Emergency Management (OEM). Various agency desks were arranged in a horse-shoe shape with a phone and an agency rep at each desk. I relieved Chief Kilduff. On a platform in the center stood a NYPD Captain looking like a circus-ringmaster with his bull horn and pointer calling out the agencies to respond to a particular request.

Calls came in for FDNY attention; hydrants out of service, people wanted to give food, shovels, and other equipment. One call came in from a car dealer in New Jersey saying they wanted to donate six new vans. I arranged delivery of them. A Police Officer came over and whispered in my ear inside the World Trade Center collapse rubble was over one thousand rounds of ammunition, hazardous materials, and a large number of weapons. I relayed that information to the WTC Command Post. I was informed there was gold-bullion stored in the cellar of 4 World Trade Center and passed this information on to WTC command. (According to the New York Mercantile Exchange: Scotia Mocatta, the bullion and metals division of the Bank of Nova Scotia was storing 379,036 ounces of gold and 29,942,619 ounces of silver in vaults under 4 World Trade Center. That's 11.8 tons of gold and 935.7 tons of silver. It was owned by people or companies who bought the metals as investments.)[38]

I sat at the FDNY desk in the Police Command Center non-stop answering question like these and got relieved at 2:00 P.M. on 9/12. I drove home. Hugs all-around when I came through the door.

My next assignment was to take command of Division 1 on Thursday, September 13th at 9 A.M. The members were reeling from the losses their companies suffered. The manpower for the Division had to be organized. The same problems existed; supplying firefighting equipment and the critical shortage of apparatus needed to be managed to get units back in-service as soon as possible.

At 6 P.M. I was finally ordered to take command of a Command Post at the World Trade Center site. I will never forget the night of 9/13. Power was out for most of lower Manhattan. The dark rubble strewn streets were patrolled by soldiers with M-16 rifles. I felt like I was back in Vietnam as I worked my way through the destruction. I was assigned to relieve a Chief at the 'West Command Post' located on West Street in front of Two World Financial Center.

The entire 16-acre site was broken into four Command Posts, one on each perimeter side of the collapse zone. The overall Staff Chief Site-Commander was quartered in Engine 10 and Ladder 10's firehouse on Liberty Street. This firehouse miraculously suffered little damage from the collapse of both towers.

Hills of rubble piles blocked direct access to 'West Command.' The best access was to walk near the Hudson River, cross through the back of the Winter Garden and come out on West Street.

Two-years prior at Christmas time my family and I enjoyed a wonderful concert by a choir in the Winter Garden. A great glass-enclosed space beautifully decorated between World Financial Center Buildings 2 & 3. It was a NYC holiday treat. We were looking forward to visiting it again. Heavy steel-beams had crashed through its ceiling shattering the glass and filling the space with glass wreckage. I carefully walked through then stepped out into a dark, nightmarish scene of smoking destruction.

Several large fires were actively burning underneath the smoke filled rubble obscuring all recognizable features. I climbed over a hill of debris and noticed a large steel-column laying on top of a pile of rubble. At the tip of this prominent steel perch was a Chief. I walked up told him I was his relief and asked for a description of West Command. He pointed out an area from where we were standing and said, "This is West Command." There were no structures only high debris piles one not much different from the rest. In the backdrop were these immense skeletal-steel-remains of the WTC buildings protruding into the night sky. Portable pole-lights powered by rumbling generators created pockets of light in the surrounding darkness casting an eerie glow on the billowing smoke.

There were FDNY firefighters, civilian volunteers, firefighters from other states, police officers, construction workers and God knows who else crawling over debris like ants. Carrying buckets filled with debris then dumping them in any available clear space. This was so different from the organized fireground chaos command operations I was used to. This was overwhelming.

I had no control over non-FDNY personnel and didn't know who was where. I rapidly asked the Chief "Who is working on the pile? What voids are being searched? Do we have any information on trapped victims?" Trying to take on the whole chaotic scene I felt uncertain and disorientated.

The height of the fallen column gave a focal point for officers trying to find the Command Post and provided a peak where I could overlook a portion of the scene.

Standing on the column behind me was the Officer in Command of NYPD Emergency-Services. I asked if police officers could organize controlled 'access-points' to limit who was coming into the area. He said he would, but it was obvious he didn't feel it was possible. Other than short conversations there were no formal meetings with NYPD. Everyone was doing the best they could to deal with what was in front of us.

I established a Staging-Area for FDNY personnel directly to my right and went out onto the pile. When I saw a Battalion Chief, I requested a 'progress report.' He told me a general surface-area search was being performed with selective debris removal in areas that might hold a trapped victim in a void. Standard operating procedures for a building collapse. I had him define the area he was working in and to report any dangerous searches to me. I contacted the other Battalion Chiefs on their radios and requested them report into the Command Post. Chiefs slowly started coming in giving progress reports and requesting various resources. I did not stop talking.

**There were FDNY firefighters, civilian volunteers, firefighters from other states, police officers, construction workers and God knows who else crawling over debris like ants.**

Communicating was difficult with anyone more than a couple of feet away. There were hose-lines operating, generators running and construction equipment creating a chaotic clatter of noise. We were given N-95 masks that slip over your mouth and nose. I had to shout my instructions to be heard and often draped the mask around my neck. We didn't have enough handie-talkies for everyone which created a problem contacting people in the distance.

Volunteers kept pouring in while incoming FDNY firefighters were standing by in the Staging-Area. I vividly remembered the firefighters in quarters watching volunteers working at the site while I tried to keep them in firehouses. Well now that would not do. I turned my bullhorn to its highest volume. Went out on the pile. Got up close and personal to anyone who was not an FDNY member and told them in no uncertain terms either go to the Staging-Area or leave my area. This was a risk assessment priority-action to obtain accountability and control of the significant risks the searchers were taking. I got many dirty looks from the sea of volunteers, but I wouldn't allow them to ignore me. I started sending in FDNY members to take over the volunteer's positions on the bucket-brigades and searching in the pile. There were police officers in the area who gave me some support in getting the response I needed from all the different volunteers many were civilians in sneakers and jackets not knowing the dangers present only looking to help.

© New York City Fire Department

The union ironworkers have my complete respect. Immediately after the attack they came to the site and went to work cutting huge steel columns with fires burning below giving off heavy smoke. This required great skill and determination. They were extraordinary and initially they weren't getting paid for it.

On September 14th President Bush came to the site climbed on top of a rubble pile with a firefighter and gave his speech. It was really something we needed to hear. We were beat up. Staggered by our loses. When he began talking, we heard what we desperately needed to hear. Never in my life had a politician made a greater impact on me. I honor and thank President Bush for that short speech which meant so much to all of us.

Late September was unusually mild in NYC this changed one night when heavy rain with strong winds blew down onto the site. Large pieces of cracked glass began to fall from the World Financial Center Buildings broken windows. The heavy glass was scaling through the night sky smashing around search teams and around the West-Command Post area. Anyone struck by it would suffer serious injuries. Also, the heavy rain in the pitch black night was further restricting vision and causing loose debris to slide making conditions even more unstable. I decided to pull all teams out of the West Command search area and moved to an area of safety. I called the on-duty Site-Commander and told him I wanted to pull my people back. He said it was my decision and shortly after I believe the other sectors stopped work as well. I used this time to meet with the officers and go over the need to keep good control over who went into voids, where they were working and who was supervising them. Once the high wind and rain stopped teams immediately went out on the pile intensely searching for victims.

As the days wore on a north to south roadway through the site was cleared which allowed an increase of activity with dump trucks, bulldozers, and excavators all going full speed. Everyone was under pressure to find anyone who was alive and trapped. There was no slacking off.

## Never in my life had a politician made a greater impact on me. I honor and thank President Bush for that short speech which meant so much to all of us.

New routine search procedures were developed. When a void was discovered, we called for a camera to be snaked down into the void. If the void could possibly hold a victim or, if suspected body parts were present, we called for the dogs to verify. If the camera and the dogs indicated a presence, then we sent in people.

The dogs proved to be very unreliable. They often falsely indicated someone was alive or there were body parts in areas where only rotting food was found. But it

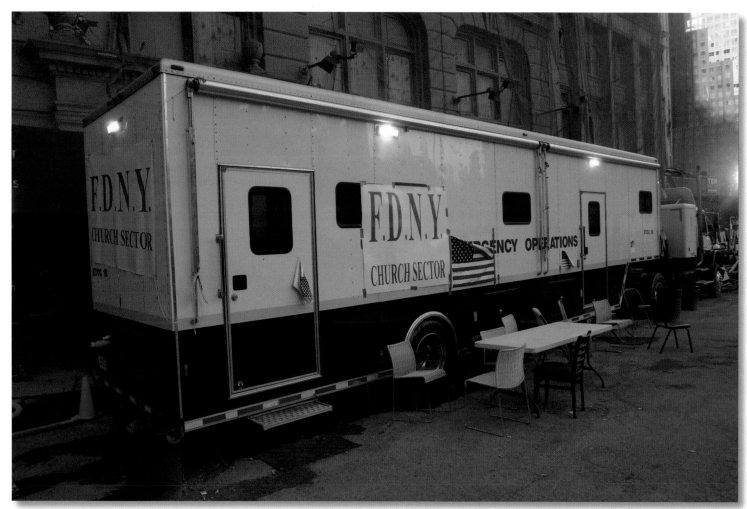

## These procedures were repeated again and again, camera, dogs, people.

was hard to do away with the dogs. They were very popular with the media. Everyone seemed to love the dogs with bandages on their burned paws from walking on the heated steel. These procedures were repeated again and again, camera, dogs, people.

On a few occasions where a void lead into another open area which needed further searching, I would be called to go down into the void to survey the next set of proposed searches and decide whether to continue. The voids were a horror. Tight, twisting, dark, stinking holes with smoke drifting around creating pockets of deadly carbon monoxide. The search crews crawled through no matter what the conditions were. Anyone performing those searches gave it all they had in their attempts to save a trapped victim.

'West Command' quickly grew from a steel girder jutting out over a rubble pile to a small shack and finally to a trailer. I liked the shack. It was a 15´ deep, 20´ long, three-sided open front with maps and team roster clipboards on the walls and a large sheet of plywood supported by two wooden horses serving as the desk. The firefighters erected a wooden, 2˝ x 4˝ flagpole giving it an 'outpost' look that suited the environment.

When the trailer first came to the site, I was reluctant to use it. I told the Army Corps of Engineers to put it off to the side to leave a clear space in front of my Command. I wanted to be out in front, able to survey the site continuously and be where the people who needed to contact me could readily find me. I kept the trailer off to the side and used it for conferences and communications.

Two weeks after 9/11 the possibility of someone being alive was getting slim and we were getting desperate. A French rescue-team technical specialist approached me and proposed a system to locate a tapping noise using triangulation. It required shutting down all operations to hear the sound and fix its location. There were reports of trapped victims using their cellphones to call for help. None of this was officially verified but the media was reporting it and rumors were circulating indicating it might be a possibility. I was ready to try anything. I called over one of our Rescue Captains whose opinion I trusted. If he said it was possible, I would call the Site-Commander and request shutting down my sector to perform the procedure. The Rescue Captain said the system had flaws in accurately pinpointing a sound and he did not believe the reports of victims using their cellphones and did not want to stop searches in progress. That was good enough for me to drop it.

Another time a woman was brought to my Command Post who told me of a dream she had. Someone was trapped but able to see a light near a green sign.

The information she provided was too general. I told her if she could provide more specific information on a location in my area, I would be willing to send personnel to investigate. I was ready to listen to any suggestion to find a victim.

Every day we expected someone would be found. We were constantly disappointed. The many long hours spent risking everything gained us nothing. It was a hard thing to take. Teams of firefighters relentlessly crawled into one dark hole after another. We found many body parts but never a living victim.

Around the end of September, the surface debris and most deep voids had been searched. Staff Chiefs determined there was a very low probability anyone could still be alive without having water. Rescue searches were generally called off unless something significant would warrant a high-risk effort. The bulk of the work now was shifting thru debris looking for the dead.

I volunteered to work a straight 30-day-detail at the site for the month of November. The 'pile' now became known as the 'pit.' New routines developed during the 'recovery' mode. Excavators would lift up rubble drop it in a clear space and firefighters would sift through it looking for body parts with shovels and hands before the rubble would be loaded onto a dump truck and taken to a landfill in Staten Island where it would again be searched for body parts by firefighters lining along conveyer belts examining the spread out debris.

After spending hours staring at a confused mass of rubble trying to see mangled human body parts my mind started imagining gruesome images especially in the evenings. I was glad my command duties kept me from constantly staring into debris looking for people I knew.

When remains of a body were found all work in the immediate area would cease. I would go out to consult with searchers to determine if they belonged to a firefighter, police officer or a civilian. If it was a police officer, I would immediately notify NYPD or PAPD and they would take over the recovery process.

If it were an FDNY member I would call for a Chaplin to perform a blessing. The remains were then placed in a stokes stretcher and an American flag draped over it. We would wait for members of the company where the victim worked to arrive which sometimes took 5 hours or more and they would carry out the stokes stretcher. Saluting firefighters lined the area from where the firefighter's body part was found to the ambulance on the access road. As the stokes stretcher passed the firefighters would remove their helmets.

## After spending hours staring at a confused mass of rubble trying to see mangled human body parts my mind started imagining gruesome images especially in the evenings.

The last procedure was to record what the remains were and where they were found in our command post journal. I don't remember how many times I did that. But it was more than I ever wanted to. It was our job for the families and the members who died to ensure we did everything possible to recover the bodies with dignity and respect. But every time we found a body part my heart sank.

I started each tour by telling the officers accountability of assigned team-members was paramount. Any officer who did not communicate where they were and what they were doing would be removed from the site. I was consumed with preventing injuries or deaths on my watch. It was a very dangerous area to work in high piles of unstable building remains were surrounded by construction equipment constantly moving thousands of pounds of rubble. Often excavators would be extended at extreme angles to remove heavy sections of long steel columns so voids could be accessed, and searches made.

There were situations that could have ended badly. A 'Firefighter Assist and Search Team' (FAST) was positioned at each Command Post. They had the sole duty of responding to any situation where a firefighter or other rescue worker needed help. All search team members repeatedly acted heroically. Undeniably risking serious injury. And they did it professionally. Good communications. Constant monitoring of conditions and maintaining safety procedures with an adequate number of members standing by ready to help if needed. This went on non-stop throughout the days, nights, weeks, and months.

In terms of respect for everyone who perished the reverence FDNY members gave a victim's remains could not have been surpassed. The families of all victims were well served. We believed the site was 'Hallowed Ground' where the remains of victims from this attack on our country were still laying buried inside.

With the FDNY being the overall supervisor of the site, no one died during the entire rescue/recovery efforts and there were no life-threatening injuries to any rescue workers that I am aware of. Chiefs and Company Officers did a credible job of controlling operations under difficult circumstances and insured people weren't getting hurt or doing things they shouldn't be doing.

All the bad news of finding only casualties beat us up. Having retired members around made me feel like I

was not alone. The retired members were looking out. Helping you work through a tough time. I would bump into a retired firefighter I used to work with and for a brief moment or two there were smiles and you'd forget the sadness. The FDNY was there big-time.

It was easy to become depressed. Hell, we had good cause to be depressed. At the end of the first week, I was home in my bathroom when suddenly I started sobbing out of control. It came on in a rush. The finality of all the death.

My cousin firefighter Eddie Rall from Rescue Company 2 died in the collapse. A wonderful man. The type of person you'd want to have coaching your kid's baseball team and coming to save you if your life depended on it. His wife, sons, my uncle and aunt, and his brothers were devastated. You never forget the losses from this murderous attack. Sights, sounds, and smells bring on memories that linger forever.

A lot of it was a blur. I wish I could recall half the things I said and did. A flood of people and agencies coming to you for directions. Myriad decisions made and forgotten. Intense and unending. The thing was it didn't stop. You got on site and did not shut up. Giving directions, asking questions, trying to control the chaos. You worried and struggled.

I thought the Chief officers were as effective as…I couldn't imagine anybody being more effective. There was a fair amount of chaos. I know that's a focal point. But I sincerely believe there was a lot more control by Chiefs and Company officers than what was acknowledged.

To limit the time spent working in that environment when the 30-day detail was over a complete change of all personnel relieved the prior months team and at the end of November we were assigned back to our normal companies. At the end of the last day on site I told the members in West Command to meet at a local bar called the 'Raccoon Lounge.' We worked hard. Cold stone sober and determined the entire time. Now it was time to back off. Drop the stress and relax amongst ourselves and we did. I have a picture of us at the bar. Piles of money the bartenders were not taking. Smiling faces instead of grim dirty ones. I am overly fond of this picture and keep it in my office where I can see it.

With my 30-day detail at the WTC site over I resumed working in Division 1. The Division suffered 99 casualties in the attack. There was a cardboard box in the Division office which temporarily held the 'fire-reports' submitted by Division 1 companies who responded to World Trade Center attack.

Normally the Division Chief who had the fire would correlate the responding company fire-reports and make the final summation of fire operations for the official record. Organizing a comprehensive report of responding companies and actions performed on 9/11 was a herculean task. Many reports had to be written by one of the officers of the company who didn't respond because everyone who responded was killed. During my downtime in the Division, I read those fire-reports. I read every single one of them. I couldn't read more than a few at a time. Reports often closed with "God rest their souls."❖

# Robert Palombo
## Union Ironworker

**I** was a Union ironworker on the Marine Parkway Bridge in Brooklyn on 9/11 working on the upper-steel structure listening to a portable radio on a clear sunny day when we heard a plane hit one of the World Trade Center Towers. At first, we thought it was an accident. A few minutes later while staring at flames and smoke a large plane came into view from the north-east then turned heading west and disappeared below some buildings. A second later we saw big red flames coming out of 2-World Trade Center and realized it was a terrorist attack.

Almost immediately the Bridge and Tunnel Authority Police notified our foreman who had one of their radios to shut everything down and leave the bridge. They were shutting down all the bridges in the city. Everyone grabbed their tools wrapped-up the job and went their own way. I went home and watched the news all day, all night.

The following morning our Ironworkers' Local Union 361, we work on bridges and high-rise buildings notified us. "We're going into the World Trade Center site with our equipment." The bridge and building work stopped throughout the city. All the Union ironworkers were going down to the World Trade Center site.

## They were shutting down all the bridges in the city.

On Wednesday September 12th at 5:30 A.M. we met at our job site at the Marine Parkway Bridge. The construction firm knew we were coming and allowed us to take their equipment. We loaded up the trucks with tanks, torches, welding machines and rode into the city. At the Brooklyn Battery tunnel checkpoint the police stopped us. After two of us showed their ID and told them "We're Union ironworkers going to work at Ground Zero." They said go in. As soon as we entered the tunnel we were scattering feet of white powder dust that continued until we stopped at Ground Zero. We walked into the rubble and started working alongside firefighters and police officers on the bucket-brigades digging with our hands.

The Fire Department had GPS (Global Positioning System) equipment to detect locations where we might find human remains or people alive buried under the rubble. The first body part we found was a woman's leg with a black high-heel shoe still attached to the leg sticking up. The Fire Department stepped in. Recorded the location on their GPS and removed it.

As we continued digging, we found more legs and arms. We didn't find anyone alive. We dug by hand with buckets no machines, no heavy equipment, no cranes. Everyone was moving small pieces of material. Then at the end of the line making a pile. Every time we found a body part we'd stop. Fire Department crew members would step in take over and remove it. They told us to watch out for open voids and shifting debris and not climb to the top of the pile. So, we worked on ground level. As ironworkers we climb all over construction steel and bridges, so we know how to climb and get around things. The only protective equipment I wore was my hard hat, safety-vest, and work gloves. No one had masks on. No one said anything about the air quality being hazardous, or anything like that.

The piles of rubble were still hot and smoldering as we continued trying to rescue anyone alive. There was an understanding a person could stay alive underneath the rubble for several days without any food or water. As that first day ended, we were only finding body parts. No one was found alive, and we were beginning to lose hope. We took breaks. Walked off the pile to drink some water. We didn't eat anything. Everywhere you went you were walking in one or two feet of dark-gray dust even on the West Side Highway a distance away. There were snowbanks of heavy dust on crushed firetrucks and passenger cars. We searched anywhere and everywhere for victims.

Several times we heard explosions and thought it might have been from gas leaks. The Fire Department would announce "Everybody off." We ran quickly across the West Side Highway. After a short while the FDNY members would start going back and we all followed them. That happened a few times.

When it got dark, they were putting up lights powered by generators and at 10:00 P.M. our foreman, who was responsible for the trucks and the equipment, said "Let's go." We drove out in a six-wheeler heavy duty truck with tanks and welding machines bolted down in the back. I was with four guys and another truck was behind us. There was 10 of us in our gang. Nobody was on the roads. The highways were empty. We went to the Marine Parkway bridge work site dropped off the equipment and went home.

## There were snowbanks of heavy dust on crushed firetrucks and passenger cars. We searched anywhere and everywhere for victims.

I showered put on the TV and watched the news hoping someone would find my cousin, Frank Palombo, who was on the Fire Department. They never found his body.

On Thursday September 13th at 5 A.M. I drove to the Marine Parkway Bridge parking lot. Met up with my gang of ironworkers. Got in our trucks and drove back to Ground Zero. Firefighters were all over the place. They were there 24-7 and knew exactly what was going on. When we had a question, we would ask any of the Fire Department members. They were taking the lead and directing 'Okay, go over on this bucket line' that kind of thing. We stayed on the West Side Highway with 20 to 30 people in the bucket-brigade lines which were getting longer as we were making progress deeper onto the rubble. There was a lot more people all over the place. The third day people were losing hope.

We communicated with other ironworkers on our radios and would come down off the pile to talk. They hadn't found anyone alive and were only finding body parts. It was a total disaster site. We all continued to dig.

Fill up the buckets. Pass it down the line. Trying to find at least one person buried alive under the rubble. We left again at 10:00 P.M. Drove back to the Marine Parkway Bridge and went home.

I was feeling anger. I felt this could have been avoided. Maybe the higher-ups in government and the politicians could have avoided it somehow or knew this was going to happen. We weren't finding any of those innocent people who went to work in these buildings. I know a lot of people from my Rockaway neighborhood who worked in Cantor Fitzgerald. Another friend of mine, not with Cantor Fitzgerald, but he worked in a World Trade Center building didn't survive. A lot of people didn't deserve this.

On Friday September14th we met at the Marine Parkway Bridge, and everybody went in again. There was a lot more security. More NYPD and Port Authority police. Army trucks with the National Guard and regular Army were there. We continued doing the same thing at the same position. Nothing really changed except President Bush was coming.

We continued working on the bucket-brigade till 10:30 A.M. when they stopped us and said, "The President's going to be arriving soon." We walked over to see him. I wasn't expecting him to come because we were still searching. It was good that he came. He gave a good speech. I felt as a country we were going to do something to prevent this from happening again. I felt better when I left there that day.

After the President came, they got organized. They brought in cranes and started moving the heavy twisted, steel-girders. Dump trucks lined the streets taking debris from the pile away. My foreman now had a sign-in sheet. You could put your name on a list and start working on the payroll with Turner, Bovis, Skanska, big contractor companies. You couldn't volunteer anymore. I said, "I'll go back to my job on the bridge."

There was nothing left for me to do at Ground Zero. Some people stayed and some went back to their jobs on the bridges and buildings. I didn't want to get paid for working at the site. I would have stayed there for months volunteering if I thought we were able to find someone alive.

On Monday I went back to work on the bridge and continued to move on with my life, but it was still all everyone talked about for months. We couldn't believe we couldn't find anyone alive and how we were attacked, by a coward, hijacking the planes instead of fighting on the battlefield like a real soldier. The ironworkers had a lot of anger because everyone knew someone who was killed, and we weren't finding them. Some people took time off work to rest and to go to funeral masses and memorials when there was no body. It took a long time to get back in the swing of things.

I met an ironworker whose father built the World Trade Center in the '60s. He was one of 250 ironworkers building the Twin-Towers. For four years they put up steel and took pride in that. There's a lot of generational ironworkers who felt they needed to be there. They took a lead role in looking out for not only a brother ironworker but also for fellow citizens volunteering down there. Even when it got organized with the cranes and heavy equipment the ironworkers didn't want to see anybody cut corners to get the job done. They cared about the work. Saving the company money and getting the job done as quick as possible that's good, but safety was first.

That whole area was sacred ground and they respected pulling out every piece of iron. Hoisting every crane and moving the steel because that was the only thing left. Twisted steel beams. I give credit particularly to the senior guys who had been around ironworkers for many years. They set the tone. Good guys.

There was nothing I would change. They needed help searching for people I went down there. Seeing the second plane crash into 2-World Trade Center then the following morning being down there had a big negative impact on me. It was horrific. It's a lot different from seeing a plane crash on TV compared to actually seeing it happen. The following morning knowing thousands of people were lost…it was a horrible day. I can never forget 9/11.

There's a lot of ironworkers involved in the World Trade Center Monitoring Program because of health issues as well as psychological issues from seeing the things we've seen. We're not like firefighters who are used to bodies perishing in fires or bringing out dead bodies. Ironworkers don't see that. We put up buildings. We bust rivets. We weld. Yeah, there's a lot of ironworkers who now have respiratory issues and bad memories of the things they saw down there. Some that left the business. Couldn't deal with going back to work.

Not only ironworkers have these types of issues but a friend of mine worked for Cantor Fitzgerald. He didn't go into work that day because he had to take someone to the hospital. He got two guys from Rockaway jobs in Cantor Fitzgerald when they came out of college and they both died that day working at Cantor Fitzgerald. Afterwards he couldn't go back to work and still hasn't worked. He has survivors' remorse and lives in Florida now. I talk with him from time-to-time. Yeah, there's repercussions affecting a lot of people. ❖

# Jerry Canavan
## Battalion Chief, Battalion 31

I was home having coffee and reading the newspaper on the morning of 9/11 when I looked at the TV and saw a photo of 1-World Trade Center with a plane hitting it. I said to my wife Vickie "Oh my god, what's going on?" My mind started racing. The reporters were saying it could have been a small plane. I said, "This was not a small plane." Within 10 minutes everybody in the world was watching live news as the second plane hit 2-World Trade Center. I said, "We're under attack. This is a terrorist attack."

Took me 10 minutes to get myself together and off I went to my local firehouse Battalion 23 in Staten Island. It was empty. I signed in the company journal which is a written record of everything that happens in the firehouse. Firefighters were coming in on 'Recall' like they were supposed to do. I tried calling the Staten Island Borough Command, didn't get any answer. Waited 20 minutes. It felt like forever with no direction standing-fast. I took a mark in the journal stating I was leaving to go to my firehouse Battalion 31 on Tillary Street in Brooklyn. I briefly stopped

Photo © 2001 by Michael Heller

home told Vickie "I'm going in." She saw 2-World Trade Center collapse on the TV and pleaded "Please be careful." I said, "I'm not even sure what's going on or if I can even get over the bridge."

The Verrazano Bridge was closed. A load of cars mostly first responders were trying to get over. I hooked up with a fellow from OEM. He went to a policeman and said, "Let this guy through he's a Battalion Chief with the Fire Department." I followed him going 80 miles an hour. I thought they'll be blowing up this bridge next! Driving over the Verrazano Bridge into Brooklyn you can see the whole skyline of downtown Manhattan and I could see 1-World Trade Center burning but still standing. There wasn't much traffic took me 15 minutes to get in quarters. That's when 2-World Trade Center collapsed.

The firehouse was empty. The engine, ladder and battalion were gone. I went upstairs to the office. Phil Burns the Division Commander was there. I said "Phil, what do you want me to do?" He said "We should try to set up emergency response plan. I don't want you to rush over there blindly. We have to start getting accountability of the firefighters and not let everybody go over unsupervised." This had forethought. He was trying to get instructions from headquarters. Everybody was freelancing. A very emotional morning. Guys were coming in. You'd tell them to stay here we're trying to develop a plan. They would do that for 15 minutes and suddenly disappear. We weren't shuttling guys in a division-van to the site or anything like that. For the rest of the day guys were reporting in without their bunker-gear stripping the racks of everybody's firehouse gear. I had my gear locked in the Battalion lockers.

I continued working with Phil Burns trying to put an emergency response plan together wondering if we could get city buses to transport firefighters to a Command Post. The day was so chaotic. You couldn't hold the firefighters back.

The phone calls from families were the worst "Where's my father?" "Where's my husband?" A very emotional period. We had no information to give them saying "We don't have any reports about who's all right and who's not all right."

By 10:00 P.M. stragglers started to come back from the site. They were walking across the Brooklyn bridge to Tillary Street which is at the base of the Brooklyn Bridge on the Brooklyn side and was the first quarters you would hit. They were covered with dust and were sticking their heads in the sink to wash off.

Deputy Chief Dave Corcoran came in and started working with Phil Burns then said to me "You come with me, and we'll go over." We went over in the division-van to a makeshift Command Post near Vesey Street and West Street and started putting teams together with an officer and a minimum of five firefighters to give them supervisory control. You didn't want to send them out with less than that. It was dark. The only lighting was from a few gas powered generators

© New York City Fire Department

tower-lighting. Teams formed bucket-brigades under precarious conditions. Fires were burning in the collapse pile pushing out heavy smoke. The unsupported remains of the World Trade Center façade looking like any second could fall on you. A million things went through my mind.

The night was very quiet. With disoriented rescue workers walking in kind of a fog without a lot of supervision trying find a void they could crawl in and search for a victim. You didn't hear much. An occasional chirp of a Scott mask Pak PASS alarm (firefighters mask safety alarm that activated if there was no movement) that ended later in the night when the batteries wore down and the PASS alarms stopped working.

I stayed overnight instructing teams to report back to us every hour and a half to let us know where they went and what they did. We tried to get team-officers a handie-talkie radio. There was a lot of radio traffic about precarious situations. With so many firefighters and officers on one tactical channel radio transmissions were stepping on other radio transmissions. It was difficult to have good communications. The radio messages blurting out "The remains of this wall are falling." "We're going down into the subway tunnel." "We're going into a deep void... "

> ## Everybody was flying American flags outside their homes. We became a real patriotic together country. It didn't matter if you were a Republican or a Democrat, conservative or liberal, everybody seemed to be on the same page in unison with this. The country was brought together for a period of time due to these horrible circumstances.

The Verizon telephone company building on the corner of Vesey and West Street was the center for telephone communications in the area. It had severe structural damage caused by the collapse of the 7-World Trade Center building. Being an older building built sturdier and heavier than lighter-weight newer building construction helped it withstand the structural instability caused by the damage. Telephone company crews were doing repairs through the night to get service back online.

We were all in a fog. Obviously suffering from the severe loss of life not only of civilians. We knew a lot of firefighters died. But nobody knew how many were missing. It was beyond comprehension.

I had 28 years on the job. You know how it is, it's a big job. You get know a lot of people from getting promoted together going to fires together. These people were dead. And not just a few of them. A lot of them. And the civilians. There were 39 parishioners killed from our local parish St Clare's in Staten Island.

In the morning I walked back to Tillary Street over the Brooklyn Bridge to quarters in my bunker gear. I was tired from working in the firehouse during the day then at 10:00 P.M. going over to the site and staying there till 6:00 A.M. in the morning. I was shot. There was a ton of people in the firehouse wives, firefighters reporting for duty. A Ladder company from New Jersey was taking in Ladder 110's alarms. Volunteers from all over taking in responses. It was out of control. I stayed a few hours took a shower had a cup of coffee, then left.

I got home at 2:00 in the afternoon on the 12th slept a little bit then went Saint Clare's Church. They had a gathering of people singing *God Bless America* and other songs. I spent a lot of time in church to have some quiet time. This was before all the funerals started which took up all your spare time.

Everybody was flying American flags outside their homes. We became a real patriotic together country. It didn't matter if you were a Republican or a Democrat, conservative or liberal, everybody seemed to be on the same page in unison with this. The country was brought together for a period of time due to these horrible circumstances.

On the morning of Thursday, the 13th I went back to the firehouse. We started making, or trying to make, the firefighters report to a staging-area. When there was a request for more manpower a city bus would take groups of firefighters and officers to the World Trade Center site. But even with this in place guys would disappear and go in on their own.

I remember talking to a guy saying "Listen, you got to stay here. We have to try and operate with an officer as a team not rushing there freelancing." He said "My brothers gone. I'm looking for my brother." What do you say to this guy? You're trying to understand the emotional turmoil they're going through. This was going on for days afterwards. They didn't want to wait at the staging-area for two or three hours before going to the site. A lot of them would sit tight for 15 minutes and then they were gone. A few days later everybody started to understand. We don't want to keep you there for no reason. We needed to get a handle on who was going into the site.

On the morning of Saturday September 15th, I went back to the World Trade Center site. I got assigned to the site's northwest area where the telephone building was. There were still hazards galore all over the place. Construction workers were cutting steel like crazy so we could remove it and search voids. I went into the underground-complex where the Path train tubes came in from New Jersey. It was fairly intact, dark and dusty. I'm sure it had been searched previously. We were performing 'secondary searches' to make sure no one was missed in the darkened shops and restaurants.

They were restocking everybody with tools and equipment. Handie-talkie radios were assigned to all Chiefs. A lot of the voids were now being searched by our special trained 'confined space rescue teams' and the Homeland Security USAR (Urban Search and Rescue) teams who had the dogs. If a dog indicated there was a body or body part, we would send people into the voids.

Some of the dogs are trained to search for survivors and there were no survivors. The handlers were saying "The dogs are really confused and despondent because there's no survivors." The dogs were awesome and that was bizarre. They had other specialized dogs they brought in that were trained to search for cadavers.

It took another week before they got logistical material to the site. The big tent where everybody went for food and good respirators. The first couple of days you were walking around with the paper respirators.

The next week they started the 24-hour shifts schedule. They were giving the Divisions a lot of leeway with that through most of September.

In October we were getting a good handle on everything. You could volunteer to leave the firehouse for a month and work at the World Trade Center site which I did. I was working in West Command. At the start of the tour within a half-hour period around 20 teams would report in. We would give them their team number designation. We weren't referring to them by their unit number on their helmet. It was team numbers. They filled out two copies of the BF-4's with the team names. The officer kept one copy and we had a copy. We gave the team leader a handie-talkie radio and their assignment and sector location and told them what their tasks were.

## Some of the dogs are trained to search for survivors and there were no survivors. The handlers were saying "The dogs are really confused and despondent because there's no survivors."

Sometimes they went down into the pit. Which wasn't the most favorable assignment. NYC sanitation dump trucks were loaded with rubble from the site by excavators and then dumped at the base of the trucks. Then teams spent hours staring into the twisted mess of rubble. Shifting through it one last time. Looking for any type of body remains or equipment like the wiring of a Scott mask or a boot. It was a horrible assignment and wasn't one of the things the firefighters liked to do so we took that into consideration and rotated the teams to do different jobs during the day. We would say 'Do this for two hours. Take a blow (leave an active area to go to a rest area). Go have a cup of coffee something to eat. Or go sit in the church where everybody was taking some quiet time to sit and think for a half-hour.'

We were finding more body remains in the pit. I don't know how many remains we brought up that pit road. Guys were always respectful. If they found a piece of bunker gear or body part, they would call the Chief on the radio. Put it in a body bag. Then put it in a stokes stretcher. Everybody would line-up on the pit road and salute as the firefighters from the company the remains were from brought the stretcher up the road. Everyone was so respectful and solemn. It's still difficult to talk about it.

I used to go into a church on Church Street to take a break quite a bit. There was a little cemetery in the back untouched by any of the rubble from the buildings collapse. A nice place to go for a half-hour break to clear your head and then have a cup of coffee.

There were Battalion Chiefs and Deputy Chiefs down in the pit supervising and making sure all operations were done as safely as possible. A lot of my time was in the 'West Hut' Command Post working with Battalion Chief Jimmy Riches who was always there. His son was a firefighter in Engine 4 and was killed there. I became very friendly with Jimmy. He never went home. Anytime I was working. Jimmy was there.

I'll tell you what. We did a great job under the circumstances. It was completely chaotic the first couple of days. But we got a handle on it.

By Saturday September15th it became tremendously more organized. We were using the non-repeater respirators which was a better face mask. With the unusually warm fall weather after an hour with those respirators on you wanted to take them off. A lot of my supervision was "Keep the respirator on don't take it off." Once all the teams were dispersed the West hut was quiet. Jimmy Riches would stay, and I would go into the pit to supervise and talk to the guys. "Did you find anything? Do you need

anything? Do guys need a break? Is everybody okay?" It was very emotional. People were breaking down. Chaplains were walking around talking to firefighters. It was crazy.

By the end of October most of the underground fires were out so you really didn't need the respirator all the time. I wore mine most of the time. And when I was around, they did. It could be we're having the problems we're having today because we weren't more diligent in wearing respirators and protective gear.

Looking back, we had that first terrorism training book come out with the picture of the World Trade Center on the cover with the bull's eye. It was ahead of its time.

By 2003 I had 30 years in, and my career was winding down. I was starting to breakdown a little bit. My knees were bad. I knew I wasn't going to last too much longer. I retired in 2005 fairly burnt out and moved away. I had lived in the city my whole life. Born in Brooklyn married Vickie a Brooklyn girl and moved to Staten Island. We lived in the same house in Great Kills for 32 years. As soon as I retired, we moved to Raleigh North Carolina. At least once a month I get together with a dozen retires from the job and we go out for breakfast.

**I would go into the pit to supervise and talk to the guys. "Did you find anything? Do you need anything? Do guys need a break? Is everybody okay?" It was very emotional. People were breaking down. Chaplains were walking around talking to firefighters. It was crazy.**

A lot of the decision to move was—I felt like I needed a fresh start. I was a little burnt out after the whole 9/11 thing. So many friends and people I knew lost their lives in that attack. I'm not exactly sure why I wanted a fresh start and left the city which I always loved. But it turned out to be a good decision. I love it here in Raleigh-Durham.

Every year on 9/11 I go to the 8:00 A.M. mass at my local church Saint Catherine of Siena in Wake Forest. It's a quiet day for me. Then I put on the TV. Sit there and watch for three hours the reading of the names. I hear names of guys I was friendly with. It's a bummer. A melancholy day for me. ❖

# CHAPTER 5
# Mutual Aid

**P**atriots didn't only come from neighboring fire departments. They came from ironworkers, bus drivers, the Sanitation Department's dump trucks drivers. An army of NYC citizens giving out food and supplies on the site. Nurses and doctors at emergency care tents. The Salvation Army's food wagons. The Canadian families who opened their doors to the people on diverted commercial airplanes. United States air force fighter pilots. All of these and more were true 'Patriots of 9/11.' And you never knew they were there. Till you needed them.

FDNY Headquarters requested and received mutual aid from Nassau and Westchester counties fire departments on September 11.[39] Mutual aid from New Jersey was also requested by Division 8.

# Theodore (Teddy) Goldfarb
## Division 8 Commander

**A**s everyone says 9/11 was a beautiful day. I was off duty preparing to take advantage of the day. My wife Barbra was in the kitchen watching the TV news when she called out "Teddy there was an explosion at the World Trade Center." I ran into the kitchen. You could see heavy black smoke coming out of 1-World Trade Center. My first impression was 'that's flammable liquid burning.' The initial report was an explosion. I was able to see a gash on the side of the building where the plane went into the upper floors and the wings went through at an angle causing gashes that covered quite a few floors. First, I thought it might've been a transformer that exploded. They have mechanical equipment floors up there. But it quickly became obvious it was a plane. A few moments later the second plane hit. I thought 'We got a problem I got to go'

> ## Patriots didn't only come from neighboring fire departments. They came from ironworkers, bus drivers, the Sanitation Department's dump trucks drivers. An army of NYC citizens giving out food and supplies on the site. Nurses and doctors at emergency care tents.

I gave my wife a kiss and headed off to Division 8 headquarters. As I was walking into Division 8 Rescue 5's apparatus was rolling out the door responding to the World Trade Center. I had a second to decide. Should I go with them, or should I see what's happening? If I went with them, I wouldn't be here now because none of those eleven members of Rescue 5 responding that morning survived. And as far as I know none of their bodies were ever recovered.

I knew this was going to be a major situation and I would have to get as much apparatus as I could into service: reserve pumpers, spare pumpers, thawing apparatus, brush fire units. Whatever I could put on the road and man them with members coming in on 'Recall'. That was my plan. I was in constant contact with our dispatchers and knew we were low on companies available to respond to other fires or emergencies.

I taught Fire Science at New Jersey Middlesex County College fire science program for 23 years. I would invite Chiefs from New Jersey fire departments that bordered Staten Island; Bayonne, Elizabeth, Linden, and others for lunch to say hello and get to know each other's resources and operations. They knew who I was, and I knew who they were. I wanted to build up relationships so we could operate on incidents simultaneously on our borders.

Lou Kelly the Chief of the Elizabeth Fire Department was the mutual aid coordinator for Union County. I called Lou up at 11:00 A.M. and said four words "Lou I need help." He said, "What do you want?" I said, "Can you give me 20 companies 10 engines, five ladders, five rescues?" He said, "Where do you want them?" I said, "Have them come to Division 8 headquarters." And he said, "I'll have them there in an hour." I then called Bill Prairie the Middlesex County Mutual Aide coordinator and asked for the same number of resources which he agreed to send. I discussed with our dispatchers what we should do when these New Jersey units arrived. We couldn't send them out by themselves. They didn't have our radios and they didn't have hose threads that matched our hydrants thread outlets. We teamed them up with the companies we had left. I took the 'Recall' firefighters and officers and put one of them on each of those New Jersey fire apparatuses. They would guide them to alarms and help with communications. The Union County Fire Department units came with their field communications apparatus. That went to Staten Island Fire Communications office. I assigned Battalion Chief Richie Olivieri to take command at the Staten Island Fire Communications office. I told him "We have to keep whatever units we have in-service for the big jobs. Use other units like brush-fire units for obvious small jobs like an odor of gas. Don't send full first-alarm assignments."

Numerous false reports were received. Other hijacked airliners. The Staten Island ferries were coming with large numbers of injured victims. I decided to set up a whole medical facility at the Staten Island ferry terminal ready to treat mass casualties that never came. I assigned a firefighter to go downstairs and stop MTA express busses. Have the passengers leave the bus and keep the driver. I wanted express-buses because they are over the road busses and have cargo/luggage compartments. I sent these busses with several firefighters on each bus to the big-box stores like Costco to load up on water and whatever first aid supplies they had. Then I sent these busses to the Staten Island ferry terminal to set up a medical facility.

I went to the World Trade Center site at 5:00 P.M. right after 7-World Trade Center collapsed. Someone in the firehouse took my boots. Stuff was disappearing. So, I'm wearing sneakers and my bunker coat walking through tons of water and dust that was like muck-mud. I was given the assignment of getting water on the heavy fire in 7-World Trade Center's collapse debris field.

I estimated height of this debris field was 12 stories. This was all that remained of a 47-story high-rise building. We had our tower ladders fully extended and elevated attempting keep the fire under control.

The thing that stood out was if a 47-story building collapse created a pile of rubble 12 stories high. Then two-110 story building collapses should create a rubble pile 24 stories or more in height. Yet the height of rubble pile caused by the twin towers collapse was not nearly that high. I considered this an amazing thing.

I worked alone at the 7-World Trade Center fire through the night and went back to Division 8's firehouse in the morning and literally, slept on the floor in the bunk room.

On Wednesday September 12th, we set up a Staging-Area at the Staten Island Home Port. It was mostly open space with a lot of buildings not being used. We used one of their buildings and assembled hundreds of firefighters. They hadn't worked at the site and were all hot to trot. Everybody wanted to work there. I had a tough time explaining the situation. We can't get

> Then two-110 story building collapses should create a rubble pile 24 stories or more in height. Yet the height of rubble pile caused by the twin towers collapse was not nearly that high. I considered this an amazing thing.

The NYPD did not initially do a good job of setting up World Trade Center site perimeter security. There were many firefighters from other areas that came on to the scene on their own. These firefighters were being interviewed by the media on TV and the FDNY guys in the Staging-Area were watching it. I was able to calm them down.

I don't know how many days I worked before taking a break. I lived in Brooklyn. As a kid we went to Brighton Beach. I always liked it there. That comfort of childhood and security. So, maybe it was three days later when I had a couple spare hours, I went to Brighton just to calm my nerves down. I sat at Brighton 15th Street the end of the boardwalk by myself. Not a plane in the sky. I spent three hours by myself. Spoke to nobody. Got my brain orientated. And put myself back together again.

It now turned into a combination of working in the Division and then working at the site. Whenever I wasn't on duty I was at the site. I didn't go home for quite a few days. On Friday September 14th, we went to the site and operated on a division level supervising the members who were finding body parts.

Eventually we graduated from a tent on Liberty Street to an office trailer. They brought in the biggest crane in the United States and set it up right next to our command post. It was a huge monstrosity of a thing that came with 20-tractor-trailers worth of parts.

Later a decision was made to dedicate people full-time to the site. I elected for reasons I can't explain I would rather work in the firehouse than work at the site. So, I did not participate much in the recovery operation.

I'll tell you who deserved recognition the steelworkers. They were unbelievable. A major force in moving everything. Early on there were bucket-brigades moving material out in small buckets and we weren't having a huge impact on getting into the voids doing that. But when the steelworkers came that changed.

Every few hours the excavators would lumber off the pile. Some with broken treads. To get re-fueled, oiled, and first aid for their damaged threads. Almost like a human being. And then went right back out on the pile again working around the clock.

Another agency that did a great job was OEM in getting the necessary resources on the scene. When I initially got on the site there were hundreds of dump-trucks lined up from numerous city agencies such as Sanitation Department, Department of Transportation, Parks Department, Housing Authority and more. There is no other place in the United States where this large number of resources could be assembled that quickly.

A dedicated traffic lane was set up from the World Trade Center site to a Sanitation Department landfill on Staten Island where all debris was taken to be saved and later again shifted through for body parts.

We ate in the 'green tarp café' on Liberty Street. Its front glass windows were blown to pieces from the pressure of the buildings coming down and it had a green tarp over the front. After a couple of days all kind of

celebrities came. They brought us good food, so we went there on breaks. Everyone we dealt with was doing more than they had to do and that kept us up and running.

The department sent out an official communique 'We were not allowed to use FDNY apparatus at the funerals.' They couldn't support the funerals on the level they used to support line-of-duty funerals. There were 89 funerals in Staten Island alone. John Ferry, the Captain of Rescue 5 walked into my office one day and says, "Chief can you get me two aerial ladders for my funeral ceremonies?" So, I thought 'Well, let me call Lou Kelly again.' I called and said "Lou, can you get me two aerials?" right away he said "Yes" and sent two aerial ladders and a pumper to the Rescue 5 funerals. I did not feel comfortable asking him to do this for all the funerals. We spoke with the head of our ceremony unit, Lieutenant Joe LaPointe, and asked him to help us out which he did. I felt a special relationship to the members of Rescue 5. We were in quarters with them. They were very supportive of the Division. And obviously super supportive at fires or any kind of emergency.

Lieutenant LaPointe leaned on New Jersey Chief Lou Kelly, and he provided these resources for all the funerals in Staten Island over a three-month period. Afterwards I spoke with Lou Kelly and said, "Lou, I have to commend you. Elizabeth New Jersey is a small fire department eight engine companies and five ladder companies and you're giving me two ladder companies and an engine company for these funerals over these three months. If somebody in Elizabeth was injured because of a lack of responding apparatus and any petty politician or news reporter found out. You would have been under tremendous stress to justify what you did for us." He said to me "9/11 raised the esteem of firefighters in the eyes of the world and only you paid the price. I'm more than willing to do this." He put his neck out for that. Yeah, nice, a good man. And I think Lou Kelly raised the esteem of the fire service in the eyes of not only New York but the entire world. He died at a fire and in return for his help on 9/11 the FDNY provided a large contingent of members for his funeral services.

That was the most important thing. The unbelievable cooperation of anybody and everybody.

The National Forest Service sent in a Level One Incident-Management Team. When that team got here the fire department poo-pooed them. What are these Smokey Bear hat guys doing here? The Forest Service was used to handling huge fires over periods of weeks and months with these Incident-Management teams. After a while our upper echelon recognized their value. About a year later the FDNY started our own 'Level One Incident-Management Team' and used the Forest Service to train our members.

One of the criticisms of 9/11 operations was the lack of cooperation between NYPD and the FDNY which led to having a police Captain detailed to fire headquarters and we detailed a Battalion Chief to police headquarters. A year after 9/11 during one of the training secessions I was having lunch with that police Captain. We used to call him 'Vinnie the Cop.' I said, "Okay Vinnie you've been in the fire department for a year now what's the big difference culturally?" He said, "You put your bosses in danger we don't." And obviously we lost every rank in the department and thought 'words of wisdom out of his mouth'.

Regarding the criticism that the fire department did not have good personnel accountability that day. I don't think it was the problem it's being made out to be. If we had a better personnel accountability system, I don't think there would have been an iota of difference in the outcome of the situation. Early on after the collapses we didn't know who was missing. We had false reports of certain companies missing that weren't and things like that. But I don't think there was any way that could have been improved in that kind of situation. Okay? Did it cause us to lose more members or anything like that? Absolutely no way did that happened.

I lost so many friends. A traumatic experience. Much on the level of when you lose a parent or God forbid children. I treat 9/11 the same way. You have to go on with your life. I did the best I could in the things I had control of that day and the following days. I don't regret anything I did. I think the department did well considering we lost the whole upper echelon. We had to reorganize a little bit and come up with a plan. I think we did it the best that we could under those circumstances. That's all I can say. ❖

# Matthew Chartrand
## Business Manager, Ironworkers Local 361 Structural Steel

I was an ironworker for eight years and a foreman on the Williamsburg Bridge setting road segments on the Manhattan side when the plane hit 1-World Trade Center on September 11th. Almost immediately we were told by the police to close our gang-boxes, get everybody secured, and shut-down the job. We were often working with the police. I had one of their handie-talkie radios because they had to close off the roadways when we brought road segments in. They told me to have my guys walk the bridge. Go up and down the cables to see if there was anything suspicious. Our guys walked the bridge from the Manhattan side to the Brooklyn side. When we got done, they shut the bridge down.

I drove home and got a phone call. A General Foreman from the Ironworkers Union told me we were sending volunteers down to the World Trade Center. To get

on the highways you were going to need your Union Ironworker card and your license. Contractors jumped in. Hey, let's get down there. We got the equipment. We want to help. No haggling as far as borrowing tools or machinery. It was coordinated. Everybody worked together. They said, 'We're not getting paid for this and you're not getting paid for this. It's all volunteer.' We said absolutely. And everybody went down to the WTC attack site. I had friends and family affected by this attack. I had to go. No choice. It was something burning in me to go there and help.

At 5:00 A.M. on Wednesday September 12th I met up with two buddies of mine who worked with me on the Williamsburg bridge. We got our own personal tools wrenches, strikers, gloves, and whatnot and were driven down to the Trade Center in a bus disembarking on Vesey and West Street.

There was a pay-loader moving cars off the site. They were going right through the car windows picking them up and dumping them out of the way. We walked into the pile set up torches, ran outlines and went to work cutting steel where they directed us. Sometimes we in-

the street saw the gear we were carrying. He didn't know us from a hole in the wall. The people from the restaurants didn't know us. Everyone wanted to help each other.

The job foreman at the Williamsburg bridge told us were going to be shut down for a couple of days. We drove to the Brooklyn bridge on Thursday September 13th. Parked our cars and walked over the bridge into Manhattan. Again, a stranger picked us up and drove us to the site. We walked into the pile and met up with ironworkers.

One building alongside the site had large pieces of steel from the collapse hanging out of its exterior wall that could fall at any time. A crane was in position with a man-basket on it. They asked, 'Who wants to go up there and work on cutting the steel down?' John and I, a guy I work with, hopped in the basket. Went up two hundred feet when they blew an evacuation whistle. They thought something was collapsing. Everybody scattered off the pile. I'll tell you. Dangling in a basket high in the air waiting to be brought down wasn't a pleasant feeling.

After a while they came back and dropped us down. We got out of the basket and that was the end of that operation.

## We hadn't eaten all day and night. A couple of restaurants were open. When they saw us looking. They brought us in. Gave us food. The whole nine yards and didn't charge us anything. Very nice.

We stayed on the ground for the rest of the day and while walking home the same thing happened. Strangers gave us a ride. In the beginning it wasn't well organized but as every day went on it got better. The collapse area was sectioned off into four distinct areas with large construction companies winning bids for each one of the sectors. Friday morning September 14th, we were getting ready to walk over the bridge when Local 40 Union, whose territory is lower Manhattan, said "They're coordinating the effort. Go to Local 40's Union Hall." I said, "Nah, I'll walk down the pile because that's what we've been doing." They said, "You're going need a badge and get signed up for it." I said, "I didn't want to get signed up." Walked down to the site and worked into the night again. That lasted one week.

On Saturday my company called said "We got the Williamsburg bridge job open." I was back to regular work. The company I was working for got part of the contract to cut steel and remove debris at the site and asked me if I wanted to go there. So, during the week I worked the bridge job and weekends worked in the pile. I did that until the end of November.

teracted with the bucket-brigades moving garbage pails full of building debris out of areas where steel needed cutting. We stayed doing this until eight that night.

Walking home towards the eastside of Manhattan somebody saws us, asked if we wanted a lift, then drove us to the Williamsburg Bridge. We walked across to the Brooklyn side and started looking for something to eat. We hadn't eaten all day and night. A couple of restaurants were open. When they saw us looking. They brought us in. Gave us food. The whole nine yards and didn't charge us anything. Very nice. The guy who picked us up from

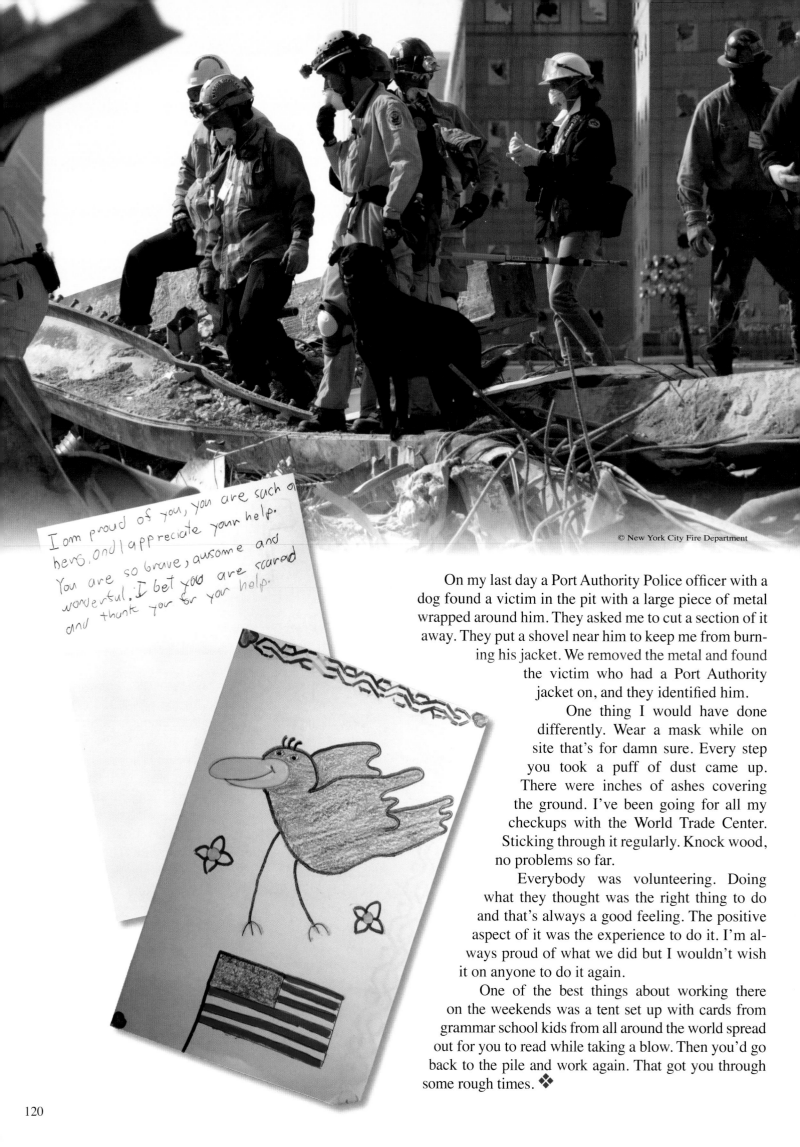

© New York City Fire Department

I am proud of you, you are such a hero, and I appreciate your help. You are so brave, ausome and wonderful. I bet you are scared and thank you for your help.

On my last day a Port Authority Police officer with a dog found a victim in the pit with a large piece of metal wrapped around him. They asked me to cut a section of it away. They put a shovel near him to keep me from burning his jacket. We removed the metal and found the victim who had a Port Authority jacket on, and they identified him.

One thing I would have done differently. Wear a mask while on site that's for damn sure. Every step you took a puff of dust came up. There were inches of ashes covering the ground. I've been going for all my checkups with the World Trade Center. Sticking through it regularly. Knock wood, no problems so far.

Everybody was volunteering. Doing what they thought was the right thing to do and that's always a good feeling. The positive aspect of it was the experience to do it. I'm always proud of what we did but I wouldn't wish it on anyone to do it again.

One of the best things about working there on the weekends was a tent set up with cards from grammar school kids from all around the world spread out for you to read while taking a blow. Then you'd go back to the pile and work again. That got you through some rough times. ❖

# CHAPTER 6

# Why Did These Buildings Collapse?

## Why Did These Buildings Collapse?

In 1998 I was a Battalion Chief in the 39 Battalion supervising units in the low-income residential areas of Brownsville and East New York in Brooklyn when Chief of Department Peter Ganci called me into his office and said he wanted me to create a Safety Coordinator course for all Chiefs in the FDNY. I was honored to undertake this assignment but didn't know where to begin particularly when it came to finding accurate information concerning the stability of a burning building. So, I started where I learned the most on the job talking to those who knew more than I did the acknowledged leaders of the department Chiefs Ray Downey, Larry Stack, Pete Ganci, and so many others who took the time to share their knowledge on all aspects of this subject.

## One of the tenets of firefighting is 'Structure Dictates Tactics.'

I reached out to people in the private sector to see what information they had to offer and contacted a well-known firm that demolished high-rise buildings and asked what they knew. I will never forget the conversation. "Well, the first thing you do Chief is take a look at the building's blueprints and find the main load-bearing structural members." I had to stop him there by saying "Wait, sometimes a Chief never saw the building before being called to the 3 A.M. fire and has no blueprints or any type of information about the building." He was amazed. He said, "You mean to tell me that before you fight the building fire you don't know anything about it?" I told him it was a rare thing to have any detailed information concerning the building's structure. And even if you did you couldn't tell how much damage had been done by the fire before you arrived because you couldn't be sure how long it had been burning and smoke obscured inspecting the interior. He didn't know what to say and had little to tell me after that.[40]

I was not surprised to learn there was a persistent lack of detailed information concerning fire-induced building collapse. A National Institute of Standards and Technology (NIST) study performed in October 2008 on fire testing of materials encountered similar problems when trying to find information on fire-induced building collapse. "Difficulties were encountered during this survey in readily identifying news and other credible sources of historical and technical information on the fire-induced collapses of buildings. The potential data sources were fragmented, often incomplete, and sometimes conflicting. This lack of data and information significantly hampered the development of a more complete understanding of the magnitude and nature of fire-induced collapse. A centralized reliable body of catalogued information on fire-induced building collapses is needed."[41]

The two main goals of all fire departments are to protect life and property. To achieve these goals upon arrival at the scene of a fire the first action firefighters perform is a 'Size-Up' to determine initial actions. One of the tenets of firefighting is 'Structure Dictates Tactics.' Different initial tasks must be performed for different building types: fireproof or non-fireproof, high-rise, or low-rise, single-family, or multiple-family dwelling, commercial or residential building.

## Very few would have had a general concept of the structural supporting members of the WTC buildings. Almost none had a detailed understanding of the design elements. Many had never been inside these buildings before.

Every Chief officer arriving at scene on 9/11 was performing their 'Size-Up.' At the initial Command Post as firefighting professionals all these Chief officers had a vast personal knowledge of how an out-of-control fire inside a building affects the buildings stability. Very few would have had a general concept of the structural supporting members of the WTC buildings. Almost none had a detailed understanding of the design elements. Many had never been inside these buildings before.

# The World Trade Center Buildings

Construction of The World Trade Center Twin Towers began in August of 1968. The first tenants moved into the North-Tower in December 1970 and the project was mostly complete by 1973.

The World Trade Center site consisted of seven buildings spread across 16 acres of land bounded by Vesey, Church, Liberty and West Streets. The Twin Towers North-Tower 1-World Trade Center and South-Tower 2-World trade Center were both 110 stories high about 1,350 feet in height and square with each wall 208 feet in length. These towers contained 10.4 million square feet of office space allowing up to 50,000 office workers. Other buildings in the World Trade Center complex included 3-World Trade Center a 22-story hotel. 4, 5, and 6-World Trade Center were all 8 to 9 story office buildings. And 7-World Trade Center was a 47-story office building built in the mid-1980s just north of the main World Trade Center site.

The Port Authority hired architect Minoru Yamasaki to design the buildings. He modeled the plaza after Mecca and incorporated other features of Arabic architecture in the building design including point arches and arabesque patterns. Minoru Yamasaki used several innovative construction techniques to design open space floor plans uninterrupted by columns. There were four major structural subsystems in the towers the exterior wall, the core, the floor system, and the hat truss.[42]

An elevator-car system consisted of express and local elevators in the structural core allowed the substantial open floor space in the Towers. This elevator system used staggered sky-lobby floors with express and local elevators. All elevators were in the core. Each Tower had three stairwells in the core which essentially ran from top to bottom.

The 1968 New York City building codes were in effect and it did not require sprinklers for high-rise buildings except for underground spaces. At the time of 9/11 automatic fire sprinklers had been installed in all the World Trade Center office spaces.[43]

I relied on the National Institute of Standards and Technology U.S. Department of Commerce (NIST) investigation of the World Trade Center towers collapse based on their long history of investigating firefighter fatalities caused by major fires involving burning buildings and their investigations being scientifically performed to accepted standards.

According to NIST approximately 10,000 gallons of jet fuel were sprayed into multiple stories quickly and simultaneously igniting hundreds of workstations and other combustibles. The aircraft and subsequent

**Approximately 10,000 gallons of jet fuel were sprayed into multiple stories quickly and simultaneously igniting hundreds of workstations and other combustibles. The aircraft and subsequent fireballs created large open areas in the building exterior through which air could flow to support the fires.**

THE WORLD TRADE CENTER
NEW HEADQUARTERS
FOR INTERNATIONAL COMMERCE
UNDER CONSTRUCTION BY
THE PORT OF NEW YORK AUTHORITY
TO BE COMPLETED IN STAGES
1970 - 1972

fireballs created large open areas in the building exterior through which air could flow to support the fires. The impact and debris removed the insulation (which was Spray Applied Fireproofing Material) from a large number of structural elements that were then subjected to the heat from the fires.

From these findings, factors, and observed performance, NIST concluded: "The two aircraft hit the towers at high speed and did considerable damage to principal structural components (core columns, perimeter columns, and floors) that were directly impacted by the

STRENGTH & HONOR

BATTALION ONE MISSING
E4                  L15              E6              E10              BC MATT RYAN
CAPT FARRELLY LT.LEAVEY   LT O'HAGAN   LT ATLAS       LT.PAUL MITCHELL
RICHES          LARSEN         BEYER           PANSINI
SCHOALES       OELSCHLAGER   JOHNSTON    J. OLSEN
TEGTMEIR      KOPYTKO        HOLOHAN
ANAYA            T. KELLEY                         L10
VILLANUEVA    BARRY                           LT HARREL
                      ALLEN                            TALLON
                      E. OLSEN

aircraft or associated debris. However, the towers withstood the impacts and would have remained standing were it not for the dislodged insulation, and the subsequent multi-floor fires. The robustness of the perimeter frame-tube system and the large size of the buildings helped the towers withstand the impact. The structural system redistributed loads in places of aircraft impact, avoiding larger scale damage upon impact. The hat truss, which was intended to support a television antenna atop each tower, prevented earlier collapse of the building core. In each tower a different combination of impact damage and heat-weakened structural components contributed to the abrupt structural collapse."[44]

The report goes on to acknowledge the World Trade Center towers would likely not have collapsed under the combined effects of aircraft impact damage and the extensive, multi-floor fires that were encountered on September 11, 2001, if the thermal insulation (Spray Applied Fireproofing Material) had not been widely dislodged or had been only minimally dislodged by aircraft impact. In the absence of structural and insulation damage, a conventional fire substantially like or less intense than the fires encountered on September 11, 2001, likely would not have led to the collapse of a World Trade Center tower.

Regarding conspiracy theories NIST found no corroborating evidence for alternative hypotheses suggesting that the World Trade Center towers were brought down by controlled demolition using explosives planted prior to September 11, 2001. NIST also did not find any evidence that missiles were fired at or hit the towers. Instead, photographs and videos from several angles clearly showed that the collapse initiated at the fire and impact floors and the collapse progressed from the initiating floors downward until the dust clouds obscured the view. The falling mass of the building compressed the air ahead of it, much like the action of a piston, forcing material, such as smoke and debris, out the windows as seen in several videos.[45]

Their examination of the cause of the high fatalities revealed: Approximately 87 percent of the estimated 17,400 occupants of the towers and 99 percent of those located below the impact floors, evacuated successfully. In 1-World Trade Center, where the aircraft destroyed all escape routes,

1,355 people were trapped in the upper floors when the building collapsed. One hundred seven people who were below the impact floors did not survive. Because the flow of people from the building had slowed considerably 20 minutes before the tower collapsed, the stairwell capacity was adequate to evacuate the occupants on that morning.[46]

Because of The Port Authority of New York and New Jersey's (Port Authority's) establishment under a clause of the United States Constitution its buildings were not subject to any state or local building regulations. The buildings were unique both in their height and in their innovative structural features. Nevertheless, according to NIST: The actual design and approval process produced two buildings that generally were consistent with nearly all the provisions of the New York City Building Code and other building codes of that time that were reviewed by NIST. The loads for which the buildings were designed exceeded the New York City code requirements. The quality of the structural steels was consistent with the building specifications. The departures from the building codes and standards identified by NIST did not have a significant effect on the outcome of September 11th.[47]

# World Trade Center Building 7

7-World Trade Center is possible the only known high-rise building (building over 75 feet in height) to collapse due to fire damage to ever occur. This distinction deserves comment.

The leading hypothesis from NIST regarding the collapse of 7-World Trade Center is as follows: The conditions that led to the collapse of 7-World Trade Center arose from fires perhaps combined with structural damage that followed the impact of debris from the collapse of 1-World Trade Center. The fires were fed by ordinary office combustibles. The fires on floors 7 through 13 heated the building structure. The floor construction was lighter than the columns and with thinner Spray Applied Fireproofing Material. The floor beams, floor slabs, and connections heated more quickly and to higher temperatures than the columns. The elevated temperatures in the floor elements led to their thermal expansion sagging and weakening which resulted in failure of floor connections and/or buckling of floor beams. Sufficient breakdown of connections and/or beams resulted in loss of lateral support and buckling of at least one of the critical columns supporting a large-span open floor bay on the eastern side of the building on or below floor 13. This was the initiating event of the collapse. The initial local failure progressed upward to the east penthouse. As the large floor bays became unable to redistribute the loads, the interior structure below the east penthouse collapsed

into 7-World Trade Center. Triggered by damage due to falling debris and loss of lateral support to adjacent interior columns the failure progressed westward in the region of floors 7 through 14 where the floors had been weakened by fires. This ultimately resulted in the collapse of the entire structure.[48] Note: The Federal Emergency Management Agency (FEMA) investigated the 7-World Trade Center building collapse and generally came to similar conclusions.[49]

> **Triggered by damage due to falling debris and loss of lateral support to adjacent interior columns the failure progressed westward in the region of floors 7 through 14 where the floors had been weakened by fires.**

# The 1993 World Trade Center Terrorist Attack

Noontime Friday February 26, 1993, a rented-van carrying a bomb drove into the public parking garage beneath 2-World Trade Center and parked on the underground B-2 level. At 12:17 P.M. the bomb exploded instantly cutting off the World Trade Center's main electrical power line and knocking out the emergency lighting systems. The greatest damage occurred on levels B1 and B2 with significant structural damage also on level B3. The blast wave was so powerful it opened a 100-foot-wide-hole, penetrated five-stories of reinforced-concrete, and destroyed hundreds of vehicles in the garage. The explosion ignited fires in many of the vehicles causing large quantities of smoke to rise to the 93rd floor of both towers. Evacuation-stairs were contaminated with thick black smoke from burning car tires which also filled the elevator shafts and caused many smoke-inhalation injuries as occupants attempted to evacuate. Hundreds were trapped in elevators, including a group of 17 kindergartners on their way down from the South-Tower observation deck who were trapped between the 35th and 36th floors for five hours.

## The Fire

On February 23rd, 1993, I was the Captain of Ladder Company 12. We responded on the 3rd alarm, which came in almost immediately, to 2-World Trade Center. While responding in the department radio dispatcher reported heavy-fire conditions in the underground parking area of the World Trade Center Tower buildings with victims trapped on the floors above. The streets near the World Trade Center were clogged with emergency responder's apparatus. We positioned our apparatus as close as we could on the West Side highway near Vesey Street.

I knew from experience with fires in underground parking garages there would be no visibility in heavy smoke from burning car tires. Limited ventilation to move the smoke out of the area. And we would not be able to search the open space in the underground garage by following walls. This would make it difficult to know where we were in relation to our entry/exit doorway.

I grabbed our search-rope as I left the apparatus and reported into the Command Post near the entrance to the underground parking garage. The Chief in Command quickly ordered us to make a primary search for victims in the cellar B-2 level. Ducking under the heavy black smoke rolling out we walked down the garage entrance driveway and found a stairway leading to the B-2 level. I left one firefighter at the doorway on the B-2 level to help us find our way out if something went wrong with the search-rope. Tied the search-rope off and entered the thick-black smoke to begin our search. We used 2, two-member teams—one on each side of the search-rope—with me in front playing out rope from the search-rope bag. As we passed burning cars, we felt the sounds of exploding tires around us. Periodically we'd stop and one member of each team would break off from the search-rope disappearing into the dark smoke sweeping a tool in front and to the sides searching for soft resistance indicating an unconscious victim while maintaining voice contact with the other member holding onto the rope who directed the searcher back after they completed a perimeter half-circle search.

## I thought 'This building could never collapse supported by these deeply-embedded enormous structural steel supports.' And I think many of us at this fire felt the same way.

We were staying low taking 'hits' off our masks when needed by putting the mask face-piece up to your face and briefly breathing in mask-tank air. Then shutting the air supply off. This procedure was strictly against official guidelines, but it allowed us to conserve air and search a larger area for a possible victim.

While progressing deeper into the garage my handie-talkie radio blared out with a 'May-Day' message for a firefighter who had fallen into the rubble below. If I was going to assist with this 'May-Day' I knew I would have to find the edge of the blast crater as quickly as possible. Rapidly crawling on my hands and knees I suddenly touched ragged edges of broken concrete with re-bars sticking out of it. I had reached the edge of the blast hole. It would have been easy to stumble into the gaping hole below if I wasn't crawling.

At the edge of the broken concrete, I could see down into a space filled with cars at crazy angles among sections of blown-apart concrete floors. The smoke was lifting into the blast-hole void above and I could see across a wide open area the size of a football field. There were massive, exposed steel columns penetrating deep into the granite bedrock below rising tall and straight to the top of the tallest building in the world and I thought 'This building could never collapse supported by these deeply-embedded enormous structural steel supports.' And I think many of us at this fire felt the same way.

On the handie-talkie radio Rescue 1 reported they were lowering members on ropes into the rubble below to remove the injured firefighter in a stokes basket. There was a lighter smoke condition near the open crater space. We took a brief break to orient ourselves. A lot of radio traffic messages were interrupting each other resulting in difficulty for someone to provide a complete report before being stepped on by another message. I kept monitoring the radio for any further information on the injured firefighter while searching for other possible victims.

We operated for approximately one hour on the B2-level until another ladder company relieved us. I briefed them on the area we searched. Left them our search-rope. Followed the rope out to the stairs leading to the street. By this time Engine companies were making good progress in putting out the car fires and the smoke was beginning to lift. I reported our search was 'negative' (no victims found) to the Chief was told to 'take-up' and left the scene.

Six people were killed, five Port Authority employees and a businessman whose car was in the parking garage. Additionally, 1,042 people were injured. Most while evacuating the building after the blast.

Ladder 12 Firefighter Mike Mullan worked this fire with me. He also responded on 9/11 and perished while searching for victims in the Marriot Hotel. Mike had the Irish healthy good looks. Always a smile on his face a beautiful woman in his arms and constantly telling jokes.

In 1992 on a bitter cold January night Ladder 12 was called to respond to a water main break in an HIV hospice. The water was 3 foot high in the basement and contaminated with the building's sewer water. If the water rose two more feet and got into the buildings electrical service it would shut down the power and people on life support equipment would die. It took 3 hours in that freezing contaminated water to put in pumps, find the water main break and seal it up. At daybreak they offered us some coffee and as we were drinking it firefighter, Mike Mullan, asked me if he could play the piano in their cafeteria. I was miserable and said sure do what you want. He climbed on the stage and banged out 'Great Balls of Fire' Jerry Lee Lewis style. Brought a smile to every face in that room.

# CHAPTER 7

# The Pile Becomes The Pit, Memorials and Funerals

## Daniel Nigro – Chief of Department

I was de facto Chief of Department on the afternoon of 9/11 but officially on the Sunday after 9/11 out on the Plaza of 9 Metro Tech we had the largest promotion of people ever to replace all the officers from Lieutenant to Chief of Department we lost and that was my tenure start. Then we all got to work keeping this department running and doing everything we could over the next year. I had just short of a year as Chief of Department when I retired from that rank on September 9, 2002, after Commissioner Scoppetta told me he wasn't going to give me tenure. Which meant I could retire or go back in rank. I chose to retire. At times I questioned that choice. I always missed the job and was kind of young to retire and thought 'maybe I was a little rash.' But all in all, it worked out. I was sworn in as Commissioner of the NYC Fire Department on June 9 2014, and continue in that position till today in 2022.

I think any people who say they were operating at 100% after 9/11 especially any of us who survived that day would be lying. It was a very emotional time. I think you lean on friends and family. Family was big for me. And they put up with my mood swings which at the time were pretty strong. I was trying to keep myself in control. I knew I had a big job to do and needed to at least appear strong. Faith, people lean on their faith. I know I did.

The Staff of the fire department pulled together. Everybody knew they had a job to do. And they did their job and a lot of times they did their job and someone else's job because that other person wasn't there anymore.

We had a lot of help. It was great to see the country unified behind us. It gave us a certain moral strength having people appreciate what we did. When the Italian Consulate contacted the Department, the call was directed to me the ranking Italian American. They had citizens who died in the attack, and I got to know the Consul-General here. In November he said to me "We'd like to send you to Rome. There's going to be a big Pro-American rally in Rome, and we'd like you and a couple of the family members who lost their loved ones to attend." I said, "You know I'd love to go but I have way too much to do." He said, "It's only two days. The Pope is going to recognize the group and after the rally there's going to be an audience with the Pope." I thought 'Well, I don't know if I should turn this down. When is this opportunity ever going to happen?' So, we went. I brought Jerry Barbara's daughter, Donald Burns son, a few fire officers, and we brought a chaplain's helmet in honor of Father Michael Judge to give to the Pope. And lo and behold there was a mass full of people at St. Peter's. My wife and I got to go to the altar and met Pope John Paul II. This was an experience like I never had before.

> We had a lot of help. It was great to see the country unified behind us. It gave us a certain moral strength having people appreciate what we did.

I came back strengthened from looking in his eyes and having him look in my eyes. I always felt he was a very charismatic man. Meeting the Pope on the altar of St. Peter's above the tomb of St. Peter himself was very powerful. I came back a stronger person. Better able to do my job. Which was to lead the department and show strength.

The funerals and memorial services we went to seemed like almost every day. I spent Christmas Eve at the World Trade Center site. Christmas Day visiting firehouses. And on New Year's Eve I was on the site at midnight.

In the month following 9/11 I visited every firehouse that lost a member. Some of these visits were very difficult.

Members of these firehouses were emotional, and people were worried more attacks were coming. They asked me "How is the department going to keep the members safe if it happened again?" Those months following the attack were especially difficult for those firefighters working in Manhattan. They were very concerned about

further attacks. Nobody knew what this Al-Qaeda group planned or what other people they had out there. There were all sorts of rumors about, chemical, biological, or more bombs. Each tour our members came in was a sign of their bravery.

We had members far away from Manhattan who volunteered to leave their unit and come to another unit to replace the members we lost. We needed chauffeurs (drivers and operators of fire apparatus) in some of the companies. People stepped up and they didn't have to. They weren't forced to. They volunteered. Which really says a lot for the department.

It was our worst time and our best time. All in one. And I don't know how that's possible.

I wish we would have been more concerned with the conditions down there and the air we were breathing. A lot of us came out of the pre-mask era in the fire department where you took credit for being someone who could take a feed and I don't think we were as concerned as we should have been. Some people blamed it on the Federal Government telling us the air was clear. But I think we knew it wasn't. Just like back in the day. We knew going into building fires without a mask on wasn't going to do us any good, but it was our duty.

## People stepped up and they didn't have to. They weren't forced to. They volunteered. Which really says a lot for the department.

## It was our worst time and our best time. All in one. And I don't know how that's possible.

Perhaps we could have protected ourselves by always wearing respirators and maybe if we did, we wouldn't be losing people in the numbers we're losing them now or having people suffer through the various illnesses because of being at the site. So, that's a regret I have certainly.

I do regret not seeing the dangers that day and putting so many people in those two towers. Being too close to the two towers and being one of the Chiefs in charge of the largest loss of life in fire department history. I'm not proud of that. It was a complete life changer.

I think there's a certain darkness I don't always recognize in myself, but some people see it. They've told me you're not as happy-go-lucky as I used to be even though I've had many moments since 9/11 of joy. Kids getting married. Grandchildren being born. All the things that my poor friends like Pete missed out on. I think there's still a cloud that hangs over you of loss and sadness and your life being... There was a life before 9/11. There's a life after 9/11. And the life after 9/11 is different.

When the anniversary of 9/11 gets near, around the middle of August, things change in my head because I know it's around the corner and that's when all these memories are stronger. Not that they ever go away. But in the weeks leading up to 9/11 anniversary each year things get worse and it's hard not to be emotional.

Some years I do better than others in our ceremony downstairs. Having to speak this year I didn't do that well in keeping my emotions in check during the ceremony for Chiefs; Bill Feehan, Pete Ganci, Jerry Barbara and Donald Burns. These were people that I knew and loved. And seeing their families and speaking with them is difficult.

Being at the site in the morning and having the names read you realize after an hour we're just up to 1/3 of the way through. It's a terrible thing. I deal with it by being with family. My family gets together for dinner after the ceremony here and then we go back to the World Trade Center for the band's event and doing it as a family is important. Both of my sons-in-laws are on the job. One's a Chief, one's a Lieutenant. My kids grew up with the fire department. It's a family business so to speak. And that gets me through it. The strength of family. ❖

# John Sudnik – Battalion Chief

On September 12th I got up early and went into the firehouse. It was somber. A lot of tears going on in the firehouse. Timmy Stackpole was recently promoted out of the Sheffield Avenue firehouse. They already found Timmy's body.

I was the Captain there. As much as I wanted to stay, I felt like I needed to get down to the site and do what I could. I got my gear. Drove to Headquarters. Went to the seventh floor and saw Dan Nigro. The first thing he did was hug me. He thought I was dead. In the first couple days, certainly not the next morning, we didn't know how many people we lost. We knew there was hundreds. There was a list going around of who was missing and I was on that list. He probably saw my name and thought 'I told him to get in my car and go to the site.' I suppose that's how he saw it. I never asked him.

Dan Nigro was now the new Chief of Department. I said to him "What do you want me to do," he said, "Well you know what, because we're going to need as much help as we can at headquarters would you stay in Operations and help us out?" I said "Of course." What was I going to say? I didn't feel it was a request. I took it more like this is what I need you to do type of thing. So, that was my assignment. I stayed and worked in Operations.

In the days following we worked on developing some type of family assistance and fielded phone calls from families asking for information about family members who were missing. They were continually calling back to find out if we had any updates or anything like that. I mean, obviously, you can imagine how our families were reaching out. They needed information. When bodies were found and identified we needed to notify them and how that was going to happen was a big concern.

Another big concern was taking control of the site. You had emergency operations being performed by people coming from all over the country trying to help and they were on the pile. Which was extremely dangerous. They needed coordination. Getting control of this was another big concern of the Staff Chiefs in Headquarters.

Then I got promoted to Battalion Chief on Sunday September 16th. I had a bunch of emotions. Obviously, to say it was bittersweet is an understatement. It's always nice to get promoted. But there was no celebrating.

In Headquarters it felt like you had to start from scratch and try to deal with something you'd never dealt with before. Everybody wanted to go down to the site and the Staff Chiefs realized at some point everybody's going to get tired and there's going to be nobody able to work at the site or, in the firehouses. We had to force people into a schedule where you'd work at the site and maintain a workforce to staff the firehouses. And then you needed to go home.

An 'AB' work schedule was created 24 hours on, 24 hours off, for the people in the firehouses and for the people down at the site. Then we went to the 'ABC' work schedule 24 hours at the site, 24 hours off, then 24 hours in the firehouse followed by 24 hours off. This was to insure we had 'continuity of operations' and we weren't burning out our members.

The hardest part for me as a Captain was getting promoted out of my company and not being able to be in the firehouse to help support them. Within short order they got another Captain in there. I had a good relationship with Timmy Stackpole. We got promoted to lieutenant together, so I knew Timmy for a long time. That he is gone still bothers me to this day. The Lieutenants in Engine 290 were senior guys. They picked up the leadership role and the truck officers as well. That's a good firehouse.

I ended up going down to the World Trade Center site a couple times on my days off from Headquarters. I considered myself lucky and fortunate to be alive and a little bit guilty as well. There was nothing I wouldn't do. When they asked, I said, "Whatever you need I'm here." This was my internal thinking.

After spending a few months in Operations, I volunteered for a 30-day detail and worked down at the site as a Battalion Chief supervising the recovery operation during the month of December. I remember meeting the mayor-elect Bloomberg when he came to the site on the day he was inaugurated.

Here I am, 20 years removed from 9/11 and I think about the immediate impact on me and the significance health wise, psychologically, emotionally. I chose to endure and re-double my efforts. To work harder. Whenever somebody asked me to take on a job in Headquarters even though I wasn't thrilled about coming off-line because I love being in the firehouse, it was very difficult for me to say no. Especially to certain people knowing what their sacrifices were.

I'm in the highest-ranking uniform position in the department and I guess that's what led me to becoming the Chief of Department. I'd like to think I'm still working hard after 9/11. I'm now, 20 years later, dealing with a pandemic. I'm certain my experience along the way after 9/11 prepared me to lead this department through this pandemic.

The first couple of years on the anniversary 9/11 I was drawn to going to services and masses for the lost members I knew well. I liked spending the morning at the ceremony at the Fireman's Monument on Riverside Drive. I've been doing that for quite some time now. The 18th Battalion does a great job there, it's a great turnout in a beautiful setting, a nice place to reflect.

At headquarters we have a 9/11 ceremony for the four members we lost here in headquarters. I've been attending this for the past seven years. First as Chief Operations now as Chief of Department.

Obviously, it's something we're all going to carry with us for the rest of our lives. I feel fortunate to be able to continue working for the period I have and of course we all know so many people who couldn't and probably

more important there are many people still feeling the impact of 9/11 with illnesses and unfortunately losing their lives. I can keep going on about how many people I was close to who got sick from being at the site on 9/11 and have passed.

9/11 was the defining moment in my career and I pray to God we don't have another that rivals it.

The most important impact from 9/11 was knowing how dangerous our job is and how fragile life is. It doesn't matter how well prepared you are. How much you train. How diligent you are. The nature of our job is such that anything can happen and be beyond your control. And the impact could be devastating.

That we lost 343 members on one day. One incident. Shows more than anything else it doesn't matter what company you're in. Whether you're in an Engine or a Ladder company. A Rescue or Squad. Whether you are busy or not busy. It doesn't matter. When you join the FDNY. Raise your right hand and take the oath to serve the people of New York City. You have to know because of the type of work we do. Anything could happen to you. ❖

> ## When you join the FDNY. Raise your right-hand and take the oath to serve the people of New York City. You have to know because of the type of work we do. Anything could happen to you.

## Elizabeth DeFazio – Secretary to Chief of Department Peter Ganci

The next morning, I drove to my husband's firehouse. The whites of all their eyes were red from being in the dust at the site. Then I drove to headquarters. When I got near headquarters a cop stopped me and wanted to know why I needed to get to headquarters. I showed him my FDNY-ID he said "The building is in 'lock-down' get back in your car. Don't get out of your car again until you reach the building."

Guys were starting to come back from being at the site all night. The lists of who was missing was not completely accurate. Firefighters used other firefighters bunker gear and if they found bunker gear on a victim, they assumed it belonged to the firefighter whose name was on it. And that wasn't the case. There were guys from my husband's firehouse I had seen that morning and they were listed as missing. I told Chief Nigro "These guys are alive. I'm telling you they're alive. I saw them this morning."

So, they had us calling firehouses speaking only to the officer working. We would get the officer's name and ask him if the names listed are missing or alive. I don't know how many days we did it for but one of the girls couldn't continue. It was too emotional for her. We had officers on the phone crying while we were trying to establish exactly who was alive and who wasn't. It was awful. That was the most frustrating part. The unknown. I remember reading off names to officers and they would say "Missing, missing, missing," and when we gave them a name and they said, "He's alive." It was such a happy feeling when we were able to cross somebody off that list and write—alive.

Everybody did their best. Jumped into it. Firefighters do what they do best they went into action. The top leaders were gone. Only Chief Nigro was in the next day. Everybody did above and beyond.

My family was in Europe trying to get home. We still couldn't get them on the phones. My husband started the 24-hour on, 24-hour off shifts. I knew he was a firefighter. But at night there was a part of me…I didn't want to be home by myself. I was never like that before.

I plowed into going to headquarters and working. We had to make an accurate list for these families. Working, that's what got me through it. The atmosphere in headquarters was oh-God awful. What happened was unthinkable. People were walking around like zombies. A horrendous time.

Calls came in from around the world. People wanting to come and help. Companies offering their machinery, equipment, anything, and everything. We took the name of the company and the contact information. My husband didn't want me to go to work. I was like 'I'm not sitting in this house watching television. We have stuff to do. I'm going to work.'

## Calls came in from around the world. People wanting to come and help. Companies offering their machinery, equipment, anything, and everything.

On Saturday I went to Chief Ganci's funeral. On Sunday, September 16th they promoted a bunch of guys. I went to headquarters to help prepare for the promotion ceremony. They were promoting guys to all the different ranks and some 'posthumously.' Chief Nigro was formally promoted to Chief of Department.

A bunch of retired Chiefs came to the seventh floor. They wanted to visit victim's homes and make a connection to support the widows because there were so many deaths the department couldn't do what they normally do.

For weeks, everybody was in shock. I would even say for months. I lived in West Brighton Staten Island. I can't tell you how many firefighters lived in the area. So many families were affected. It was an awful time.

It's still tough on 9/11. September rolls around and you know what's coming. I can't stand it and I don't want to go to the headquarters ceremony. Then I go and it makes me feel better. But it's awful. I can't wait for 9/11 to pass. I try and block it out of my brain, but you can't.

I remember earlier that morning on September 11th Chief Ganci was sitting in his office. He was on some kind of diet when he handed me this cantaloupe he hadn't opened saying "Here, I don't think I'm going to be able to eat this today. It's going to be a long day. You take it and enjoy it." I remember staring at that fruit. I didn't want to eat it. How fragile life is. ❖

## Patrick McNally – Deputy Chief, Division 14

What got me through. Helped me do what I had to do. Was the brotherhood. The teamwork. This is our job. This is what we were trained to do. Nothing was too unusual. I reported into the Command Post. The Command Post got knocked out—set up another Command Post. That's what we were trained to do. And we relied on our training. The other thing was we made all the proper searches and did the best we could. That's the brotherhood part of it. At an 'All hands' fire you always wanted to make sure everybody does their very best. And we would do our very best at the World Trade Center. As terrible as it was. That day was the worst thing that ever happened to the FDNY. And I believe. It was our finest hour.

In retrospect with all the sicknesses and other medical problems we have. We could have rotated the personal more. Maybe that would have cut down on it. There were Chiefs who lost their sons who came every night to aid in the search and that went on for months. Certain guys I know worked there the whole time and a lot of them ended up with one form of cancer or another. I have multiple myeloma, a form of bone marrow cancer. We never had trouble getting firefighters to go to the site. There were plenty of guys willing to go. That's our strong suit. But it might have been a weakness.

Given the job of doing the 'rescue and recovery' I don't know what we could have done differently. Having been given the task. I thought we did it well.

The last couple of weeks we were sifting through the debris. Almost by hand. An excavator would pick it up. Then spread it on the ground. And after it was searched move it to another spot where it was picked up and searched again. Then it was taken to the Staten Island land fill and gone over again so there would be no doubt. That was a dedicated attempt to find whatever remains we could. I understand one night a firefighter found a fingernail in all that debris. That's how closely the firefighters were looking. Nobody was shirking this tough miserable work. I think that was our strength. These were our brothers and that's the way firefighters treated it.

As far as any serious injuries the only one I heard of was a broken leg. That could have been the most serious injury in the whole recovery operation. You have to give tribute the Chief assigned to Safety for the entire site Chief Ronnie Spadafora. He created safety procedures making things very strict about how dangerous things got done. He later died from a World Trade Center related cancer.

Particularly during the first couple of months we used a lot of Chiefs in situations which would normally require a Company-officer's supervision. We didn't want freelancing. We put a big burden on the Battalion Chiefs, and they did a good job. I don't want to be patting ourselves on the back but I think using Chiefs like Company-officers made a difference. And they all stepped up. We did almost nothing without a Chief in charge of it.

Unfortunately, in addition to the 343 there's all the illnesses and 9/11 related deaths. Some of those illnesses could have been caused in the beginning. But I don't know what we could have done differently. I heard Battalion Chief Orio Palmer's handie-talkie transmissions about getting hose-lines in place and the progress in making searches. We were treating it like a fire. Nobody was saying 'Let's get out of here.' Initially we felt if we could get water on the fire, we could put it out. I don't think the Chief officers in charge knew the devastation caused by those jet fueled planes. We had no point of reference to compare it to. There isn't much history of how high-rise buildings could collapse. How much damage they could take. So, it's hard for anyone to look back and say you could have done this, or you could have done that.

I worked the last night we operated at the site. We knew family members would be attending a ceremony in the morning. A weird thing was. I kept thinking 'There were water puddles and not knowing how deep a puddle was I didn't want any of the family members thinking their loved ones could have been missed because we didn't search under the water.' I got the Sanitation Departments street-sweeper to make the ceremony area puddle free and 'broom clean.'

## That day was the worst thing that ever happened to the FDNY. And I believe. It was our finest hour.

I never planned to be a Staff-Chief. I always thought if I was the 6th or 3rd Division Commander. I'd be a happy guy. But after 9/11 whatever they need me to do from here on out I will do. It made my sense of dedication even stronger. Things were going to be different now. There were so few of us close to the top levels of the Department. You knew it after Chief of Department Pete Ganci's funeral. We lost a whole part of the job. When Chief of Operations Sal Cassano called me to go on the Staff. I didn't even ask him what my job was going to be. I thought 'I lived' and so many guys didn't live. I was at that Command Post. Standing next to Pete Ganci, Bill Feehan, Eddie Geraghty, Dennis Cross, Timmy Stackpole, Ray Downey. They all died in the collapse. I'm lucky to be here.

When 9/11 comes around, well it's my wedding anniversary. While I was working, I would always go to the formal ceremony at the site. I did that until I retired in June of 09. I moved to Long Beach Long Island and there's a nice 9/11 memorial in Point Lookout. I've gone there many times and I go to church in the morning with my wife. Then we spend a quiet day together. ❖

# Herbert V. (Ted) Rolfing
### Assistant Chief of Department,
### Bureau of Fire Prevention, retired

I was in the kitchen when the TV reported an aircraft had hit the World Trade Center. I saw the towers come down and like everybody else my first thought was to go there. But I didn't. I was still trying to get used to the effects of a heart-attack and understand what I could do and what I couldn't do. I felt I owed it to my wife. She put up with worrying for 35 years of my career and long story short, I did not go to the Trade Center that day.

A friend of mine retired Chief Pete Hughes got involved in running a thing to help the families at Pier 94 on the West Side docks. I called him but they didn't need any help there. I was beside myself. I was home and doing nothing.

> ## The volunteer firefighters in the areas where the families lived were great. They went way overboard. Doing everything they could at these funerals and memorials.

Then I went to a meeting at the training academy concerning FDNY notifications to the families where we all signed up to have an FDNY Chief officer notify the families when they found remains. We went through the list of who was still missing and who wanted to go to each family.

One guy I knew was Joe Angelini a firefighter from Rescue 1. His son was also killed so the family had two deaths. I met Joe through work. He was one of those guys you met and your best friends. Like you have known each other for years. I signed up to visit his family. We went to the local church where he lived in Long Island and got the pastor to come with us to the house. We knocked on the door his wife answered and said, "Can I help you?" You could see the look on her face. She knew what was coming. I said, "The Fire Department found the remains of your family member." It was as you can imagine a very solemn thing. We were at Joe's house for a while when they asked if I could go and notify his mother. Naturally you can't say no to a thing like that. We went over to his mother's house, and it was a short and sweet visit. I only got called to do this twice.

At some funerals where they didn't have an FDNY Staff-Chief at the church I would go up to the family and say, "On behalf of the Commissioner of the New York City Fire Department...." This was out of hand too. But I didn't think it was right by the family not to have a Staff-Officer represent the department at their loved one's funeral. My conscience motivated me to do it.

There was a lot of retired Chiefs attending the funerals one said, "How the hell are we going to bury 343 guys?" Yeah, I attended a bunch of them. A song often played at a funeral was 'You Are The Wind Beneath My Wings.' To this day it drives me so deeply sad. The volunteer firefighters in the areas where the families lived were great. They went way overboard. Doing everything they could at these funerals and memorials.

I spent a day at the site once in February. I probably should have gone more often. It was very emotional. I never went back. While I was there, they found a civilian's body part. Everything stopped. They placed the body part in a stokes stretcher. Covered it with an American flag and carried it up the ramp. Out of the pit. I saw it being handled well. They were particular about doing it with respect. The aura. The way everyone was treated. The attitudes of everyone working there. Was like a religious thing. ❖

---

## John Casey – Division 3 Commander

As the days went by four command posts were established one in each of the four sides of the site and you could see progress as we got organized. Excavator equipment was moving the steel cut by ironworkers and dump trucks were removing debris. The construction guys were very good. We didn't find too many bodies that's for sure. What little was left of people was unbelievable.

Everyone still wanted to be down there, but they realized the need to have firehouses staffed. After a week or so we started having the funerals and with each new month we were going to 'memorials' with an empty casket because many of the victims didn't have any remains and empty caskets couldn't be buried. We'd line up with only a hundred guys whereas before there'd be thousands. A lot of retired guys helped by coming to these funerals and memorials in uniform which was good. It gave an FDNY presence to the families who loved their firefighters. You wouldn't have a full FDNY band. Maybe only a couple of pipers. Other departments sent their bands. One from Boston and other cities too. It was beyond the capabilities of headquarters to do anything like what was normally done with so many memorials and funerals.

The companies took over. You couldn't beat that. You saw it in the firefighters. How good this job is. They did it. The officers and firefighters stepped up and took care of the families. There's nothing you can compare it to. It was on a scale that we never experienced in the past. The camaraderie we have in this department is unbelievable. Some houses lost 14 firefighters and officers. Gone.

Firefighters from other units that these firefighters didn't even know took the ball and ran with it by working in those firehouses so the firefighters who suffered losses could take care of the families.

Outside of the firehouses flowers piled up placed by people in the neighborhood. A little story of all the people bringing food to the firehouse. I was standing outside of a firehouse when a car pulls up and a guy comes out with trays of food. One of the firefighters says to another "Gee, we hardly have any room in our refrigerator." The guy that brought the food heard this and left. An hour later he comes back with a refrigerator in his truck. People were unbelievable. The public was so good.

A year later when I was the Staten Island Borough Commander, I contacted the retirees who volunteered to work. They did so many different tasks. I had a little ceremony for them. They did a great job. Even when we're retired, we feel we are still part of the job no matter what.

I know the complaint. The firefighters and officers who came in from home weren't organized when they went to the site. Now, I don't know how we could have stopped that then or in the future. If there was God forbid something like that tomorrow and firefighters are trapped or hurt. They would still leave home and go to the disaster. You're not going to prevent that. They saw the buildings come down on television. Knew hundreds of firefighters would be dead or injured and responded. Cannot be prevented. Could controlling the firefighters from responding in prevented some of them from possible being killed? I don't know. Who knew those buildings were going to come down. Nobody thought they would come down so soon like that.

We learned a lot about truss construction over the years. Knowing construction is an important part of firefighting. Today a big part of training is building construction.

9/11 was a defining moment in my fire department career. Nothing compares. It's world history. A sad time in my life. I think of it a lot. So many good people I worked with were killed. One of them was Battalion Chief Orio Palmer. Everybody thought so much of him. A man with a bright future in the department.

I was standing outside of a firehouse when a car pulls up and a guy comes out with trays of food. One of the firefighters says to another "Gee, we hardly have any room in our refrigerator." The guy that brought the food heard this and left. An hour later he comes back with a refrigerator in his truck. People were unbelievable.

Photo © 2001 by Michael Heller

The only regret I have is I didn't do more training with the members. Some guys went to the Rock (FDNY Training Academy) and worked there. That's important. The training I mostly did was in the field. That's your job to train and make them safe. Seventy five percent of this job is getting experience going to fires and learning what you had at a fire. Seeing what the fire did. How it burned. Where the problems were. And afterwards going back into the fire-building. Everybody in the firehouse. Wringing it out like a rag. Looking and seeing what happened because that's the experience to learn from.

I hate the 9/11 anniversary day. I hate it. I retired in 2004 and on the 10th anniversary I did suit up and go to the First Battalion. I can't wait for the day to be over.

On occasion over the years, I've gone to the memorial of Flight 93 in Shanksville Pennsylvania honoring the 40 passengers and crew aboard the plane who took actions to stop the attack on the United States Capitol. One day in January I was going to drive myself, but I decided to take my twelve-year old grandson Christopher with me. The memorial is in the middle of a mile square field with no trees. It's 4:00 P.M. starting to get dark. We were at the memorial alone. There was a foot of snow on the ground. Suddenly ten cars pull up filled with men and women. I went over to this older guy and said "What's going on? What's this?" He says, "I'm a retired Marine Corps General working with returning veterans from the war and I bring these veterans here to show them what they went to war in Afghanistan for." Then he proceeded to make an unforgettable speech. I turned to my grandson "Christopher, never forget this moment." It was unbelievable to see what these soldiers were doing and what this General was doing for the troops that went over to fight in Afghanistan. A very powerful moment.

I think about all those guys whose lives were cut short. It's so sad. And the victim carry-outs at the site. We found remains of so many firefighters. How very sad it was waiting for their companies to come so they could carry the body parts out. ❖

## Rochelle Jones
### Captain Engine 4
### (promoted to Battalion Chief)

I was on vacation in New Mexico with my husband when we got a phone call from my stepson who said, "A plane hit the Towers." We immediately turned on the TV and watched the whole horrible scene unfold knowing perfectly well as Captain of Engine 4 they would have obviously responded to the scene we were watching. When the buildings came down, I said to my husband "Everyone in Engine 4 working today is dead." He said, "You don't know that." I said, "They would be there when those buildings were coming down. They're going to be dead."

I called the firehouse and spoke with a firefighter at the house-watch. He went over a list of people he had seen and told me there were eleven missing. Then he called me back and said, "We're also missing these three." Which included one guy who was rotated out (probationary firefighter rotated to work for a period to time into another firehouse to gain knowledge of different areas in the city). So, I knew before I left New Mexico there was 14 lost in our firehouse (Engine 4 and Ladder 15).

I thought I was going to get a flight out on Wednesday but there was no air travel. Thursday morning, I packed up the car and for the first time had to journey back to New York City by myself. I brought my dog a 160-pound mastiff in the backseat of a two-door Honda Accord and headed East. I slept for an hour or so here or there in the rest areas. Coming across country all I could think about was the firehouse, my people, and New York City. Thinking about it as a very microcosm scene. Once I started hitting the cities there were signs and flags on all the overpasses 'United We Stand' 'God Bless America' 'We Love New York.' I realized it was bigger than just my guys or my city. On a Pennsylvania highway where you're directed to merge right because a lane is closed a traffic sign was flashing, 'Merge Right, United We Stand.'

I arrived in New York City at 5 A.M. on Saturday September 15th and called the firehouse. Division 1 put me on the 24 hours-on, 24 hour-off, work shift as of Sunday morning. So, Saturday I tried to get some rest.

Sunday morning Andy Graf one of my lieutenants Bob Kemp a senior firefighter from 15 Truck, and Tom Bailey a brand new proby, picked me up and drove me to the firehouse. When I got to there, I had rollcall. You never knew the words "I'm so glad to see you" could mean so much. One of the guys gave me a big hug and said, "Somehow it feels like Mom is home and things will get better." That was pretty much where it stood.

Right after roll call an engine company pulled up in front of quarters. I asked, "What are you doing here?" They said, "Dispatchers are relocating companies into your quarters on 24-hour shifts." I'm thinking 'So, we're going to have strangers in the firehouse for 24 hours.' That was a shock to me. Both of our companies were 'out-of-service' (not responding to alarms). Then Ladder 159 came. A company where I had been a Lieutenant. That's the first time I let myself cry at the firehouse. Seeing them and thinking, 'At least, it's people who know me and won't be....' Quite often it's like 'So what's it like having a woman boss?' 'What's it like working with a woman? 'or 'How is she at fires?' These guys in Ladder 159 knew me. I was feeling less judged. And that felt good. I had ten-thousand other things in my head.

> ## Once I started hitting the cities there were signs and flags on all the overpasses 'United We Stand' 'God Bless America' 'We Love New York.' I realized it was bigger than just my guys or my city.

We held a firehouse company meeting with the officers and firefighters from Engine 4 and Ladder 15. We were trying to make plans about families who lost their loved ones. Already we were understanding we weren't getting people out alive and wanted to move forward towards having services.

Lieutenant Andy Graf, who was the senior man, was trying to protect me and said "I don't want you to go straight to work (going to the site). I want you to be able to handle it and I don't want you to deal with a bunch of

Photo © 2001 by Michael Heller

people." I think he was afraid I was going to break down. But instead, I was in job-mode. At 11 A.M. we took a van to the site. I couldn't comprehend it. I knew the area and was trying to figure out where I was. What corner would this be? Then my job-brain kicked in. Okay, what do we have to do? What can we do?

It was surreal and real at the same time. We didn't report-in to a Chief or anyone else. We walked out on the pile and were approached by a large group of Chicago firefighters who felt they weren't being used. They asked me if I could get them put to work. They felt they had more experience than some of the out-of-town firefighters there. But there was nothing I could do. I was trying to make sense of it all and spoke to a Chief who said, "No, we don't need those guys now." We did some bucket-brigade work and surface-searches on the pile. At 5 P. M. we went back to the firehouse.

The first family I met was Lieutenant Joe Leavey's family who came into the firehouse on Sunday. I had met them at the Christmas party and was familiar with his wife and ten-year-old daughter. They were amazing. I thought 'Okay if they're handling it this well, that's a good sign.' Thinking about facing the families became a little bit easier. Lieutenant Joe Leavey's funeral was our first funeral. Until then we had only had memorial services. It was planned as a memorial on his birthday but turned into a funeral when a week before they found some remains and were able to identify them as Joe's.

Later Sunday night we were back at the site again. On our own. Doing surface-searches and moving buckets of debris. We weren't being assigned a specific task and there was no one I had to check in with. Everyone was doing what they could, yet it was a robotic scene. You were doing something and didn't know if it was going to make a difference. It was hard.

Monday morning before rollcall we had a meeting with officers of the incoming 24-hour shift. I wanted reach out to the families of the Engine members lost and start finding out where we were. Who was accepting and who wasn't? Some thought their loved ones were in the underground shopping area waiting to be saved.

Getting a grasp on the family situations of each of the guys. Who was married? Who was living with somebody? Who was single? Which firefighters had dads on the job? How are we going to get the families together so they could lean on each other? How the surviving guys were doing and where we stood with being back in-service. During those 24-hour shifts, everything went 100 miles a minute.

We didn't have a rig and weren't assigned any specific tasks. We were on our own. I didn't know what was going on every place else. I just knew what was going on with us.

Ladder 15 was responding when an air-line broke and it came to a stop before they got into the site. The chauffeur stayed with the rig working to fix it was saved. The rest of the company was killed.

We lost 14 people. Thirteen were assigned or on rotation and one who was rotated out and died while working in another company who responded to the attack. We had probies who hadn't finished probie school working in the firehouse. We realized a lot of these families didn't know each other because they hadn't been to company picnics, Christmas parties or other functions together.

After the meeting on Monday a couple of the guys picked me up and we went to visit the Staten Island families who had lost their husband or son. It was a whirlwind. I'm sure everybody feels the same way. You can't remember everything because it was so crazy. We visited at the home of firefighter Tom Kelly's widow Kitty. She was good and gracious. Everybody was still in disbelief. It was hard. The Barry family lost their son.

Paul Tegtmeir's wife Cathy was a volunteer firefighter in their town and had been to the site. They were taking families to see the site from a distance. When I spoke to her, she said "I know he's not coming home and I'm going to start making funeral arrangements." She was the first one I met who totally had her feet on the ground. Some of them accepted it mentally but emotionally they were still holding out hope. She was like "Okay, nope."

I was in the firehouse most of the time. Making phone calls. Meeting with people. So, I didn't spend a tremendous amount of time at the site. It was a mix of trying to get a hold of everything and figure out the next steps. A big thing was the liaisons (firefighters taken off the work chart to assist the families) who helped with the families. One of ours was firefighter Dan Barron who was on rotation in Engine 4 stepped-up and did an excellent job. With 14 deaths in the firehouse, we had three liaisons.

Also, there was the home-companies of rotators who died and who didn't lose anyone else. They were helping the families. But it almost became a competition. After few weeks I made a call to all the companies we shared somebody with. Going over who was going to have the honor-guard for the wake and pallbearers at the funer-

als. I realized because our Battalion was so devastated, we couldn't always get guys to cover these funerals. So, what were we going to do?

I said to the home-companies "This is a very hard situation. Obviously, we've never been in this situation before. Could we possible share the duties of the funerals?" I didn't have people who could do those things. Our roster was pretty bare.

I remember calling John Graziano. I was in a study group with John for both lieutenant and captain exams. It was such a relief to have somebody say "I understand. Don't worry about it. It's all going to be fine. It's all going to work out."

One of Ladder 15's assigned firefighters was on rotation in a truck company in Brooklyn. Every tour he was scheduled to work there he'd show up here because they would fill-in his tour so he could be with us. That was incredibly generous of them.

I tried to get the rotators who were assigned to our firehouse but rotating in other firehouses back so we would have a complement of people assigned here dealing with these families for weeks, months, and years to come. I called the officer at the transfer-desk and said, "Listen, I want to get these guys on rotation back." He goes "We can't do that there are a lot of things going on give me one guy you really want back." This was the first time I got snarky and bitchy. I said, "I want Sergio Villanueva back." He goes "Where is he?" I go "Ladder 132," he goes "Okay, I'll do it." I go "You can't do it he's on the bottom of that frigging pile." I know there's paperwork and headquarters procedures but understand what's going on here. I've got rotators who are going to leave our firehouse in January and never see these families again after they had been in contact with them for the worst days of their lives.

We did get our guys back in the end. It wasn't easy. It was a hard time. Doing things for and being with the families was mostly wonderful.

I love Captain Tim McKinney of Ladder 15 to death. All the officers in our firehouse were great. Tom Gainey, Andy Graf, Jim Milone, and John Viola all great guys. The 1st Battalion Chiefs were head and shoulders above the rest. They were great. To help they sent me an administrative officer. This guy was so on the ball it was scary. A family would come to quarters and a question would come up. He'd be like "All right, I'll look into that." He was shadowing me. If I said I need to call the Division by the time I got upstairs he's like "I called the Division they're taking care of it." You didn't have to ask him he was listening and doing.

People would come by with food, to pray, and to tell you how bad they felt. It was a constant flow of people in the firehouse. These teenage girls from California had traveled across the nation with their mom's selling 'a dollar a Band-Aid.' Where you could write something on the Band-Aid then they sealed the Band-Aids together and had this ticker-tape type thing in a big-roll that they were selling like raffle tickets. So, they're making me, and Tim McKinney stand there with this roll of Band-Aids going across our hands so we could see this wonderful thing they did when Tim whispered, "I hope they're not used Band-Aids."

There was bizarre stuff going on. We had street performers from San Francisco come. We had left quarters to get the meal from the supermarket and when we come back there was this circus with flaming batons, tricked-out fairy-type costumes and acrobatic stuff being played out on the apparatus floor! People with kindness in their hearts but at times—not good judgement.

All the members of the house whether they be rotators or assigned stepped up to fill in the empty spaces for us. These guys kept me going. And I hope and I think. I kept them going. I realized even before I left New Mexico to head back as the Captain of the company there was a lot of things I was going to have to be, the counselor, the mom, the friend. I knew my role had expanded exponentially at that point.

I always credit Ladder 159 with teaching me how to be a boss in many, many ways. I was the first woman to be promoted to lieutenant and worked in Ladder 159 as a new lieutenant. The job wanted me in the Battalion 33's 'R group' (relief group that covers vacancies in the battalion companies only) and not leave the battalion so the Chiefs would know you and you'd only be dealing with one set of Chiefs. It turned out the companies I worked in always gave respect to the rank. So, I wasn't really concerned about getting respect. Guys know what it takes to become a lieutenant the competition and the studying that goes into it.

And I've been blessed with working with wonderful Chiefs. Particularly in Battalion 33 which covered the Marine Park/Flatbush area of Brooklyn. I grew up in Sheepshead Bay Brooklyn and a lot of guys lived in Gerritsen Beach which was the neighborhood near me. They were, I don't know, irreverent, but respectful at the same time. I learned to balance the line. Not take everything too seriously. And not to worry about the small stuff. They taught me a lot about being a boss. It's not always easy. I'm not going to lie to you. No doubt about it good people. Yet constant testing. Especially in the beginning.

When I was promoted to Captain I got the UFO (Until Further Orders assigned to a particular company) spot in Engine 4 and before my first tour was over Chief John Coloe from Division 1 asked if I was interested in the spot. I'm like "Can I finish my first tour before I decide?" Chief Coloe, who I worked with many years ago. Good guy. Said "Well if you're not interested, we'll take you out and put somebody else in." I said, "Okay, then I might be interested." I was like, 'Okay, I can do this spot.' I had the stress of—this is going to sound very girly—you're always a girl going into the firehouse and it's always someplace in your head...I don't know if a man on the job can grasp that. And I thought this is the first firehouse when I walked into the kitchen, I didn't feel like Oh, that's the girl. It was no big deal. I found that odd and comforting, all at the same time.

One morning I was in the firehouse having a regular morning in the kitchen drinking coffee having breakfast chatting it up. We were actually laughing. The typical firehouse bantering going on when I get a call from the dispatcher. I picked it up in the kitchen and the dispatcher said, "They found one of your guys at the site we will send you a response ticket." I hung up the phone. Went to the office and cried. You almost feel like you're having a normal day and then you're reminded. This horror is not over.

We went to the site. Tommy was a rotator. Guys from Tommy's original company were there, and I said, "Do we know if it's Tommy for sure?" A guy said "Yes, he has our company shirt on." His dad was a Chief in the Bronx, and we were going to wait until he could come down with his other sons to escort Tommy's body out. So were waiting. It was a miserable day rainy and crappy. The guys were mulling around. I was like 'I can't leave Tommy's body here.' I was getting very upset. There were a lot of eyes on me. Then a guy who had been assigned on rotation to 4 Engine and was digging in the pile that day came over and said, "I'm not letting you stand here alone. I'm not letting you cry. So, we're going to talk about something else." He saved me that day. I think the whole shock of having a normal firehouse morning then suddenly to be smacked back to reality….

Over a year later, maybe two, I was finishing up a night-tour in the 2ⁿᵈ Battalion when Chief Jay Jonas came in with bagels and said, "This morning is the first morning I felt like it's a pre-9/11 morning." So that's the way it is. This is never going to be over.

On the anniversary of 9/11 there's good years and there's bad years. I always go to Engine 4. I want to be with the families who come to the firehouse so they will see a face they know. The job is changing so quickly. I guess it always does. There's only a handful of guys still in the firehouse who were working with me then. Some of the families come every year. Some, maybe their widows don't come and instead the extended family comes Cousins, Uncles and Aunts. I always feel that's my place. And have never been any place else on 9/11. I'm shocked when people don't recognize September 11ᵗʰ and think "Oh, people have a normal day on September 11ᵗʰ?" I still can't grasp that. I don't know where else I would be on September 11ᵗʰ. Engine 4 that's where I belong. ❖

## Ralph Bernard – Lieutenant Supervising Fire Marshal, Multi-Media Unit Supervisor

On Saturday September 15ᵗʰ, our task was to record the first of the funerals for Chief of Department Peter Ganci, Assistant Commissioner William Feehan and Father Michael Judge all on the same day. I knew Chief Ganci. Worked with him. He was somebody I respected. It was a very sad day and a terrible loss for the fire department. One funeral is terrible to begin with. How do you respectfully do 343?

There were times where on one day there were 12 funerals. I have a limited staff. There was no way my unit could accomplish this without help. The members from the companies who lost a firefighter or officer. The municipal or volunteer Fire Departments where the members lived. All stepped-up helping with services. They couldn't do enough for us.

I find the plaque-dedication worse. Funerals are fresh. It just happened. Everybody's in shock. You haven't had time to process it. A year later you do. At a plaque-dedication the wife, the mother, a sister or child, somebody gets up and talks about their loss. It's so personal. It really hits home. They've lived a whole year without the person they love.

The FDNY is so supportive of the families. Members in the firehouses, EMS stations, they are—all there—for the family. And I know from going to so many of them it's appreciated. Definitely needed. It's all part of the healing process. They're not alone.

We were documenting 'ground-zero.' Taking pictures and filming pretty much every day. Walking down West Street into the site all you see is devastation. You don't see anything not damaged. It's an original vision you would never have imagined. Walking through the pile members were lined up on bucket-brigades or resting. Exhausted from working. Drinking water and eating in this contaminated environment.

When President Bush came to the site on September 14ᵗʰ, he was personable to everybody. He's visiting the worst terrorist attack on United States soil. And then he made the speech on top of the destroyed fire apparatus with a firefighter which everyone has seen. It was emotional. A powerful moment. We needed guidance and hope and I think he did a good job being there talking to the members. The boots on the ground. It was well received.

9/11 made America united. Everybody was on the same page. You saw people from all over holding up signs USA, FDNY, NYPD, PAPD, 'We love you.' The streets were lined with these signs. The people of New York City were so appreciative.

We did whatever needed to be done for documenting and recording 9/11. So many events. The supply of blessed funeral urns for victim ashes. Rigs being donated. We had a high school group from Hawaii who sang then presented this surfboard they had custom made to commemorate 9/11. So much stuff was given. I remember two nozzles with all the 343 names engraved on it. All kinds of artwork. Money was being given to the FDNY to help rebuild. We lost our members, and we lost a lot of equipment and apparatus too. There was always some sort of event with items being donated needing to be documented.

Around the beginning of December, the Fire Commission had a holiday party for the people at headquarters and their children to show support. Everybody needed the reassurance. we're all family. It was a nice holiday event. And still there were the normal fire department ceremonies going on, hiring firefighters and promotions.

On November 12ᵗʰ we had two major incidents on the same day in addition to the World trade Center operations; There was a 5ᵗʰ-alarm fire in St. John's the Divine church and the plane crash in Rockaway. We videotaped and took still-photos of all these events.

We digitized all the 911 dispatcher-recordings of the calls that came in. Everybody wanted a copy of the fire-ground communications and apparatus-radio communications with the dispatchers. It was my job to put together a day where all the families could get together and listen to the recordings before we gave it to the media.

The atmosphere around headquarters was different. Everyone wasn't themselves. A lot of tension and anger. You did what you had to do. Everybody I worked with — went above and beyond. They wanted to make sure the families got everything they needed. My hours were always long. What kept me going was 'what's next?' I knew if I kept busy, I wouldn't have to think about it. Doing one battle at a time. Not thinking about it. It's when I was not busy, I started thinking: 'Wow, what a terrible thing happened'. So, I kept busy.

I would have liked to have gotten there earlier to document some of the stuff I didn't get. But, on the other hand if I had my vehicle, I would have gotten there earlier and might not be here because I would have been in the lobby of 1-World Trade Center getting shots of what was going on at the Command Post. I would have filmed Chief Ganci at the 'Command-Board' with Commissioner Feehan. These are the kind of things we were always looking to get at major fires.

## 9/11 made America united. Everybody was on the same page. You saw people from all over holding up signs USA, FDNY, NYPD, PAPD, 'We love you.' The streets were lined with these signs. The people of New York City were so appreciative.

The 9/11 anniversary ceremonies are tough. We have two ceremonies at Headquarters on 9/11. One in the morning and afterwards we have a ceremony for the families of members who have passed from 9/11-related injuries. All the families and company members come to Headquarters. It's a very nice service. We do a video-scroll with the photos of the members who have passed away the previous year then the families go into the lobby of Headquarters where they lay a white rose on a beautiful mahogany tribute-table made by the shops with a plaque stating, 'We Will Never Forget' showing 343 firefighters marching down Fifth Avenue with American flags. Some of the families do a rubbing of the member's name on the 'Memorial Wall Plaque' in the lobby of Headquarters. It's emotional and supportive. ❖

# CHAPTER 8

# Lessons Learned

The FDNY prides itself on training. The Training Academy has a sign on its wall "Let no man's ghost come back to say my training let me down." After every fire or emergency of consequence the firehouse kitchen becomes the training center with discussions arising from the events played out to determine the 'Lessons Learned.' If there were errors in judgement or mistakes made, they are passed on in informal conversations with members in the firehouse. And if thought necessary, the officers will conduct drills on the tactics and skills that need going over. Sometimes an officer or firefighter will write a story about the incident for the departments WNYF (*"With the New York Firefighters,"*) magazine so everyone in the department can benefit from ideas to improve operations. Constant drilling is the hallmark of how firefighters respect their profession.

## McKinsey & Company Report on Recall Procedures

At the Fire Department's request McKinsey & Company, a well-respected international consulting firm, offered their services for free and spent five months working with Department personnel to develop recommendations for change to enhance the FDNY's preparedness. Here is how they introduced their findings. "Never before had a single terrorist act caused such a massive loss of life. It was the worst terrorist attack in the history of terrorism. In the aftermath of this extraordinary event, the enormous heroism of the members of the Fire Department of the City of New York stands out as an inspiration in the face of calamity. Three hundred forty-three FDNY personnel sacrificed their lives while trying to save others. They facilitated the safe evacuation of more than 25,000 people, the largest rescue operation in United States history."[50]

**It was the worst terrorist attack in the history of terrorism...Three hundred forty-three FDNY personnel sacrificed their lives while trying to save others.**

McKinsey & Company had unlimited access to FDNY records and worked closely with FDNY personnel who responded to the World Trade Center attack. Their 'Lessons Learned' included a review of requesting mutual aid from departments outside the city to support fire operations. And, improving coordination between FDNY and NYPD command and control functions.[51]

## The 911 Commission Analysis

The National Commission on Terrorist Attacks Upon the United States, '9-11 Commission' was chartered to prepare a full and complete account of the circumstances surrounding the September 11th terrorist attacks including preparedness for, and the immediate response to, the attacks. They reported the following: During FDNY North-Tower Operations Command and Control decisions were affected by the lack of knowledge of what was happening 30, 60, 90, and 100 floors above. According to one of the Chiefs in the lobby: "One of the most critical things in a major operation like this is to have information. We didn't have a lot of information coming in. We didn't receive any reports of what was seen from the (NYPD) helicopters. It was impossible to know how much damage was done on the upper floors, or whether the stairwells were intact or not." As a result, Chiefs in the lobby disagreed over whether anyone at or above the impact zone could possibly be rescued, or, whether there should be even limited firefighting for the purpose of cutting exit routes through fire zones.[52]

The 911 Commission on Terrorism further noted Civilians at or above the impact zone in the North Tower had the smallest hope of survival. Once the plane struck, they were prevented from descending because of damage to or impassable conditions in the building's three stairwells. The only hope for those on the upper floors of the North-Tower would have been a swift and extensive air rescue. Several factors made this impossible. Doors leading to the roof were kept locked for security reasons and, damage to software in the security command station prevented a lock release order from taking effect. Even if the doors had not been locked, structural and fire radiation hazards made the rooftops unsuitable staging areas for a large number of civilians; and even if conditions permit-

ted general helicopter evacuations—which was not the case—only several people could be lifted at a time.[53]

At 9:32, a senior chief radioed all units in the North-Tower to return to the lobby, at the same time, a Chief in the lobby was asked to consider the possibility of a rooftop rescue but was unable to reach FDNY dispatch by radio or phone. Out on West Street, however, the FDNY Chief of Department had already dismissed any rooftop rescue as impossible.[54]

The FDNY now has official procedures for serious fires in a high-rise building. An FDNY Battalion Chief responds to the NYPD aviation unit heliport, boards a responding helicopter to survey the scene, decides on whether or not to attempt a Rooftop-rescue and provides information regarding exterior structural damage.

## 2006 Plane Crash Into Building

As the On-Scene-Incident Commander when Yankee pitcher Cory Lidle and his flight instructor's plane crashed into a high-rise residential building in Manhattan on October 11, 2006, I benefited from having a discussion concerning the exterior damage to the building with the FDNY Battalion Chief in the NYPD helicopter.

Although there was heavy fire on the 29th and 30th floors of the building with structural damage to the exterior and interior walls caused by the plane impact there was no discussion concerning a Rooftop-Rescue. To my knowledge this procedure has never been performed for a fire in a high-rise building in NYC. The two floors of fire involving several apartments on each floor were extinguished using FDNY Standard Operating Procedures for fires in fireproof high-rise residential buildings which is an aggressive interior attack. All visible fire was knocked down in less than 40 minutes, timed from arrival, with no further injuries to civilians.

Outstanding efforts by FDNY first alarm units resulted in successful extinguishment with minor injuries to members. 9/11 was still on everyone's mind and I remember the look of concern on the faces of officers reporting into my Command Post. And I also remember, after giving them their assignments, they proceeded without hesitation dodging falling bricks as they entered the building. Several companies were awarded a unit citation in recognition of their actions.

## I remember the look of concern on the faces of officers reporting into my Command Post. And I also remember, after giving them their assignments, they proceeded without hesitation dodging falling bricks as they entered the building.

## Office of Emergency Management (OEM) Response

After the South-Tower was hit OEM senior leadership decided to remain in its "bunker" in 7-World Trade Center. At approximately 9:30 A.M. a senior OEM official ordered the evacuation of the facility after a Secret Service agent in 7-World Trade Center advised him additional commercial planes were not accounted for. Prior to its evacuation, no outside agency liaisons had reached OEM. OEM field responders were stationed in each tower's lobby, at the FDNY overall command post, and, at least for some period of time at the NYPD command post at Church and Vesey.[55]

## It is impossible to measure how many more civilians would have died but for the determination of many members of the FDNY, PAPD, and NYPD to continue assisting civilians after the South-Tower collapsed.

Regarding the evacuation process the 9/11 Commission on Terrorism report stated: In other instances, intangibles combined to reduce what could have been a much higher death total. It is impossible to measure how many more civilians would have died but for the determination of many members of the FDNY, PAPD, and NYPD to continue assisting civilians after the South-Tower collapsed. It is impossible to measure the calming influence that ascending firefighters had on descending civilians or whether, but for the firefighters' presence, the poor behavior of a very few civilians could have caused a dangerous and panicked mob flight. But the positive impact of the first responders on the evacuation came at a tremendous cost of first responder lives lost."[56]

The 9/11 Commission recognized how critical the lack of a comprehensive evacuation of the South-Tower immediately after the North-Tower impact occurred and states: No decision has been criticized more than the decision of building personnel not to evacuate the South-Tower immediately after the North-Tower was hit. A firm and prompt evacuation order would likely have led many to safety. Even a strictly 'advisory' announcement would not have dissuaded those who decided for themselves to evacuate. The advice to stay in place was understandable however, when considered in its context. At that moment no one appears to have thought a second plane could hit the South-Tower. The evacuation of thousands of people was seen as inherently dangerous. Additionally, conditions were hazardous in some areas outside the towers.[57]

High-Rise buildings egress-systems are not designed to accommodate an initial 'full-building evacuation' of occupants at a fire or emergency. In addition to injuries, which often are incurred by civilians evacuating multiple floors, there is the negative impact of having large numbers of occupants in and around the Lobby Command Post and/or being struck by debris if outside near the building's perimeter.

The 9/11 Commission went on to state: Whether the lack of coordination between the FDNY and NYPD on September 11 had a catastrophic effect has been the subject of controversy. We believe that there are too many variables for us to responsibly quantify those consequences. It is clear the lack of coordination did not affect adversely the evacuation of civilians. It is equally clear, however, that the Incident Command System did not function to integrate awareness among agencies or to facilitate interagency response.[58]

## Thomas Galvin – Deputy Chief, Division 3

The week following 9/11 the city was establishing a 'Family Assistance Center' on Pier 94. A firefighter came back from there walked into my office and started screaming at me "You guys don't know what you're doing. I took Carl's wife down to Pier 94 and nobody there is helping anybody from the fire department." I said, "Hold on let me track it down." I called headquarters and told them "I don't know what's going on a firefighter just went to Pier 94 with a deceased firefighter's wife. Is the city doing something? Is the fire department aware of this? The Chief said, "Let me call you back." Another Chief from headquarters called back and said, "We just heard about some type of 'Family Assistance Center' the city set up on Pier 94 could you check it out?" Exasperated I said, "I was the one who called." I get to Pier 94 and a lady from City Hall starts yelling at me. "Where are your guys? Your guys are supposed to be here." I'm like "Listen, I'm just finding out about this. What are you doing and what do you need?" She explains how they are providing various resources from around the city in one location Pier 94. I said, "Okay, I can have people here tomorrow."

I put it out to the members of the Division and several members stepped up to help. Just like everything the FDNY does these guys went down there on the blind and before you know it, they are the premiere resource group in the city to assist families of the FDNY and families from other agencies. They did a tremendous job.

As I look back, we were confronted with an expanding catastrophic incident. Our plans didn't fall apart but control did with multiple, sudden, collapses of high-rise buildings. The fire service never experienced a single collapse of a commercial hi-rise structure due to fire conditions before. Look at the command level Chief officers we had at the scene in the North-Tower Chiefs Peter Hayden, Joe Callan and in the South-Tower Chiefs Donald Burns and Jerry Barbara. All of whom had high-rise fire experience. At the main Command Post we had; Chief of Department Pete Ganci, Assistant Commissioner Bill Feehan, Chief Ray Downey, and Chief Sal Cassano.

But as we conducted a 'Post Incident Review' there were areas of command and operation we revised and took actions to address. Some of these were:

- To improve communications within high-rise buildings a Post radio was developed by Captain Mike Stein and Chief Pete Hart.

- Provided a cache of equipment to properly staff 300 firefighters.

- New Recall procedures to control Recall events.

- Concerning Accountability, we established a 'Planning Unit' and our own 'Incident-Management Team.'

- The 'Special Operations Command' was expanded to provide improved technical-rescues and hazardous-material-mitigation capability throughout the city.

- We were greatly assisted by the 'Southwest Wildland Fire Incident-Management Team' during our time at the site and learned their procedures.

When you're in a Command Chiefs position you are accountable for everyone's safety. From that day forward I was always thinking 'how can I make things better' and make it clear to people how we want them to operate effectively and safely. We have a responsibility to get these firefighters home at the end of the day. As a Chief you have an impact on their whole life. Not just the time when they're on-duty.

On the anniversary of 9/11 normally the first stop is 4 Truck. I was a Captain in 4 Truck and a Deputy Chief in Division 3. They do a nice ceremony right across the street from the firehouse followed by a mass at Saint Patrick's Cathedral. Carl Asaro and Dennis Devlin were in Division 3 on light-duty, and both were assigned to the Ninth Battalion. From there I go to the 18th Battalion's ceremony at the firefighter's monument. Those guys do an unbelievable job. There are no politicians. It's the fire department running everything for the firefighters and their families. It's well done. My next stop is to headquarters for the four Staff Chiefs. That's my last firehouse and I always made it a point to make it.

We suffered a tremendous setback. But fortunately for this department we have so many quality people. At my retirement I talked about the pleasure and honor of working in the greatest organization in the world. And it's not because of what we do. It's because of the people who make up the FDNY. We were able to survive 9/11 through hard work and quality people. The civilians and the firefighters. Literally thousands of people stepped up. The 'Shops' (Apparatus Repair Unit) civilian workers, I had no idea the workload they got hit with getting those rigs back in-service with a limited staff. They're as dedicated as firefighters.

While suffering through this tragedy we were all fortunate to work for an organization with so many quality people and be able to bounce back as well as we did. ❖

## NYC Local Law 26 Emergency Action Plans

In 2004, New York City Mayor Michael Bloomberg signed into law Local Law 26 which required high-rise buildings to incorporate, improved sprinkler systems, better exit signs, additional exit stairways, and other features to protect occupants during fires or emergencies. NYC Local Law 26 also mandated 'Emergency Action Plans' for all high-rise commercial buildings. And for new high-rise buildings an 'Auxiliary Radio Communications' system must be installed which provides high-powered boosted radio repeater communications system for first responders. The fire protection systems in NYC high-rise buildings are the best in the world and they are the safest buildings to live in as acknowledged by long existing records regarding injuries and loss of property in these types of occupancies.

## The fire protection systems in NYC high-rise buildings are the best in the world and they are the safest buildings to live in

There is an after-effect from 9/11 that has remained persistent. When a fire occurs in a high-rise building no matter what instructions occupants are given 'They are leaving the building!' This is the result of what occurred from the collapse of the World Trade Center Twin Towers where the people who did not evacuate and 'Sheltered in Place' subsequently died.

There must be an understanding of the uniqueness of that event and the dangers occupants will encounter by self-evacuating from floors remote from the fire floor. There must be trust in fire department capabilities to effectively mitigate dangerous fire conditions. Fire departments routinely extinguish fires in high-rise buildings. Their efforts can be hampered by self-evacuating occupants leaving doors open as they evacuate, crowding limited stairs and sustaining injuries which occur with regularity during fire condition evacuations. It's a dangerous mistake based on a lack of knowledge of the hazards involved and a lack of trust in the ability of first responders to protect them.

I was Chief of Fire Prevention when Mayor Bloomberg also required the complete revision process of NYC's Building and Fire codes. These codes had not been completely updated since 1968. We went over, line by line, every word of these codes. A considerable task which took over a year. The Building Department opened their doors for input from us which was not common prior to 9/11. It was an open exchange of ideas to build safer buildings. I give the Building Department a lot of credit in providing this forum and Mayor Michael Bloomberg for initiating and supporting this work.

## Post-Radios

I vividly recall the first time I was offered to use a 'post-radio.' On a cold January night sometime after 9/11 I was operating at a high-rise residential building fire in the Chinatown section of Manhattan. My Command Post was in the crowded lobby with far too many self-evacuated occupants excitedly talking. Fire was blowing out windows on the upper floors when a Battalion Chief brought in the 'post radio.' My first response was "Not Now." After the fire was under control. I performed my own test of the 'post radio' and it definitely improved communications. At the next high-rise fire, I quickly notified a Battalion Chief to set up their 'post radio' immediately.

Some of the efforts the FDNY made to improve command and control was to equip every firefighter with a handie-talkie radio which identifies their assignment for the tour, and the company they are working in. This information is captured electronically at the scene. The department also mandate's 'emergency roll-calls' procedures to be regularly practiced at routine fires once the fire is under-control.

# CHAPTER 9

# Aftermath

The cost to New York City based on overall economic loss was estimated at between $82.8 and $94.8 billion USD with the lower number being consistent with the NYC Partnership's November 2001 estimate and the high-end consistent with the New York City Comptrollers October 2001 estimate.[59]

The money banks might have been emptied but the blood banks were filled from the giving hearts of New Yorkers with blood donations souring in the weeks after 9/11. According to a report by the *Journal of the American Medical Association* the number of blood donations in the weeks after the September 11, 2001, attacks was markedly greater than in the corresponding weeks of 2000; 2.5 times greater in the first week after the attacks.'[60]

Everybody wanted to help in any way they could. It especially affected young people as expressed by my nephew.

## Justin Mastriano
### Firefighter Ladder 155

When 9/11 occurred, I was in my girlfriends now my wife, Molloy College apartment. We woke up to a phone call from Colleen's brother who was going over the Whitestone Bridge he said, "You got to turn on the news. A plane just crashed into the World Trade Center buildings." We popped on the TV and were in disbelief of what was going on. We watched the whole thing unfold on the television the rest of the morning. From that moment on, seeing the bravery, unity, and camaraderie I knew I wanted to become a firefighter in the FDNY.

What the FDNY did during 9/11 looked like that's what it's all about when the chips are down and everything's going bad. 9/11 was the reason why most of the probationary firefighters in my class wanted to be a part of the FDNY.

After 9/11 the instructors in the probationary training classes focused on keeping the traditions and legacy that the department was built on alive. The sentiment during our training was 'You're replacing legends on this job. It's a big responsibility.' They pounded it into our heads, and we ate it up because it's important to all those guys who died to keep these traditions alive. Everything they built we need to keep it going and not let something like 9/11 destroy the greatest job in the world. That bravery when someone needed help. Being there to step up and help in times of crisis that's what I believe in. Hopefully we'll never see something like 9/11 again. But if it does, I know we are going to be there to help people.

It's a great thing about the FDNY. When push comes to shove—we're going to get the job done. If we're ordered to do something we're going to take those orders and follow them to the best of our ability. ❖

**What the FDNY did during 9/11 looked like that's what it's all about when the chips are down and everything's going bad. 9/11 was the reason why most of the probationary firefighters in my class wanted to be a part of the FDNY.**

## Tom Curti – Fleet Maintenance Deputy Director

Everybody pitched in. No complaining about the apparatus covered in dust or anything like that. We got all the "line-unit companies" apparatus back in-service by operating 24 hours a day, working 12-hour shifts, seven days a week for three weeks. We had support from the Long Island and New England's "Association of Emergency Vehicle Technicians." They sent 40 certified fire apparatus mechanics who volunteered to help, and we brought them in.

> **We had support from the Long Island and New England's "Association of Emergency Vehicle Technicians." They sent 40 certified fire apparatus mechanics who volunteered to help, and we brought them in.**

We had a total of 98 destroyed rigs: 19 pumpers, 18 ladder trucks, two Rescue trucks, one Tactical Rescue Support unit, two Rescue Support units, two High-Rise Support units, one Satellite Hose Wagon unit, one Mask Service unit, two Fleet Maintenance field service units, 10 ambulances, 24 sedans, 16 Suburban's—all totally destroyed.

Performing preventive maintenance on a regular periodic schedule to on-line units, spares, and reserve apparatus insured they were ready to go in-service. The 500 series reserve fleet was created after the 1977 Blackout when the FDNY found out they had the recall manpower but no available apparatus and equipment. A fleet of 25 reserve pumpers was created and positioned in firehouses throughout the city. This fleet saved us. After 911 we added 10 ladder apparatus to this fleet.

The FDNY also maintains about 10% of its active fleet to be used as spares when an assigned apparatus is undergoing repairs. Good inventory, standardization, and the personnel to put it all back together really paid off. An outstanding job. And the manufacturers Seagrave and Salisbury helped. We had a lot of apparatus on order. They stopped producing for other people and turned their production of apparatus completely, one hundred percent, to build FDNY apparatus. Plus, they donated some apparatus.

We decontaminated our entire fleet. Millions of dollars were spent. This decontamination was performed on all fire apparatus, support vehicles, cars, and ambulances.

We're kind of unique to the fire industry. We have an 'Apparatus Committee' where mechanics, supervisors, firefighters, and officers, all put our two-cents-in to come up with rigs that worked for everybody. Our specifications also consider the extremely high call volume and the conditions of the city roadways. If we have continual problems, we always do a 'failure analyses' to conclude what is causing it and how to fix it. And we put that

With all the damaged and destroyed apparatus there was the possibility of companies being out-of-service which would have resulted in less fire protection and further peril immediately after 9/11.

Photo © 2001 by Michael Heller

into the specifications for future rigs. I can't say enough about the fleet maintenance people and the support we got from Headquarters. Anything we needed we got.

A couple of guys that worked in the 'Shops' have sadly passed away from 9/11-related cancers. With all the damaged and destroyed apparatus there was the possibility of companies being out-of-service which would have resulted in less fire protection and further peril immediately after 9/11. My people put themselves at risk to protect the people of New York City by working in that environment. Job well done! ❖

## The FDNY Counseling Service Unit

The FDNY Counseling Service Unit (CSU) staff visited every firehouse and EMS station and added satellite locations to provide mental health services to members and their families. Prior to 9/11, CSU consisted of 11 full-time counselors mostly providing counseling for family issues, personal stress, or bereavement. They were all working at one Manhattan location. Post-9/11 Trauma Groups were available at several FDNY CSU locations in members' communities. Peer counselors were deployed throughout FDNY. Two weeks following 9/11 CSU facilities were operational in Staten Island, Queens and later in Suffolk and Orange Counties. The FDNY WTC Health Program annual monitoring exams have helped identify mental health concerns and their relation to work done at the 9/11 disaster site.[61]

## Dennis Asher
### Captain Engine 28

My son Brett, an EMT in Harlem, was off that day and my other son Tommy was working in Engine 75. Thank God they had a fire at the time of the attack and did not respond to the site until after the collapse of both buildings. I was on light-duty. Brett and I managed to get into Engine 28's empty firehouse located on 2nd street in the lower east side where I picked up my gear and drove to the site.

Beat-up firefighters were sitting down on the rubble in the streets around the site. We found some water bottles and were giving them out when I met guys from my company. There wasn't much you could do with so many fires still burning. The smoke and thick dust filled the air.

After a while Brett stayed and I went back to the firehouse to figure out how to organize getting in touch with the family members of those firefighters still missing believing they were going to be rescued. We knew the location of Ladder 11 from the response-ticket directing them to the Marriot Hotel so we were thinking it was a possibility they would be good. Families started coming into the firehouse for information. I ended up staying in the firehouse throughout the night.

Brett stayed on the pile during that first night until after the collapse of 7-World Trade Center. He came running through the firehouse door devastated. He couldn't find his brother Tommy and thought maybe he got buried under the building when it came down. We ended up finding Tommy the next day.

You know it was helter-skelter that day. My son Tommy got hooked up with this Marine guy who had a dog. They ended up doing something almost beyond understanding. They went eight stories below ground-level under the pile. My son had a couple of water extinguisher cans and was trying to keep the fire away from the rescuers involved in pulling out three Port Authority Police Officers who were trapped in the rubble. One guy died early on. The other two guys survived. My son's oxygen level was so low when they finally pulled them out, he collapsed. They took him to Bellevue Hospital and put him in a hyperbaric chamber. He was in the hospital for the rest of the day. We didn't know where he was. I thank God every day having had the three of us working in the FDNY at that time and we survived as a family.

The way it went down for our firehouse was Engine 28 was inside the North-Tower when they heard this rumbling sound. They were not aware the sound came from the South-Tower collapsing. They thought it was the floors above the fire collapsing. Eventually they got radio communications to evacuate the North-Tower and started to come down.

When they got to the lower-level debris from the plane crash hitting the building and people jumping out of building was falling around the exits. The officer was

> **They went eight stories below ground-level under the pile. My son had a couple of water extinguisher cans and was trying to keep the fire away from the rescuers involved in pulling out three Port Authority Police Officers who were trapped in the rubble.**

on the radio trying to contact Command to get information on another way out of the North-Tower. Trying to protect his firefighters from being seriously injured. Firefighter Roy Chelsen looked around to see what was best for the company when he grabbed the officer and screamed "Get off the radio. We've got to get out of here now. The South-Tower has collapsed!" They immediately exited the building. Roy Chelsen saved their lives. On January 9, 2011, Firefighter Roy Chelsen died because of the injuries he sustained while operating at the World Trade Center. This kid was a spectacular firefighter.

The members of Engine 28 survived. The Lieutenant and six-firefighters from Ladder 11 did not. Some families were coming to the firehouse, and we were figuring out who was going to communicate with the families of missing members. I spent the next day going to our families' homes in Long Island and Queens. Telling the wives, we're still in a rescue mode. Giving them hope. Everything was going to be good. We were going to get them out. And we didn't.

> **We had assigned firefighters to a particular firefighter who was lost. On the days the members weren't working in the firehouse or down at the pile they were going to the family homes trying to do what they could as best they could, while looking to recover the remains of their loved ones.**

Matthew Rogan was a firefighter in Ladder 11 who was killed. I had worked with his father John Rogan and made a special effort to be with him. Years before my son Dennis was killed in an auto accident so, I felt his pain. I had this need to be with him and his wife and the firefighter's wife. I visited with them several times.

We had assigned firefighters to a particular firefighter who was lost. On the days the members weren't working in the firehouse or down at the pile they were going to the family homes trying to do what they could as best they could, while looking to recover the remains of their loved ones.

The Uniformed Fire Officers Association was trying to get as many members as possible to show up at an American Legion Hall. They were discussing what we could do. A person in charge of the Counseling Unit was making a presentation asking for anyone interested in helping firefighters in firehouses who lost a member to please come down to the counseling unit maybe we can find something for you to do. As soon as he finished speaking with the members, I presented myself to him. Being on light-duty I said, "I'd like to think I could do something to help." I told him what was going on in our firehouse and I had previous training with the Marine Corps on PTSD. He took me right away saying "I'll make the phone calls." That's how I ended up getting detailed to the Counseling Unit on Lafayette Street in Manhattan.

At first it was a mess. Trying to organize and coordinate the effort to help all these people who were suffering was overwhelming. No doubt about it. There were people from the Chicago Fire Department, the Boston Fire Department, the Department of Veterans Affairs. There was a 'Peer Intervention Group' from the New York City Board of Education. The Saint Vincent Catholic Medical Center had psychologists and psychiatrists looking to do work with the family members.

Then somebody got the idea to try to recruit professional mental health people who might want to volunteer to help, and I thought 'that's something I could get involved with.' I made appointments with them at their place of practice and filled them in on what it was they were dealing with regarding the kind of life we live in the firehouse and what we're basically about. If they were still onboard, then I would make arrangements with each of them to be introduced into a firehouse that had suffered a loss.

We tried to do it when the Commanding Officer was there, whether it was a Lieutenant who had seniority because they lost the Captain or the Captain who had survived. We would introduce the psychologist or psychiatrist to the firehouse. The counseling was done in the firehouses. That was the program. There were firefighters hooking up with the counselors one-on-one and the counselors were deciding to meet with them in their private office and were doing that pro bono too. That wasn't in the program.

Then it grew. They got involved with many of the families. There was a lot of funding being made available because it was a big undertaking. The FDNY counseling unit was branching out. Making satellite-offices in all the boroughs to make it easier for families to address their situation with a counselor and not have to come into the city. That was amazing.

Malachy Corrigan was a spectacular guy when it came to the counseling part of the job. Diane Caine too. These were the people already working in the Counseling Unit and they hired people from all over to provide care where needed. They created 'Out-Reach' programs for the children and parent who lost their firefighter. During the holidays they provided an opportunity for kids and their family members to go to Radio City Music Hall or go to a play during Thanksgiving, maybe see the tree. Do things inspiring to the children and at the same time difficult for the wife without her husband being there.

> **The FDNY counseling unit was branching out. Making satellite-offices in all the boroughs to make it easier for families to address their situation with a counselor and not have to come into the city. That was amazing.**

I don't know who oversees the counseling unit now, but I would suspect they are more in-tune about the psychological aspects of our jobs. I believe our Lord provided an opportunity for us to do a job so quickly and efficiently without having any other things hindering us. I met some remarkable people who care about others in this world.

I have to say part of having the courage to go into those firehouses I didn't get it on my own. There was lot going on there. End of story. ❖

# Epilogue

The Terrorist were all about death. For themselves and innocent others. They thought by their actions they would put fear in our hearts and make America weaker. Their attack had the opposite effect. It made our country stronger in every way. It brought us together. 'United We Stood' to face hatred and evil. And, we had the free world countries by our side.

You'll find stories of how 9/11 inspired us to accomplish our goals to help others and persevere through life's hardships everywhere. I found the following while casually reading a magazine: "…I had an appointment to call a former Army Ranger named Neil Forbes. We went through the training only a year apart and we're soon trading Ranger School stories and joking about mutual friends. Before we finished, I asked him; "How did you stay motivated during the dark times every Ranger student experiences?" He pauses for a considerable time, then it becomes clear that he choked up. I have no idea why. He takes a few deep breaths before telling me he wrote the initials JQ, followed by 9/11/01, inside his Ranger School patrol cap. He did so in honor of Jimmy Quinn, brother of a close friend we realize we have in common Joe Quinn. Jimmy lost his life in one of the World Trade Center towers that day. Neil says when times get tough at Ranger School, he would look at those initials, remember Jimmy, and think to himself, how bad can this be? I am still here, still breathing, and this pain is a reminder that I am still pushing myself.[62]

All of New York City pulled together to improve conditions for everyone who lived here and for those who come in to work or visit. And it was not just Americans helping.

In Berlin, 200,000 Germans marched to show their solidarity with America. The French newspaper of record, *Le Monde*, ran a front-page headline reading "*Nous sommes tous Américains*", "We are all Americans." In London the US national anthem was played at the Changing of the Guard at Buckingham Palace.[63]

NATO, (the North Atlantic Treaty Organization an intergovernmental military alliance between 27 European countries, 2 North American countries, and 1 Eurasian country) on September 12, 2001, the day after the terrorist attacks at the World Trade Center and the Pentagon, invoked Article 5 for the first time in its 70-year history. Committing its members to stand by the United States in its response to the attacks in a four-paragraph resolution, that passed unanimously.[64]

I represented the FDNY at the 9/11 ceremony in New Zealand in 2019. After all these years the New Zealand Fire Department was still honoring those who made the sacrifices on 9/11 by walking up a high-rise building in their turnout gear and holding a ceremony reading the names of the 343 FDNY firefighters killed on 9/11 and the names of their members who were killed in-the-line-of-duty. It amazed me how half-way around the world it was important for them to honor us and realized it wasn't

© New York City Fire Department

just Americans but people around the world who will help others in their time of need. Doing what they can. Each in their own way no matter what nationality or race. And you never thought—this would happen in our time.

On October 18, 1783, at the end of the revolutionary war, General George Washington issued the last general order to his troops. I felt he described the world we lived in during 9/11 when he said: "No one who had not been a witness to the event could imagine that the most violent local prejudices would cease so soon, and that men who came from the different parts of the continent, strongly disposed by the habits of education to despise and quarrel with each other, would instantly become one patriotic band of brothers." [65]

© New York City Fire Department

160

# References

1-History.com 21 century 9-11-2001 attack updated 9/11/2020

2-The National Commission on Terrorist Attacks Upon the United States, 911 Commission report Chapter 1 We Have Some Planes. Hijacking of American page 4

3-Ibid Chapter 1 hijacking of American page 5

4-Ibid Chapter 1 hijacking of American page 5

5-Ibid Chapter 1 hijacking of American page 6

6-Lynn Spencer, 2008 Touching History, The Untold Story of the Drama That Unfolded in the Skies over America on 9/11, page 24-25

7-The National Commission on Terrorist Attacks Upon the United States, 911 commission report, Chapter 1 Hijacking of United 175 page 7

8-Ibid Chapter 1.1.1 Hijacking of United 175 page 8

9-Ibid Chapter 9 Heroism and Horror, FDNY Initial response page 302

10-Ibid Chapter 9, Heroism and Horror, FDNY Initial response page 290

11-Ibid Chapter 9 FDNY Initial response page 291

12-Ibid Chapter 9 FDNY Initial response page 301

13-Ibid Chapter 9 FDNY Initial response page 302

14-Ibid Chapter 9 FDNY Initial response page 300

15-Ibid Chapter 9 Summary page 293

16-Chapter 9, Heroism and Horror, FDNY Initial response Chapter 9 page 305

17-Ibid Chapter 9, 9.2 page 308

18-Ibid Chapter 9 page 307

19-Ibid Chapter 9 page 309

20-Lynn Spencer, 2008 Touching History, The Untold Story of the Drama That Unfolded in the Skies over America on 9/11, page 108

21-Ibid page109

22-Ibid page 153

23-National Commission on Terrorist Attacks Upon the United States 911 commission report Chapter 9 page 286

24-Ibid Chapter 9 page 287

25-Ibid Chapter 9 page 287

26-Ibid Chapter 9 page 287

27-Ibid Chapter 9 page 289

28-Ibid Chapter 1 page 18

29-Ibid Chapter 1 page 20

30-Ibid Chapter 1 page 23

31-Ibid Chapter 1 page 31

32-Ibid Chapter 1 page 35

33-Ibid Chapter 1 page 35

34-Ibid Chapter 1 page 39

35-Ibid Chapter 1 page 45

36-McKinsey and Company the Final report page 10, www.nyc.gov/html/fdny/pdf/mck_report/executive_summary.pdf

37-'OSHA Publications Dangerous Worksite The World Trade Center' report

38-NEW YORK (CNN) Precious metals buried under debris September 22, 2001, Posted: 5:36 AM EDT (0936 GMT)

39-McKinsey report page 10 http://www.nyc.gov/html/fdny/pdf/mck_report/executive_summary.pdf

40-Hill, Howard. Failure Point: How to Determine Burning Building Stability, PennWell, Fire Engineering 2012, pg. 2

41-NIST GCR 02-834-1 paper. Analysis of Needs and Existing Capabilities for Full-Scale Fire Resistance Testing. 2008

42-Robert Grudin (April 20, 2010). Design And Truth. Yale University Press. p. 39

43-NIST NCSTAR1, Federal Building and Fire Safety Investigation of the World Trade Center Disaster page 12

44-Ibid Events Following Collapse Initiation 6.14.5 page 175

45-Ibid 8.2 Summary page 176

46-Ibid 8.2 Summary page 176

47-Ibid 8.2 Summary page 178

48-NIST NCSTAR 1A 1/29/09 Section 3.2 The Leading Hypothesis page 25

49-World Trade Center Building Performance Study: Data Collection, Preliminary Observations and Recommendations FEMA 403, May 2002 Chapter 8. Section 8.2.5.1

50-McKinsey and Company Final report www.1.nyc.gov/assets/fdny/downloads/pdf/about/mckinsey_report.pdf page 1

51-Ibid Recall mobilizes additional off-duty firefighters

52-The National Commission on Terrorist Attacks Upon the United States, the 911Commission, Chapter 9 page 298

53-Ibid page 317

54-Ibid page 299

55-Ibid page 305

56-Ibid page 316

57-Ibid page 317

58-Ibid page 321

59-Thompson Jr., William (September 4, 2002)."One Year Later; The Fiscal Impact of 9/11 on New York City" (PDF). Comptroller of the City of New York Office.

60-Glynn, Simone A. December 1, 2010, Journal of the American Medical Association pg. 289, 2246–2253.

61-Health impacts on FDNY rescue/recovery workers from 2001 to 2016 CSU Counseling

62-Outside magazine 05.20, Why the hell am I standing here, shivering on a remote mountain trail in the Appalachians? by Will Bardenwerper

63-Jenkins, Nash (November 14, 2015). "How Paris Stood With the U.S. After 9/11". Time. Retrieved 2019-06-03

64-History.com www.nytimes 2001/09/13

65-A New Age Now Begins by Page Smith, Volume Two A people's history of the American revolution McGraw-Hill Book Company New York 1976 pg. 1784

162

# National 9/11 Memorial & Museum

# Index